Body, Self, and Soul:

Sustaining Integration

Also by Jack Rosenberg:

Total Orgasm

Body, Self, and Soul:
Sustaining Integration

By

Jack Lee Rosenberg, D.D.S., Ph.D.

With Marjorie L. Rand, Ph.D.,

And Diane Asay, M.A.

Humanics Limited   Humanics New Age
Atlanta, Georgia

PRINTED IN THE UNITED STATES OF AMERICA

Library of Congress Cataloging in Publication Data

Rosenberg, Jack L., 1932-
 Body, self, and soul

 Bibliography: p.
 Includes index.
  1. Mind and Body Therapies.   2. Self.   I. Rand,
Marjorie L., 1944-   II. Asay, Diane.   III. Title.
RC489.M53 R67   1985   616.89'14   85-2293
ISBN 0-89334-082-0

Humanics Limited ● Humanics New Age
P. O. Box 7447/Atlanta, Georgia 30309/(404) 874-2176

Acknowledgments

Many people have affected my life and, indirectly, the development of Integrative Body Psychotherapy. This list doesn't include all of them, by any means, just those whose contributions have been particularly striking.

My parents. My wives: Patricia Connolly and Lynn MacCuish. My children: Andrea, Melissa, Erik, Katherine, and Mariya.

Rev. Karl Boterman, Jean Pouteau, Fritz Perls, Jim Simkin, Robert Hall, Loren Borland, Phil Cucuruto, Anna Halprin, Michael Murphy, Elaine Kepner, Kati Breckenridge, Victoria Hamilton, Gil Segel, Joanne Segel, Hal Stone and the others at the Center for the Healing Arts, Richard Alpert, Covert Bailey, Marilyn Ross, and Jack Downing.

All the students I've ever had, especially the infamous Monday group.

Marjorie Rand, without whose drive, intellectual integrity, charm, tenacity, utter reliability, and good humor, this book never would have been written nor the Rosenberg-Rand Institute established.

Diane Asay, whose early push to write down what I taught resulted in the first draft.

Valerie Cooley Murphy, who saves my life repeatedly, bills me for "house-wifery," "money-juggling," and "mothering," and who finally overcame her suspicion of psychologists to edit this book.

Jack Rosenberg

I would like to acknowledge:

My mother, father, husband and children for teaching me about relationships.

Eric Marcus, Alan Brovar, Jack Zimmerman, Joanne Segel, Judith Broder, Jeffrey Trop, and Ellen Jacobs, my teachers and trainers.

My clients and students for the opportunity to learn from and teach them.

My friends for putting up with me.

Jack Rosenberg, my teacher, therapist, friend, co-author, and partner for having faith in me and for being in the right place at the right time.

Valerie Cooley Murphy, my roommate at Esalen and our editor, for making deadlines and frantic phone calls, and for her fabulous sense of humor.

Diane Asay for her help on the first draft of the book and for her wonderful dream.

Marjorie Rand

I would like to acknowledge my great debt to Jack Lee Rosenberg who taught me about my breath and its unifying function to body-mind-spirit. Because of his teaching, I participated in the conceptualization and early writing of this book, so that others would benefit as well.

I offer great thanks to Margie Rand who unstintingly organized us and grounded us through the writing of this book, and who as a colleague from the beginning of our graduate student days has shared in the discoveries, pains, and lunacies while we grew together.

To my family I give my love and thanks for the joy, love, and true friendship that have sustained me always. And to my Teacher, Swami Chetanananda, who daily teaches me what it means to grow, I offer my deepest gratitude.

Diane Asay

Contents

Introduction   11

1. Integrative Body Psychotherapy: What and Why   13
   The Primary Scenario   18
   The Sense of Self   20
   Energy   22
   Other Manifestations of Energy in the Person   24
      Intellectual Energy   25
      Sexual Energy   25
   The Therapeutic Process   26
   Reliving the Past   28
   Obsolete Responses to the Past   31
   The Healing Relationship   32

2. The Beginning: The Basic Tools
   of Integrative Body Psychotherapy   37
   Physical History   37
      How We Take the History   41
   Nutrition and Emotions   54
      Drugs   61
   Exercise and Emotions   64
   The Journal Process   65

3. The Source: The Primary Scenario   69
   Gathering the Primary Scenario   74
   The Necessity of the Primary Scenario   86

4. Looking In: Contraction and Expansion   89
   Basic Concepts of Body Therapy   95

Cathartic Release   96
Reich's Notion of Orgastic Potency   100
The Charging Process   100
The Breathing Process   106
Autonomic Nervous System   107
Interruptions   108

5. Looking at the Body   115
The Segments   115
Release Techniques   118
  Verbal/Cognitive   118
  Muscular   118
  Energetic   118
  Stress/Movement   119
  The Subtle Energy Level   119
The Face   119
  Band I: Top of Head and Forehead   122
  Band II: Eyes; Ocular Segment   123
  Band III: Jaw and Mouth; Oral Segment   125
  Band IV: Mouth and Throat   127
Cervical Segment   128
Thoracic Segment   129
Diaphragmatic Segment   132
Abdominal Segment   133
Pelvic Segment   134
  Orgastic Reflex   136

6. Growing Up: Development of the Self   141
Stages in Development of the Self   144
Attachment Stage (Birth to 4 or 5 Months): Bonding   145
  Bonding Injuries   148
Reflection Stage (6 Months to 1½ Years): Mirroring   150
  Mirroring Injuries   151
Solipsism: A Special Kind of Injury   156
  Rebellion and Spitefulness   158
  Withdrawal   159
  Compliance   159
  Polarizing   160

The Solipsistic Relationship: The Next Generation   162
Healthy Introversion/Narcissism Stage
   (1½ to 3 Years): Reinforcing Self   163
   Reinforcing Injuries   164
Rapprochement Stage (1½ to 3 Years): Reality Testing   166
The Constituted Self   168

7. **Hanging Out: The Therapeutic Process   169**
Fragmentation   170
Boundaries   175
Containment   178
Defensive Character Styles of Relating   179
   Splitting Off   179
   The As-If Personality   180
   The Super-Trouper   190
   The Never-Enougher   196
Treatment Methods   205
   Releasing and Replacing the Negative Introject   205
   The Good Mother Messages   207
   The Good Father Work   215
Transference and Counter-Transference   216
   Stages of Transference Relationship   217
   Negative Transference   224

8. **Getting Off: Sexuality and Sexual Counseling   227**
The Physical/Energetic Level: Methods of
   Building Excitement   231
   Presence and Contact   231
   Breathing   232
   Containment and Boundaries   233
   Thinking and Fantasy   237
   Sensuality and Pleasure   239
   Genital Stimulation   239
   The Language of Sex   241
The Intra-Psychic Level: The X-Rated Movie   243
   Critical Stages of Sexual Development   245
   Incest   249
   Traumatic Sexual Experiences   255

Summary of the X-Rated Movie   260
The Interpersonal Level: Relationships   263
    Projection (Projective Identification)   264
    Re-owning Projections   265
    Sexually Expressed Energetic Blocks   268

9. **Turning On: The Transpersonal Experience   273**
    Archetypical Transpersonal Insights   279
    Dreams and Myths   293
    Body Experiences in the Transpersonal Process   299
        Centers of Energy (Chakras)   299
        Physical Manifestations of the Transformational Process   304
    Traps in the Transpersonal   308
        What You Believe is What You Get   308
        The "Messianic Explosion"   308
        The Entrance of the Demonic   309
        Transference and Counter-Transference Traps   310
        Constellation Around Psychic Powers   310
        Satsang Effect   311
        Head Trip   311
        Fallen Angel   311
        Sane/Insane/Unsane   312
    Meditation   313
    The Journey of Life   316

Glossary   319

Appendix: IBP Release Techniques Chart   325

Notes   337

Introduction

This book is about growth — personal and internal growth — and about Integrative Body Psychotherapy, the exciting new therapy that helps achieve it. It's written for people interested in furthering their own growth or in helping others with theirs. We have thought of our readers as therapists, of course, but also as teachers, parents, doctors, managers, writers, coaches, actors, and so on. To them, whoever they are, we hope to convey our excitement about a therapy that *works!* A method that deals with the whole person, integrating the body, mind, emotions, and spirit! A method that brings about profound and lasting changes!

Not one element of it is new. In fact, you may recognize everything in this book and know exactly where it came from before we tell you. What *is* new is the combination of ideas, treatments, models, and techniques into a new form, one that is vastly more effective for our purposes than any of the sources from which they are drawn.

These sources have been many and diverse, found in the course of our personal and professional explorations. They come from the East and the West: Tantra and Hatha yoga; Freudian, Jungian, Reichian, and Gestalt therapies; Rolfing, chiropractics, and movement therapy; medical models and acupuncture; meditation and dance; object relations and the human potential movement; developmental psychology and work with death and dying; and more.

Every exploration has led to valuable discoveries. Sometimes we thought we had found the perfect therapy, the total answer; other times we knew we had found just part of the answer, a piece of the puzzle. Always, the concepts — ancient and modern, Eastern and Western — have questioned, augmented, supported, and contradicted each other, constantly sharpening our thinking and understanding.

From these explorations have emerged our beliefs and working principles:

We believe that everyone has an essential Self and that this Self is the substance with which we work.

We believe that this Self comes from the soul, the universal energy embodied in the individual and made unique by its presence in that body.

We believe that this energy flowing through the body gives a feeling of well-being, of harmony with oneself and with the universe; that the awareness of this well-being and harmony is the sense of Self; and that this sense of Self is inextricably lodged in the body.

We believe that this sense of Self, lodged in the body, derives from pre-verbal experiences and that the relationship patterns determined by these experiences can only be altered by working through the body.

The process by which we have come to these beliefs has led to a new appreciation of — and reverence for — the human body, mind, and soul. We treat their integration as the natural state of the human being and we work to achieve and sustain this state with an effective assortment of techniques.

Our methods worked so well that they soon attracted the attention of therapists who wanted to learn them. From their interest grew both the teaching manual that evolved slowly into this book, and the Rosenberg-Rand Institute of Integrative Body Psychotherapy in Venice, California, co-directed by Jack Rosenberg and Marjorie Rand. In 1985, the Esalen Institute will start a residential training program in IBP at Big Sur, California.

Chapter 1

Integrative Body Psychotherapy: What and Why

Everyone knows the old story of three blind men who were trying to identify an elephant. Each one of them approached the elephant from a different direction: one came upon the trunk, the second explored the feet and the sides, and the third examined the tail. Each one was certain he knew what an elephant was. One swore up and down that an elephant was a long, thick undulating animal with two moist orifices at the lower end through which air, food, and water were taken in and often snorted out. The second adamantly disagreed. He said that an elephant was a huge tree-like structure, firmly planted in the ground, which widened to the size of a building. It was very rough to the touch. The third man laughed at the lunacy of the first two. He, in his wisdom, described his experience of the elephant as finding a snake-like creature with a tuft of coarse hair at one end. All three men were right in their observations, but limited in their explorations.

Something similar has happened in the field of psychotherapy. Brilliant explorers into the psyche have described the importance of the unconscious, the spirit, the body, and the emotions. They have taught us the mechanism of repression and the power of their very particular areas of interest, but as with the elephant, vast areas of human behavior have been untouched. With the concentration of increasing numbers of explorers on as many separate areas of study, more energy has been spent in defending different viewpoints than in sharing information. To merely increase the numbers of theoreticians is like increasing the number of blind men around the elephant — if they don't share their discoveries in such a way as to enable each other to see the whole, they are just increasing the number of limited viewpoints, no matter how brilliant or profound each is.

Because of the limitations of the many fields of study in psychology, we have gradually developed a powerful method of psychotherapy of our own, borrowing from a wide array of theories, methods, and philosophies. Our foundation, of course, has been Western psychology, including Freud, Reich, Jung, and Perls, as well as object relations theorists. In addition to the Western approaches, we have studied and applied many Eastern techniques and philosophies — acupressure, yoga, Tantric yoga, and meditation. And, as we have worked, we have explored our own sections of the elephant, trying to understand them in terms of other studies, our own personal experience, and our professional work with clients.

We have had to borrow from so many sources because psychotherapy, up to now, hasn't been able to offer a consistent way out of the human dilemma. It has consisted mainly of "head talk," ignoring the human body and, except for Jung, the spirit. The various "body therapies," attempting to solve that lack, neglect, in turn, the cognitive processes. We have found, both in our personal therapeutic experiences and in our work, that it is necessary to integrate the different parts of the human being — mind, body, emotions, and spirit. Our success has come from recognizing that our being, our Essential Self, is *grounded in the body*; that ignoring the body is to have very limited lasting success in treatment of psychological pain.

We have found, through our eclectic approach to psychotherapy, that despite the proliferation of ideas in Western psychology, there really isn't anything new; there is only rediscovery of old ideas. Sometimes they are forgotten truths from our own culture. Sometimes we find them in primitive cultures and sometimes in ancient and sophisticated philosophies. Perhaps the re-discovery is easier in a foreign context. It doesn't matter that the ideas are old; what is new in our system of therapy is that we have integrated what we have learned and developed a coherent picture of human behavior — an overview of the whole elephant, so to speak.

The importance and power of this integrated method of therapy strikes us each time we see a client who has been treated partially by one school of therapy or another. No matter how sincere that work, the client is still desperately seeking relief from emotional dilemmas. We have many examples of the failure of incomplete, one-sided therapies.

Sylvia, for instance, was a lively looking woman of forty with a cloud of wavy red hair and a twinkle in her eye. She had had six years of Freudian analysis and made good natured fun of herself, spoofing her problems with exaggerated use of the psychological jargon she had learned.

Behind her roguish charm, unfortunately, lay a long-standing depression. The years of therapy had given her the intellectual tools to shore up a failing marriage. They had helped her handle her grown-up children's leaving home and her return to the working world, but she was still depressed.

"There are weekends when I don't even open the drapes," she said. "I'm still having Victorian sex with a man I barely know after twenty years, and I'm uncomfortable calling my friends by their first names. . . What good has it all done me?" she wailed, with a twist to her smile.

Her therapy had dealt with her mind alone. It gave her the materials for wildly funny tales of her aberrations and enough insight to conduct her life fairly well. It didn't touch her body, though, and here she was only half-alive, unable to feel her sexuality and unable to feel close to her friends. She masked her depression with mood elevators and with a delightfully wry, usually self-deprecating sense of humor.

Eventually, in the course of our therapy, she got in touch with her body and began to understand its role in her psychological problems. First she worked on her lackadaisical attitude towards diet and exercise. As she continued, she tied her intellectual insights to a new awareness of her body and was able to free the sexual and emotional energy that had been blocked for so long. She found more warmth and affection in her relationships with her husband, friends, and family. Gradually, the outward impression of a charming, lively woman became, instead of a mask, a picture of the real thing.

James' background was entirely different. He had been through seven years of body therapies, having intense emotional releases in his weekly sessions. He had a slim, lithe body that moved with astonishing grace, and an abundance of sexual energy. He treated his body with respect, ate simple, wholesome foods, and exercised regularly. There was a certain animal charm about him as much from the grace and simplicity of his physical being as from a certain intellectual vacantness. He slid effortlessly away from any sustained relationship with man or woman. Despite a respectable college record, his wide range of jobs — from training dogs to building hang gliders — had in common a lack of intellectual involvement. There were as ephemeral as his relationships with people.

Unlike Sylvia, he had no need to get in touch with his body; instead he had to link his emotions to it by developing the cognitive understanding that Sylvia had worked on for so long. In his previous therapies he had neglected his intellect, and he had no relationship whatever with his therapists. He would simply go in, lie down, close his eyes, and do any physical exercise the therapist told him to do, expressing any emotions that surfaced. The emotions, thus released, were forgotten because they were never tied to any cognitive process. There was no eye contact with the therapist, no verbal communication between them other than instructions. This complete lack of a relationship was just as important in the failure of the therapy as was the neglect of the intellect. We consider the therapeutic relationship a vital necessity in the healing process.

While James was in therapy with us, his father died. The man had been a tyrant, and, of course, James's emotions rose freely to the surface. With guidance, he was able to see how they related to his lifestyle and behavior patterns. He learned that he had felt a great deal of anger at his father, anger that masked considerable pain. Only when he was able to see how his feelings about a tyrannical father had affected his behavior was he able to begin to change that behavior. He gave up the latest of his undemanding jobs and started a business of his own. He stayed with the challenges and made a successful business, one that continues to grow. He stopped eluding relationships, too, and announced one day that he was getting married. "I'm too busy to try to learn a new name every few weeks," he explained, laughingly justifying his departure from his old habits.

We often see people such as James who have undergone body therapies where the therapeutic relationship isn't stressed, and emotional release is the only goal. In these people, integration of the various parts of their selves doesn't occur. Without this integration, their lives simply can't run smoothly and comfortably.

Bill was tall, dark, and handsome and was always surrounded by women. Nobody could understand why he was depressed. He had what many men dream of: abundant sex with a string of attractive young women. He himself was in his late forties, graying slightly, successful as an upper-manager and attractive despite a casual disregard for his health. Underneath, Bill was extremely unhappy and couldn't remember when he hadn't been. He moved from place to place, from woman to woman, seldom settling down enough to unpack. He was completely dependent upon sex to provide any sense of well-being, but even sufficient sex and ever-present women couldn't save him from a sense of isolation. "If I go to bed alone, it's the end of the world. But when I wake up in the morning and see someone next to me and I'm not sure of her name, then I feel more alone than ever."

Bill's background in therapy was in the human potential movement, where emotional release was the goal, but the body wasn't involved. He was able to bellow out his anger, but found it impossible to bellow out his depression. With our method of therapy, he learned to contain his emotions within his body. He began to exercise and eat properly. His health improved, and for the first time in his life, he began to experience a sense of well-being in his body. These good feelings he was able to maintain in his body instead of discharging them. Feeling so good about himself and within himself, he was able to settle down, unpack, consider marriage, and watch his depression disappear.

Our last example of the failure of one-sided therapies is Ranga Pur, a gentle, holy-looking member of a spiritual group with whom he had lived for most of his adult life. Ranga Pur spent his days meditating and teaching yoga for a livelihood. Although he was young— thirty— and not unattractive, he had never gotten any closer to a woman than he would have to a sister. He was warm and loving with the group but there was nothing sexual in any of his expressions of love. His boyish appearance and lack of apparent sexuality suggested that he had never really grown up as, indeed, he hadn't. He was troubled by this. Not only could he not keep an outside job for long, nor take a wife, but he couldn't separate himself from the other members of the community. People took advantage of him, using his room, taking his belongings, disturbing his meditations. Unlike most people, he had never learned to establish the usual boundaries between "you" and "me," between "yours" and "mine." The ashram, while keeping him safe from the outside world, had limited his development of an individual sense of identity.

"Sometimes," he said, "I don't know where I leave off and the others begin, and . . . ," he added guiltily, "I don't always like it." Living in the community had meant that he was never able to individuate nor to establish the boundaries that normal people have.

His task in therapy was to re-claim his rightful feelings as a human being, including his sexuality. Then he had to learn from his own experiences who he was, to establish boundaries between himself and others, and to carve out an existence of his own.

The dangers and consequences of giving up one's ego before one has it, as Ranga Pur did, were described by Ram Dass in the Journal of Transpersonal Psychology:

"Psychologically there were whole parts of my being that I

was afraid of and didn't accept. . . (I tried) getting rid of them by becoming holy. . . but after a while. . . I was trying to live in the projection that other people were creating for me. . . . Then I had to be alone and when I was alone I'd go into very deep depressions which I hid.

"... the problem. . . was that the doorway to the intuition is through the human heart, and I was trying to leap into cosmic love without dealing with emotionality because emotionality was a little too human for me. . . . I pushed away my humanity to embrace my divinity. . . . The intuition. . . had to come from a blending of humanity and divinity. Until I could accept my humanity fully, my intuitions weren't going to be fully in harmony with the way of things."

Steven Hendlin, speaking of this problem of individuation within a spiritual community, says that a person who has not yet transcended ego can be trapped by a "pernicious oneness." One can mistake states of blankness, "spacing out," lack of boundaries between oneself and others, muscle relaxation, and trance for "oneness" with the spiritual group. The person assumes by this that a firmly established ego has been transcended, but the attempt at identification with the ego-level needs may be premature. It can result in the strengthening of both ego and ego-level attachments. The strengthening of ego attachments is unconscious "patch-up" work and provides shaky foundation for a threatened ego. [1]

These four examples show people who sought to escape their emotional dilemmas or ease their pain through one form of therapy or another. Each, until he learned how to integrate his mind, emotions, body, and spirit, was unable to lead a full and satisfying life, because some important part of his being was overlooked.

At this point most people want to know "what happened to these people in the first place to make them so unhappy, so incomplete?" The answer usually is to be found in early life experiences.

The Primary Scenario

The sum of early life experiences is known as the Primary Scenario. It is the collection of physical and emotional events we went through in our early years and includes everything our parents did to us and for us, as well as everything their parents did to and for them. It includes the whole milieu into which we were born — the time and place, the culture, and the sub-culture. This collection of experiences is what formed our basic characters.

In IBP you will find that we use the term "character" in a somewhat different sense than the common one. By *character*, or character structure, we mean the fixed muscular patterns, emotional responses, and belief systems that are lodged in the body and behavior. One commonly thinks of character as moral structure, not muscular patterns, but they are really much the same thing. A moral structure, as with our use of character, is a rigid structure. It allows for no spontaneous choices. It is based on rules and judgments learned in our past and applied appropriately or not to situations in our present. It is the very basis of human behavior and is lodged, inextricably, in the body. You can see why, if you consider one example in the development of an infant.

The infant comes into the world as a mass of neurological responses. His emotions will develop soon, in response to his body reactions, but his language and other intellectual skills follow significantly later. Right now, at birth, he's a pure physical entity. He becomes aware of pain immediately from the shock of being born; later he feels pain from hunger, cold, dampness, fear of falling. His pleasure comes from being fed, from warmth, from cuddling, and from stroking. His first relationship is with the person or persons who are responsible for relieving his pain, who feed him when he is hungry, dry him off, and get him warm. *The way this is done* (more than the *fact* of its being done) *will affect him for the rest of his life.* If he cries because his stomach hurts from hunger and he is soon picked up and fed, and this happens consistently, he learns important lessons. One is that he needn't fear pain, that pain is all right because it will go away and he will feel comfortable again. He learns that another person cares about his pain, that something that matters to him matters to someone else. Even as adults, the realization that another person cares about us can bring tears to our eyes. We can understand, though, when others don't care as much about our problems as we do; we can accept a lack of concern as well as feel great appreciation of sincere concern. The baby can't make any of those intellectual judgments; he is aware only that his needs are being met or are not. Those needs are not just physical needs, but emotional ones as well; both must be satisfied for proper development.

Now if another baby cries because he is hungry and no one feeds him, and this happens consistently, he too learns some important lessons. For him, pain *is* to be feared because it won't be relieved by the person responsible for him. He doesn't learn that another person cares about his pain. What he does learn is how to handle the pain himself. While he can't feed himself, he *can* seal off the pain, separating himself from it. Although he gets fed eventually, he shuts down the pain until he does. Perhaps the meal doesn't taste as good when he finally gets it because he has blocked off his hunger. Because being fed doesn't satisfy an intense emotional need, he might not associate the person who feeds him with tremendous satisfaction. After all, where was she when he really needed her? Unlike the baby who is fed promptly, he doesn't have a chance to sense that his pain is very important to another person; it is important only to himself. Babies who are consistently allowed to cry for long periods tend to give up crying, but in so doing, they have to handle their physical and emotional discomfort by learning not to feel it.

The Sense of Self

Knowing the Self and honoring it is the basis of our work in IBP as well as a goal. The sense of Self is a non-verbal experience of well-being, identity, and continuity that is felt in the body. If a child's needs aren't satisfied in a loving, caring way, he doesn't develop a strong sense of Self. The potential Self— the undifferentiated mass of energy within the child— remains more or less undifferentiated, fragmented. It lacks the cohesiveness that gives "form" to a person's sense of Self, his identity. This doesn't develop because he doesn't have a pattern of feeling good and comfortable in his body. What he does develop is the character structure of a person who seals off feeling. It is a defensive character structure and the defenses are erected between the Self and the outside world. They are useful in that they allow one to grow without further pain to the Self, but they also maintain the Self in the primitive state it was in when the character structure formed to protect it. The baby who is picked up soon after he cries and is fed in a warm, loving way when his hunger pangs are sharp, does develop a sense of well-being in his body and, therefore, a strong sense of Self.

A sense of Self is vital in one's life. In our four examples at the beginning of this chapter, you saw people who, for various reasons, had little sense of Self. Sylvia was bright and intellectually aware, but her body was only half alive. James had a lively body, but it didn't help him in his relationships. Bill kept women around to ward off his loneliness, as if constant sexual satisfaction as an adult could somehow ward off an early hunger. Ranga Pur's sense of Self had not developed fully as a child, and he didn't separate his identity from that of his parents when he was a teen-ager. When he joined the ashram, he brought with him his still unindividuated Self.

Now, remember what we said about character, that it's the fixed muscular patterns, emotional responses, and belief systems held in the body. The fixed muscular patterns get set up early as defensive mechanisms. The child, sealing off his unsatisfied pain, tightens his body to keep the pain from penetrating too deeply. He learns to seal off pain almost before it starts. The response is not a selective process, so he seals off *feeling*, not just pain, with the result that, as an adult, he may not even be aware of the pleasure his body is capable of.

Researchers have stated that "muscle tension is of fundamental importance as an expression of the personality's *habitual defenses* and that these defenses are revealed in postural attitudes, voice, and, in fact, any persistently contracted muscles."

> "This paper has tried to show: first, that patterns of muscular tension and overt activity are valid indices of attitudes and personality, and that changes in tension patterns are adequate indicators of the progress of therapy; second, that frustrations of various sorts or the interruption of strongly motivated goal-directed activities are the "reason for being" of persistent tensions, and that these tensions reflect a continuous state of readiness of which an individual may often be unaware. Freud (39) has pointed out that "the true aim of repression is to suppress the development of affect," and that "repression demands a constant expenditure of energy" (40). From the point of view developed in this paper, repression is indicated by the existence of chronic muscle tension; and a constant supply of energy is needed to maintain this condition. Thirdly, continued muscular preparation acts as a continuous source of internal stimulation, the energy of which is handled by some sort of an "overflow" mechanism. Besides chronic muscle tension being causally related to many physical illnesses, it has also been found to be associated both with neuroses and psychoses. A new definition of normality might be proposed: freedom from chronic muscular tension." [2]

IBP work intensifies the experience of emotional and muscular patterns. When these patterns are released, early experiences are relived. Most of us have consistent patterns of holding tension in our eyes, for example, or the back of the head, shoulders, or stomach. Our musculature becomes stuck in certain response patterns corresponding to defensive (protective) habits developed in our early lives.

These patterns persist throughout life, unless they are interrupted.

At one time we thought of people going along a more or less straight line from birth to death. Then we saw that people were repeating patterns over and over, "going around in circles" or "being stuck in ruts," that they were locked in their bodies, in their characters, compelled to repeat their behavior. They do this through time, so now we see them spiralling their way through life from birth to death pretty much along the same path.

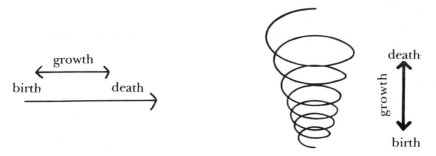

Energy

The concept of energy is fundamental to IBP. We have energy in our bodies, in our thoughts, and in our emotions. To physicists, mystics and contemplatives, energy is simply energy, existing as energy throughout the universe. Trees and rocks are masses of energy. Ocean waves and electricity are also energy. It's all a matter of vibrating waves and particles, sometimes going faster, sometimes slower. The slower it goes, the denser it is. Thus, our bodies are the densest expression of human energy.

We are constellations of energy. The energy that each thinks of as his essential "Self" is contained in his physical body, itself a mass of energy more or less contained in a solid form. The containment isn't complete, though, for we also have a field of energy outside our bodies, and this field is affected by others even as we affect theirs. We all know people who carry such negative energy that they make us feel bad as soon as they walk into the room. Likewise, there are people who make us feel good, whom we instinctively like or trust, whose presence radiates from across a room. They are described popularly as "vibrant," "charismatic," "magnetic," or as having "good vibrations."

Now, if you think of a person as being, in essence, a constellation of energy, how would you envision a healthy person? We picture him as a mass of free-flowing energy. The energy moves on all levels, through all layers, in all directions at all times. It is instantly accessible to the person whenever he needs it for any purpose.

The unhealthy person has blocks in his system and the flow of energy is impeded. We must remember at all times that we *are* energy. The essential Self of each of us is both energy itself and the awareness and appreciation of that energy. If something happens to our energy early in life, then the sense of Self develops poorly, buried under defensive blocks.

In our descriptions of hungry infants we said that the baby with a sense of well-being in his body developed a strong sense of Self. This sense of well-being comes from the free flow of energy in the body, from the natural state of things happening as they are meant to happen.

The baby whose needs aren't taken care of and who seals off his feelings, is forming blocks to his energy flow. Since all his reactions are in his body, the blocks are his growing muscular tension. Because his mass of energy isn't flowing freely as it should, he doesn't experience his Self. In blocking off feelings, he stifles the flow of energy and the core of his being — his sense of Self — lies hidden within. The sense of Self is a consciousness of the internal flow of energy. If one is disconnected from the flow, there can be no awareness of Self, or, at best, only an incomplete awareness. He will identify instead with his defensive character structure and this becomes a false sense of Self overlying the real Self.

People commonly think in terms of having a good or bad self-concept. We feel that there is no good or bad to the sense of Self; a sense of Self is inherently good and that only its lack of emergence is bad.

The people in the four case histories presented earlier expressed the undeveloped sense of Self verbally in statements such as "I really don't know who I am" and behaviorally by lack of direction, self-defeating activities, and sexual dysfunctions. Physiologically, the energy blockages inhibiting the growth of the Self can also contribute to ill health and emotional imbalance. Contacting the blockages through IBP, relaxing the tensions that produced them, and thereby releasing the energy to flow freely, allows the emergence of the stunted Self buried within. With the energy flowing unimpeded, a person can have the sense of well-being in his body that should have been his natural condition as an infant.

Through this process the client begins to experience the natural flow of energy within him, to learn how he is connected to the universe through the common energy. When this energy is blocked, the person becomes isolated from the world and from his essential Self. We believe that the essential Self remains alive deep within each of us and that we have found a way to help people make contact with it. The body and the spirit are not separate entities, and when working through one, we are really working with both. The body is the support system from which we move. When physio-logical responses to emotional conflicts are changed simultaneously with mental insight, the way is made clear for the emergence of the sense of Self. **The honoring of one's essential self is both the means and the end of this therapeutic method.**

Other Manifestations of Energy in the Person

We use our energy — blocked or not — in different ways, for different purposes. There is emotional energy, intellectual energy, sexual energy. Each is powerful in its own way, and each is subject to dysfunction through the blockages in our bodies.

Access to our emotions is in the body. Emotional expression is a body experience, not an intellectual one. The constant interplay between our emotions and our bodies is almost a cliche:

"She's making herself sick over exams."
"I always feel better after a good cry."
"She's climbing the walls."
"He died of a broken heart."
"He's in love and feels ten feet tall."
"Keep a stiff upper lip."
"This guy's got such a chip on his shoulder, he's a real pain in the neck."
"Yeah, he always gets my back up."

Emotions fire the nervous system which triggers the release of hormones which, in turn, affects and produces the emotions. Fear and anger, for instance, shoot the body full of adrenalin, enabling us to flee or attack with far more than normal power. Love relaxes us, allowing the energy to flow more easily, extending our awareness to other energy fields, and making everything easier. Hate turns us inward, stifles, and makes us sick.

Most people recognize this intuitively, but more and more it is being recognized as something that can be pursued systematically. Experimental data from many sources supports the usual effects of emotions and body. Chronic depression is treated successfully by daily running, and regular aerobic exercises are an essential part of IBP.

We can, for instance, change our feelings by changing our breathing patterns, which in turn change our neurological and endocrine systems. [3] An article in the Brain Mind Bulletin (January 3, 1983 Volume 8, No. 3) reports the discovery of a direct relationship between brain activity and the breathing cycle. "EEG responses have shown a consistent relationship between nasal airflow and cerebral dominance on all frequencies: alpha, theta, delta, and beta. . . . It also implies, for the first time, a demonstrable relationship between states of mind and specific metabolic functions. *The evidence suggests that feelings are subject to alteration by appropriate breathing exercises.*" (*italics ours*).

Intellectual Energy

From the beginning of his language development, a person applies his intellect to justifying and explaining the world to himself and to directing his own behavior. By "intellect" we mean a person's native cognitive abilities with no implication of any academic overlay. We may use the words interchangeably, but we want it understood that we're talking about the basic human cognition — the process of knowing or learning. This process starts early and soon falls into a pattern. The patterns a person habitually follows may indicate whether he's using his intellectual energy effectively or if it's hampered by emotional problems.

Although we seek emotions in the body, we confront them with the intellect. It is the person's cognitive processes that have to make sense out of the past, see the effect on the present, and work out the changes for the future.

Sexual Energy

Reich believed that the root of neurosis is repressed sexual energy. We have broadened his concept to include all forms of energy. Repressed energy, whether it is intellectual, emotional, physical, or sexual, causes neurosis. Freeing the energy so we can feel it moving in our bodies lets us use it for any creative purpose.

Sex, however, deserves special attention in IBP. Exploring a client's sexuality is an integral part of therapy. We try not to be intrusive in our exploration, but we have found that a person's sexuality is more symptomatic of his behavior than anything else. The orgastic pattern is related to breathing and muscular holding

patterns, and beliefs about sexuality are related to the Primary
Scenario. We bring together the separate aspects of a client's life and
re-frame them so that sex is included as part of the whole picture
rather than split off from the overall patterns.

For instance, Phil's "scenario" (the spiral pattern he follows through
life based on his Primary Scenario) is that he initiates things but
doesn't follow through. For example, he may enthusiastically sign
business contracts and then cancel them abruptly. The pattern
shows up in all aspects of his life: his work, his relationship, and in
his sex life, where he consistently initiates sex with his wife, only to
become impotent.

In therapy we seldom treat the symptom of impotence per se
because we find that it reflects in some way the behavior patterns in
other areas of life. It is a helpful guide. Suffused as it is with
enormous emotion, it is often the problem that got the person into
therapy in the first place. However, the problem is never just a
sexual one, but one of identity — that is, of knowing and expressing
the Self.

Our approach to sexuality parallels the Tantric approach to
energy. That is, we see ourselves as containers for the life force.
Tantra, by the way, is a type of yoga of which we had a partial
knowledge when we met Ajit Mookerjee, author of *The Tantric Way*.
He had heard of our therapy and had many questions about our
work. He asked, in particular, "How do you make the energy
move?" When we told him that we moved it with special breathing
techniques and the use of pressure points, he excitedly told us that
he, too, used pressure points to open the energy channels. Without
knowing it, we had been paralleling methods that Tantric yogis had
been using for centuries.

The Therapeutic Process

When a client first comes into therapy, he usually has one main
concern called his "presenting problem," the problem that drove him
to seek therapy. Although the client may see this as his only
problem, we see it as a symptom. Furthermore, it is a sympton that
cannot be resolved in the present situation.

As we have said, each person builds up patterns of behavior early
in life and repeats them from then on. The situations that established
the patterns were pre-verbal and pre-intellectual and are lodged,
therefore, in the body, in habitual muscular tension. The tension
also represents "unfinished business." We say "unfinished" because

the situations were never resolved by integrating the body's responses, the resultant emotional reactions, and a cognitive understanding.
This tension and the presence of "unfinished business" are part of
the "character." The compulsion to repeat patterns developed in
childhood to avoid pain is established early, and leads to similar
unfinished situations in the present. People repeat behavior that is
destined to failure, such as marrying series of spouses who resemble
— disastrously— the parents, or repeatedly taking on the same
sorts of unsatisfying jobs.

Therefore, we use the presenting problem as a vehicle for discussion, as we did with Anthony, who came into therapy complaining
of impotence. At thirty-five he was a respected attorney, but he
discounted his successful career. All that mattered was that he
couldn't have an erection. It didn't even matter that his girlfriend
didn't mind. As therapy progressed, he began to see that he
characteristically didn't "stand up" for himself with his boss or
girlfriend or anyone else of importance. Then it emerged that he
had never "stood up" to his mother, a necessary stage in separating
himself and becoming independent. Instead, he had become a
"good boy," trying all his life to "please mother," even after leaving
home at twenty. Underneath, of course, he needed to *not* please her
but, as he grew older and passed the acceptable age of open rebellion, the only way he could rebel was to unconsciously refuse to
be the "good boy" he had been. He accomplished his rebellion in
the perverse way of the unconscious by refusing to "stand up" by not
having an erection with the only mother-figure available, his girlfriend. When he finally saw that his current behavior— especially
his inability to have an erection— was repeating the pattern of his
relationship with his mother, he was able to see some humor in his
symbolic rebellion. With a solution in sight, he became less depressed
and more alive. His relationships with others improved as he
learned to "stand up" to them. Ultimately his sexual problems
disappeared, too, as he broke the unconsciously spiteful pattern with
which he met demands of people who were important to him.

Another case of sexual symptoms as the presenting problem was
Jose, a pleasant man in his mid-thirties. He suffered from premature
ejaculations as well as great generalized anxiety. In the course of
therapy, he relived a situation in which his father was beating him
and his mother was holding him, a terrified child, tightly to her
breast in an attempt to protect him. As he relived the beating, he felt
suffocated and immersed in anxiety, both his and his mother's. It
became clear to him that the intimacy of sex reactivated the old fear

of smothering and made him so anxious that he unconsciously ended the experience as soon as possible. He recognized further that the suffocation he had endured from his mother was far more pervasive than was the far more conscious anger he had always felt towards his father. However, the fear incurred by his father in this isolated incident had served to "set" the sensation of suffocation, making it easier to retrieve in therapy. Understanding his symptom, he was able to release his anxiety and resolve his anger. As the anxiety left him, so did his need for premature ejaculation, without ever having been treated specifically.

After the session in which he relived the experience, Jose reported: "I listened for a long time to the tape of that session, it was so important to me. It got to the soul of my being, so much that it gave me a chill. It dealt with my saying no and being invaded, my fear and my moaning and breathing. Each time I listened, I found new meaning and was so overwhelmed by emotion that I couldn't listen longer than fifteen or twenty minutes. Then I'd stop and try to integrate it. Maybe one of the reasons I drift away and tune out is that I'm not accustomed to a great deal of emotion, of real feeling.

"Whenever I listened to the work that resulted in my expression of anger, I felt a tremendous sense of grounding. *It was so real I felt as though I were three years old, like it was happening right now.* When I heard the breathing portion, I really got in touch with the holding in my throat and wanted to spit or cough. It was really hard for me to stay with that part; it was almost more than I could take. But I did stay with it and what I learned was *how much interconnected the feelings are with my whole point of view, the way I meet the world, and have since I was very, very young.*"

Reliving the Past

Notice that we said that Jose "relived the experience" from his Primary Scenario. We say "relived" because, unlike remembering, which is most a verbal, cognitive process, it is a profound body/mind experience involving all the senses — sight, hearing, smell, taste, touch. Simply remembering doesn't reach most of our early experiences because we had them before we had language. We retain the feelings in our bodies, feelings of warmth, of being loved, of feeling fear, of unrelieved or inflicted pain. When the feelings are negative ones, they have often been more or less blocked off by our defensive muscular holding patterns. Therefore, they are doubly hard to retrieve — not only are they unavailable verbally as are later memories, but they are hidden by the body itself. The process is like that of an oyster, which, irritated by a grain of sand, coats it with minerals till it's smooth and non-irritating. At the time of the initial irritation, the oyster didn't know any more than a small human child would what caused the pain, nor could it have explained why or how it was sealing it off. We sometimes think of these hidden, encapsulated experiences as "treasured tragedies," our personal pearls.

There are advantages in the effective way oysters deal with their pain, but the human parallel has its drawbacks. Year after year, the sealed-off irritant blocks the free flow of energy through the body, and it may restrict the normal range of feelings. The more painful the initial wound, the tighter the muscular defense and the less accessible the feelings hidden there. Because the energy is blocked by this knot of muscles, it's unavailable. So are the feelings. This makes for a more or less unnatural set of reactions to the world and other people. The pattern becomes established early in life and persists throughout it. It's visible in some people: hunched shoulders, a tightly held body that can't relax, a chronic stiff neck. But often it's not that obvious physically, and we have to look for the patterns in their behavior.

It's easy to give examples of the consistency in holding, repetitive patterns. Mabel, a dignified lady of fifty, was clearly "strait-laced." She could hardly breathe. her chest had an old, massive scar on it, leading us to suspect a traumatic injury or surgery, but she dismissed it as trivial. She had chronic bouts with asthma, but the tightness in her chest wasn't limited to her lungs. Her "heart" was involved, too, if you will, for she had never felt much love or affections for other people, nor much sexual energy. In therapy sessions, especially the breathing sesions (described later under Methods), she invariably "split off"; that is, her attention swerved away from the feelings evoked by the process. When a person splits off, he has reverted to his normal defensive pattern. This is a clue that overwhelming feelings are emerging, and the therapist must coax the client slowly back to the point at which his attention veered away. One day Mabel was able to stay with the breathing exercise, and, as a result, confronted a terrifying sensation of dying. This wasn't a sensation caused by the breathing exercises, but was her very own feeling of dying, a feeling she had had forty-seven years before and kept buried her entire life.

The situation wasn't an uncommon one in the days before antibiotics. Mabel's mother was treating her badly congested chest with a mustard plaster. The plaster was too hot, but the mother's thoughts, always easily distracted, were already far away from her little girl. The little girl, shocked into terror by the pain, was unable to cry out. Even at three she knew the futility of trying to get her mother's attention under normal circumstances, and she lay under the mustard plaster, burning, sure that death was near, and just as sure that her mother could care less. Her mother was actually horrified and contrite when she discovered the burn, but Mabel was far more traumatized by the psychic scars than by the physical ones.

Reliving the trauma as an adult, she could accept the harsh reality that her mother never had been really there for her as a child. She understood her lifelong feelings of isolation. The tension in her chest began to release and with its release came the flow of energy she needed to express love and sexuality.

Another example was Ginger. At thirty- seven, she had the body and mannerisms of a child. She spoke in a high, little girl voice and had a rigid torso and pelvis that barely moved at all. Her clothes were a little too ruffled and too cute for a woman her age; she didn't wear her childlikeness well. She had had many years of conventional therapy, but the cause of her undeveloped body wasn't uncovered until she came into IBP. It turned out that she had had a severe childhood disease requiring her to be in a full body cast from the time she was four till she was six. She was carried everywhere or moved about in a baby stroller. When she was able to relive this highly inhibiting experience, she was able to get back into her body and release it from the cast. She herself broke away from its confinement.

When a person relives an experience, feeling again exactly the fears, pains, and doubts, he takes with him something that makes a difference— his adult perspective, intellect, ego, and his language. While he is putting himself back into exactly the same spot, he now is a different person, a person with powers the small child didn't have in the same spot. As an adult, in the same wretched predicament as a child with limited powers of awareness, strength, or language, he is able to extricate himself. For instance, Sam, at three, had fallen in a stable and landed in a space between two bales of hay. He was too small to climb out and the hay muffled his cries for help, so he spent a frightened half- hour before someone came to look. As an adult, casting himself back into the stable, he relived that time. He smelled the rich, dusty fragrance, heard the flies buzzing, felt the prickly hay, saw the high walls of the bales, and tasted the bits of hay that had stuck in his mouth when he fell. With it, he felt the panic, the sense of abandonment, the hopelessness of his position. Once he had recaptured the feelings, we asked what he was going to do — let the kid languish there or get him out? "I'm getting him out," he announced, and being his adult self, climbed easily up over the bales and out to freedom. It doesn't matter that it's not entirely logical. What's important is that, in the presence of the therapist, the person relives a point of extreme emotional discomfort with his adult perceptions and skills. This allows him to cope with a situation that was devastating to himself as a child. While he may not be able to ease a physical problem, like the little Ginger forced to be in a body cast, he *can* deal with the emotional aspects of the problem. Mabel, for instance, in reliving her unfortunate treatment with the mustard plaster, accepted her mother's detachment, but didn't allow it to result in emotional injury.

This technique breaks the spell of the past. The tension in the body and the associated feelings are finally released and the character structure loses its rigidity. This is a basic assumption of IBP — that, although a person seems trapped in repetitive patterns for life, the patterns are actually interruptible through therapy.

Obsolete Responses to the Past

T.S. Eliot, in *The Cocktail Party*, said that "people are a set of obsolete responses." We think he must have seen the same things we see in people: their character structures, fixed at an early age, programming them throughout life in the same patterns, over and over, whether appropriate or not. Our work is aimed at interrupting these patterns and changing the programs. Another basic assumption in our work is that, although the past cannot be eliminated, the present can begin to include new responses. Through IBP, a person can understand what his past meant to him in terms of his present behavior. He can relive it and begin to break down its effect on the negative parts of his behavior. He can't eliminate it, but with awareness, it can be a useful signal to stop his easy slide back into his spiraling pattern. When he meets a situation in his adult life that makes him lapse into self-defeating behavior, this signals him that he learned that behavior as a child and it is no longer necessary. The grown-up Sam who had fallen among the bales of hay as a child, for instance, found that apparently unsolvable problems at work made him want to cry hopelessly. Now, confronted by such a problem, he remembers that he *was* hopeless as a kid. The hopelessness stemmed from his early realization that his mother didn't pay much attention to him. Whether he was trapped in the hay or in any other trouble, he was pretty much on his own. In reliving one such situation, he first acknowledged the pain his mother's neglect and then helped himself get out of trouble. "What happens now," he said much later, "is that I first feel the despair and maybe even the tears in my eyes but, instead of just collapsing, I remember myself climbing out of the hay. It didn't matter that my mother didn't know or care where I was because I got myself out. And it doesn't matter now. I'm not dependent on her at all because I'm perfectly capable of taking care of myself. Of course, I still wish she'd cared. . . ." Sam uses his new awareness to trigger his choice of new responses over the obsolete responses from his past.

It's also important for our clients to relive experiences of great pleasure, contentment, and happy endings. Immersing oneself once again in the dizzy excitement of childhood games, the thrill of Christmas morning, the warmth of bedtime stories, the security of family gatherings, or the serenity of evening walks down the road helps build a sense of well-being. The adult perspective of such simple pleasures never diminishes them. "It's funny," said one lady, "when I told you about climbing the hill to watch the sunset, I said it was something we *always* did, and it was one of the dearest memories of my childhood. But now that I look back and do some figuring, I realize that we couldn't have done it more than ten or twenty times in my life, yet it's as important as if it were really the way I remember it."

The Healing Relationship

Another basic assumption in IBP is that a necessary aspect of the healing process is the relationship between client and therapist. The Primary Scenario occurred within a relationship and it is within a relationship that a person must learn to deal with or transcend his Primary Scenario. Merely reliving early negative experiences isn't sufficient, or one could simply do it alone. Doing it alone won't work because the character structure built into his body that has determined his behavior patterns won't let him get very far away emotionally from the situation. Despite the distance in time and additional skills of the adult, he is still the adult that grew from that traumatized child. He needs the different perspective and the different emotional context provided by the therapist.

Remember that a child's problems develop within a relationship and that relationships differ. Two years in a body cast were devastating to Ginger but might have affected another child no further than the actual physical effects. The effects are partly individual and partly due to the relationships between children and their parents. A fearful parent will teach a child fear while another one will teach him that things will probably turn out all right. Ginger's mother, instead of despairing aloud that her child might never get well, could have talked about how much fun they would have when the cast was cut off for good. Ginger retained her mother's attitude as part of herself and never allowed herself to grow up until she was thirty- seven years old.

That's why the therapist's role is necessary. We all carry our parents around inside of us. Their presence is always felt, still nagging, praising, threatening, judging, advising. To the extent that our parents were wise and loving, their presence is useful, as well as pleasant company, In therapy, we call this the "positive introject." When the parents are unwise, insensitive, harsh, unloving, or misguided, their presence is detrimental (the "negative introject"). They stop us from doing things we would like to do, hinder our actions, stifle our reactions. They prompt our habitual responses, whether appropriate or not.

In the therapeutic reliving experience, the therapist guides his client through his early feelings and stays with him as a positive presence to counter any negative presence. For instance, when Sam was reliving his helpless sense of abandonment in the hay, the therapist provided a sensitive, empathetic and supportive atmosphere in which Sam would not feel inhibited in reliving the painful experience. The therapist said, "tell me what it's like down there."

"I'm scared," said Sam. "Scared and alone. . . very alone."

"Tell me more," the therapist said.

"No one is around," he replied in a weepy, trembling voice.

"That must be terrible for you," said the therapist.

"Yes, I've always felt alone," Sam said. "This is not a new feeling. My mother was never there for me." He continued, "She doesn't love me. . . she doesn't care. . . ," and he cried, not in the resigned sadness of an adult, but in the wrenching sobs of a small, neglected child.

The therapist stayed with Sam, showing that he understood how Sam was feeling and how it made perfect sense for him to feel that way. Now that Sam was an adult he could look back and feel compassion for the little boy, but at the same time, he could realize that the overwhelming helpless feelings of the abandoned child need not be brought into the present situation. The therapist pointed out

that the uncaring mother whose presence was with him as a child was
still with him. He substituted a new, positive introject for the negative
one — his own caring and encouraging voice. Gradually, a positive
sense of Self emerged in Sam, and at the same time, a strong sense of
well-being was developing in his body. He no longer needed to cling
to the unfulfilled longings of the past.

The ideal result of therapy is to free a person of the blocks to his
energy, to make a clear channel in which that energy flows freely.
This gives him a sense of identity or Self, a knowledge of "who he is,"
and lets him express that self in a creative, fulfilling way. He
becomes able to live his life for the moment, fully, as though each
day were his last.

There are many tools used in therapy, some mentioned already
and others to be mentioned later on, that aid in the process just
described. The body work is essential in locating holding patterns and
relating early experiences to present behavior and developing a sense
of Self and well-being in the body. Keeping a journal is a powerful
tool. The therapist follows the process, listening with sensitivity and
understanding. As we said earlier, one person's energy field can
affect that of another person. The tone and manner of the therapist
— his entire response pattern — can create an atmosphere of acceptance that fosters openness and self-acceptance and trust in the
client. His energy can trigger the client's own flow of energy.

Once triggered and allowed to flow freely, a person's energy lets
him feel, not only whole, but connected to his fellow man, to the
whole universe. With clarity, he can see more meaning in life and live
it in a fuller and more satisfying way. To the extent that he can
sustain this clarity, he experiences "enlightment," and walks the
same path as Buddha or Christ.

Therefore, we believe that enlightenment occurs as a neurophysio-
logical event. There is no place to go; there is only here and now;
here and now is in our bodies! We open the body and awaken the
energy within. This reveals the potential for growth of the arising
consciousness of the sense of Self. We have added to Reich's theory
the concept of the universe and the transformation of consciousness.
Transformation of consciousness occurs not as an idea, but in the
body. As we release the body's character armor, as our emotional
responses become more flexible, as we broaden our concept of who
we are, and as body, emotions, and mind become integrated, we
experience the transformation of our being. The content of our life
remains the same, but it is experienced from the new context of
integrated mind/body and of the constituted Self.

We hope in this book to share our knowledge, to expand current psychological thought, and to offer a unique and powerful psychotherapeutic method, which has been very exciting for us to develop.

> To come from my core of essence
> the center of being and significance
>
> And to share that inner light and joy
> with my fellow man by my own
> expression and form
>
> All else in accomplishment
> is shallow and of little lasting
> significance
>
> *Jack Rosenberg*

Chapter 2
The Beginning: The Basic Tools of Integrative Body Psychotherapy

The first step in IBP is getting acquainted: we must get to know each new client and set the atmosphere for a new journey inward in which the client learns to take care of his emotional and physical health and develops a working alliance with the therapist. To this end we have a few basic tools. These are not our therapy techniques, which we discuss at length in subsequent chapters, but some simple diagnostic tools for building a foundation for therapy. With these tools we begin to get to know a person and his body. We learn to see the effect that emotional and physical trauma has had on him and how it has formed the character structure lodged in his body. We start by taking a physical history, and then we look at what foods and drugs he puts into his body and how he exercises, if at all. To the end of re- acquainting him with himself, we ask him to start keeping a journal.

Physical History

A woman named Anne brought home to us the necessity of taking a physical history. She came to an IBP therapist shaking so badly she could hardly light her cigarettes. She complained of extreme nervousness and irritability, insomnia, and difficulty in getting along with people. It turned out that Anne had gone to a psychiatrist a year before for the same complaints. He had diagnosed her condition as an anxiety disorder, prescribed Valium, and had her come in for therapy four times a week. By the end of the year, in addition to her original complaints, she was not only a lot poorer, but also hooked on Valium. Questioning revealed that Anne drank at least twelve cups of coffee and smoked three packs of cigarettes each day and relied heavily on the Valium, which was now an additional concern.

With the gradual cessation of these toxic indulgences and a medically supervised withdrawal from Valium, her initial complaints were greatly reduced in a matter of a few weeks. She still had difficulty getting along with people, though, and her interpersonal relationships became the focus of her therapy.

Because we work with the body as well as the mind in IBP, it would be not only impossible but irresponsible to attempt to work with a person without knowing what has happened to his body in the past, as well as what is happening to it in the present. Therefore, we take a physical history, similar to the medical history that a physician takes, but with a different purpose: to learn the psychological implications of physiological trauma. This history does not replace a medical history, but is an adjunct to it. If a client hasn't had a medical examination in the past year, and we have any reason to suspect that he might need one, we might require that he have one, referring him to a physician with a body-mind orientation.

The physical examination should include an electrocardiogram to ascertain cardiovascular difficulties and a complete blood count to find out about thyroid, cholesterol, and triglyceride levels, anemia, and any infections. IBP is a powerful therapy and, as such, can be stressful. Before stressing someone's body, we need to know its limits.

If a person is currently under a physician's care, we might want to consult with that doctor before the client begins body therapy. Sometimes we discover conditions that we think need to be treated by a physician. For example, some examples of anxiety can be very severe: shortness of breath, nausea, tachycardia, and loss of consciousness. If there is any question at all, we want a medical doctor to rule out an organic cause before we proceed with the body work. Only then can we proceed with confidence, knowing that the body work, though stressful, won't be dangerous. We also supplement our treatment, when necessary, with treatment by adjunctive professionals such as speech therapists, educational therapists, gynocologists, chiropractors, Rolfers, nutritionists, and dentists.

Besides physical conditions themselves, we pay careful attention to the timing of illnesses. We want to know what was going on in a person's life at the onset of any illness — where was he living? What was his family doing? What was the economic and political climate? National and worldwide conditions and philosophies can affect even the young person whose life is bounded by his family— the Depression, for example, and the second World War. The child-rearing practices of the culture affect one, whether it's the "feed-every-four-hours and don't-touch-in-between" rule of the thirties in America or the immediate immersion of newborns in cold water that some primitive tribes practice. Famines, holocausts, civil wars, and social welfare plans affect children and adults alike.

Besides the milieu in which a person was living when he became ill, we need to know what was happening in his personal life. Had he graduated from college recently? Had he been married or divorced? Had a parent or good friend died? Had he had any car accidents or seen his house burn down? Had he won the Nobel Prize? Very often, as life changes occur, physical disease or symptomology follow, sometimes immediately, sometimes within the year. The Holmes scale (Figure 1) which lists significant life events and offers a rating of their contribution to susceptibility to illness, supports statistically what we see again and again in our practice: physical illnesses are often an attempt on a physical level to regain equilibrium after an emotional event, even such positive events as marriage or the birth of a child. People tend to repress or attempt to erase from memory the emotional trauma surrounding illness or injury, but the emotion continues to influence behavior. We must ask questions, even when they are painful, because our clients need to be aware of the emotional component of their physical illnesses, since that may be a source of repetitive patterns in their lives.

Jolene, for instance, always seemed to be getting sick. She didn't seem miserable about it. She seemed slightly worried, perhaps, about running out of sick leave or missing parties, but in general, she seemed to enjoy it. She talked fondly about her husband coming in to fluff up the pillows and bring her orange juice, and about which neighbors had brought in the chicken soup. She knew six specialists by their first names and exchanged crochet patterns with their receptionists, but she denied that she liked being sick. During her physical history, however, she told us about recurrent attacks of sinusitis that had started when she was a child. She recounts her first memory of a severe sinus attack:

> "My grandmother had died suddenly. She took care of me when Mother worked, so everything was in an uproar. I was sent off to summer camp while Mother looked for a nanny, but I got so sick the second day that they sent me home again. Mother had to stay home after all and put warm washcloths on my forehead to ease the pain."

Figure 1: The Holmes Social Readjustment Rating Scale
*A list of significant life events with a rating of
their contribution to susceptibility to illness.*

RANK	LIFE EVENT	LIFE CRISIS UNITS
1.	Death of spouse	100
2.	Divorce	73
3.	Marital separation	65
4.	Detention in jail or other institution	63
5.	Death of a close family member	63
6.	Major personal injury or illness	53
7.	Marriage	50
8.	Being fired at work	47
9.	Marital reconciliation	45
10.	Retirement	45
11.	Major change in health or behavior of a family member	44
12.	Pregnancy	40
13.	Sex difficulties	39
14.	Gain of new family member	39
15.	Business readjustment	39
16.	Change in financial state	38
17.	Death of a close friend	37
18.	Change to different line of work	36
19.	Change in number of arguments with spouse	35
20.	Taking out a mortgage or loan for a major purchase	31
21.	Foreclosure of mortgage or loan	30
22.	Change in responsibilities at work	29
23.	Son or daughter leaving home	29
24.	Trouble with in-laws	29
25.	Outstanding personal achievement	28
26.	Wife begins or stops work	26
27.	Begin or end school	26
28.	Change in living conditions	25
29.	Revision of personal habits	24
30.	Trouble with boss	23
31.	Change in work hours or conditions	20
32.	Change in residence	20
33.	Change in school	20
34.	Change in recreation	19
35.	Change in church activities	19
36.	Change in social activities	18
37.	Mortgage or loan less than $10,000	17
38.	Major change in sleeping habits	16
39.	Major change in number of family get-togethers	15
40.	Major change in eating habits	15
41.	Vacation	13
42.	Christmas	12
43.	Minor violations of the law	11

Reprinted with permission from Holmes, T.H., and Rahe, R.H., "The Social Readjustment Rating Scale," *Journal of Psychosomatic Research*, 11: 213–218, 1967, Pergamon Press Inc.

In remembering her childhood illness, Jolene uncovered her pattern. The child's heartbreaking loss of her grandmother had been overlooked by her mother in the desperation of finding a replacement babysitter. The mother not only didn't soothe the child's feelings, but she sent the child away from home when she most needed the comfort of familiar things and people who should have been able to share the pain over the grandmother's death. The eruption of sinusitis brought Jolene the nurturing she needed. It was an effective lesson, one she used well into adult life, until she learned better ways to get soothing care from other people.

How We Take the History

We have organized the IBP psycho-physical history to follow the body segments in Reich's scheme and to correspond to the body's physiological systems. If we look at the body this way, it becomes clear that trauma in each segment is important, because protective armoring will occur where there has been an injury, surgery, or illness. This armoring or chronic tension will block the flow of energy in the body, predisposing that body segment to disease. For example, we may find a diaphragm block in a person who has an ulcer or other digestive problem. Conversely, an illness may develop in an area that is blocked. The physical history gives us clues as to what to look for.

A simplifed way to collect and organize data is to begin at the top with the head and work down the body, asking questions as you go. The following diagram and lists of systems with their possible complications serve as aids in our questioning.

Figure 2: The Body Systems and Related Problems

1. Brain, Nervous Systems: Epilepsy (seizure disorder), dizziness, fainting, syncope, light-headedness, headaches

2. Vision: Myopia, hyperopia, cataracts, glaucoma, other vision problems

3. Auditory: Hearing problems, hearing aids, chronic ear infections, inner ear imbalance

4. Respiratory (nose, trachea, bronchi, and lungs): Chronic throat infections, allergies, sinusitis, bronchitis, rhinitis, chronic colds and/or coughs, asthma, other breathing disorders

5. Digestion (mouth, throat, esophagus): Communication, aggression, nutrition, sexuality, thumb-sucking, nail-biting, oral surgery, oral appliances, thyroid and parathyroid glands, neck and shoulder pain and tension

6. Circulatory (heart, veins, and arteries): Heart problems, heart attack, tachycardia, varicose veins, irregular heartbeat, heart murmur, blood pressure, chest surgery, breast lumps

7., 8., 9. Diaphragm and Abdomen: Ulcers, gastritis, hernia, intestinal inflammation, appendicitis, colitis, irregularity, diarrhea, constipation, abdominal surgery, kidney, liver or gallbladder problems, nutrition and diet

10. Pelvic (reproduction, genitals, lower abdomen, lower back): Sexual trauma (rape, incest, abortion, etc.), sexual dysfunction, cystitis, pelvic surgery (hysterectomy), vasectomy, menstruation, menopause, pregnancy, miscarriage, prostate problems, urinary infections

The head. At the head, for instance, we ask about migraines and other headaches. What time of day or night do they occur? When did you begin having them? What was happening in your life at the time they began? What part of your head hurts? Is it unilateral or on both sides? The location of a headache tells us where the blockage or tension is. Pain in the front or forehead may have to do with the eyes; at the back it might mean tension and holding in the neck and back. True physical symptoms tend to occur in only one place, while hysterical symptoms are more generalized and do not follow neural pathways.

Many people accept headaches as normal ways of dealing with the stress of premenstrual tension, overwork, and the stress of daily living. These headaches are often learned responses to stressful situations and are excellent clues to the person's own ways of dealing with stress.

People have learned to accept their headaches and to see them as medical problems, to be treated with drugs, rather than to see them as physical manifestations of emotions and to deal with the emotions directly instead of with the symptoms they produce.

We ask about any history of dizziness, fainting, lightheadedness, or loss of coordination or consciousness. These can be cases in which we need a physician to rule out organic explanations. We need to know if the client has ever had a seizure. Epileptic seizure can be triggered by emotional stress or by increased oxygenation, and the breathing work, therefore, would be contraindicated by a history of seizure. If there were a history of seizure, we would ask when he had his first seizure, what was going on in his life at the time, when was his last seizure, and so on.

The eyes and ears. Trauma and tension in the head may also be

Figure 3. The Body Systems and Reichian Segments

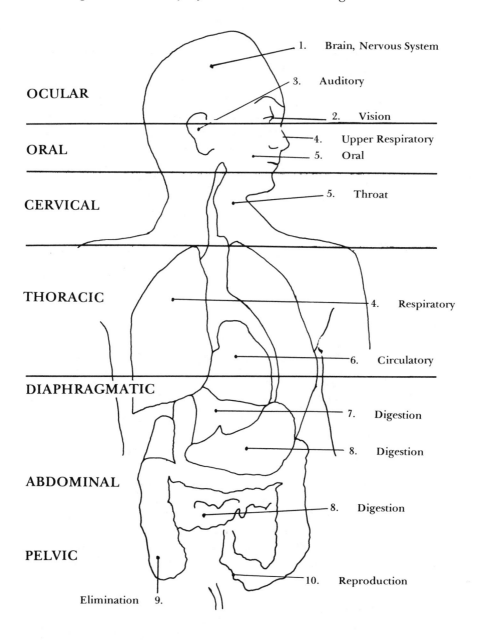

OCULAR

1. Brain, Nervous System

3. Auditory

2. Vision

ORAL

4. Upper Respiratory
5. Oral

CERVICAL

5. Throat

THORACIC

4. Respiratory

6. Circulatory

DIAPHRAGMATIC

7. Digestion

8. Digestion

ABDOMINAL

8. Digestion

PELVIC

10. Reproduction

Elimination 9.

related to hair transplants, mastoid operations, ear infections, hearing aids, cosmetic surgery, dental problems, or problems with vision. Most people are reluctant to admit that vision problems may be emotionally related, but it is common to find that changes in vision occur at such times as divorce, death of a parent, birth of a sibling, etc. The same thing is true of hearing problems. People choose not to see or hear things that disturb them. We want to help them find less destructive ways of dealing wtih problems, hopefully before an irreversible process of somatization has begun. Chronic eye or ear infections, cataracts, strabismus, and muscle weakness suggest how a person may be dealing with emotional problems. Even blurred vision and loss of central vision, though normally associated with physiological problems, may also be emotionally caused. The fact that parents may also have a history of similar symptoms may not reveal a hereditary physical problem so much as a learned response to dealing with emotional problems. It's also useful to know if a person is myopic or hyperopic (nearsighted or farsighted). This provides a small clue as to how a person uses his energy in relation to the environment.

The nose. Here we start the questions about the respiratory system. "Do you have a history of sinusitis? Bronchitis? Rhinitis (or head cold)? Allergies? T. B.? Punctured or collapsed lung? Anything else? A positive history tips the therapist off to a possible holding pattern. A history of asthma is especially interesting because asthma usually has a strong emotional component. Even if a person has outgrown asthma, the body regresses during breathing work and the old patterns may emerge, raising the likelihood of his having an attack during breathing work. This is not particularly dangerous if the condition is not severe. IBP therapists are trained to help clients learn new breathing patterns that relieve asthma if and when it occurs and to work with the underlying emotional problem. Anyone currently using medication for asthma should bring it to therapy. An attack during a therapy session is more a felicitous occurrence than a dangerous one, for it helps recover the trauma that may have triggered the asthma in the first place. This happened to Dana, a man of about forty-five who hadn't had an attack in years. When he was able to quit gasping and wheezing, he related a story about himself when he was five.

> "My mother was always very busy away from home. She didn't work, but she was always going out to lunch or shopping or somewhere. She'd promised me that we'd make cookies one

afternoon that week, but she kept going away till the week was almost gone. It must have been a vacation of some sort because I really felt that the week was going to be over and there'd be no cookies and no mother, either. Then she got in the car, again, scraping me off her skirts, and drove out the driveway. The car belched and bounced down the block and I chased her, pathetically trying to keep up. . . reaching my arms out to her. . . calling God knows what in an attempt to get her back. But instead of stopping at the corner as I'd prayed, she kept going, and I thought my heart would break as I watched the Model A travel away from me. I was out of breath and had this terrible pain in my chest and I just threw myself down in the gravel and cried and I couldn't catch my breath and started gasping. She *couldn't* have *heard* me gasping — that old car made way too much noise — but she came back. It must have been a miracle for nothing less would have deflected my mother from her intended course. She came back and took care of me all afternoon. She called the doctor, made me rest, and we finally made the cookies!"

To this day, Dana deals with separation anxieties the same way. The difference is that the minute he starts to wheeze and gasp, he recognizes his pattern. He takes a look at what is causing the anxiety and deals with it directly. If it is his girlfriend leaving town to visit an aunt or his secretary taking a vacation, he laughs ruefully at himself. He wouldn't dream of forcing them to stay, so there is no need for an asthma attack and he doesn't have one. He uses the symptom as a way of recognizing that his abandonment anxiety has been triggered.

The mouth. This is an important area related to personal expression, communication, sexuality, aggression, and nutrition. We'll discuss nutrition in the next section of this chapter. Here we ask about injuries to the mouth, thumb-sucking, nail-biting, dental braces, and oral appliances or dental protheses.

Infantile sucking past the normal time for it to cease (about six years), might be a clue to the problems in the early mother-child relationship. This oral pattern is a child's attempt to soothe his emotional pain. Even after it ceases, it may reappear in the face of pain — when the mother goes to the hospital to have another baby, for instance, or when the client confronts his emotional past during IBP work. Few adults suck their thumbs in normal circumstances, but sucking pipes, smoking cigarettes, chewing on cigars, or "just having a coupla' drinks" may be the socially acceptable equivalent. Unless the therapist has a body orientation and systematically elicits this information from the client, these behaviors may not be seen as relating to deep psychological needs. Many important behavioral clues are missed because this type of information isn't asked for. Such clues can shorten therapy and help a client deal sooner with the emotions underlying his behavior.

Dental braces often cause people to develop distortions of the face in order not to show them. They stop smiling altogether or they tighten their lips to hide the braces or otherwise react to their presence. Ill-fitting oral appliances also cause people to develop fixed muscular patterns in their mouths to compensate. Trauma of oral surgery and any missing or discolored teeth may also underlie fixed expressions of the mouth. During body work, these patterns are released and a person's whole expression can change for the better.

From a procedural point of view, we must know about any oral appliances, bridges, or dentures because body work may involve biting or clenching the teeth which could damage the dentures.

The throat. There are many vital structures in the throat. We ask about throat infections, tonsilitis, tonsilectomies, hoarseness, tightness and constriction, difficulty in swallowing, and voice changes in adolescence, some of which could have strong emotional components as well as physical ones. We also want to know about glandular imbalances. Many people are taking thyroid supplements unnecessarily to make up for a low output, for weight reduction, or as a mood elevator. This can inhibit the functioning of the thyroid gland itself. It becomes dependent on the supplement and slows its output. In IBP, with our focus on nutrition, exercise, and on breathing work, a person's energy and aliveness return. When this happens, the thyroid supplement may need to be reduced to prevent hyperthyroidism (shaking, tachycardia, etc.).

The parathyroid gland regulates the calcium levels of the blood. Nervousness or hypersensitivity may be a symptom of calcium deficiency. Since breathing influences blood calcium levels, muscle spasms may occur during the breathing work, suggesting possible calcium deficiency or parathyroid problem.

The neck. It is imperative that we work with the back and the front of the body at the same time, so, after we finish with the throat, we start with the neck. This is an area of chronic tension in most people.

It's also vulnerable to injury such as whiplash. Any tension or misalignment can cause problems all up and down the spine, for the head is a heavy load and must be perfectly balanced atop the spine. For IBP work we need to know about any injuries or chronic pain because body work can be strenuous and we must be aware of any area that's already sensitive.

The back. For some reason, the back seems easy to forget, but it has enormous importance, as anyone knows who has ever had a backache. We make sure we know of any spinal or muscular problems before we begin body work so as to avoid re-injury. Tension in the back can reveal problems in the front and vice versa. Tense shoulders indicate held emotions such as fear and a protective attitude, as well as a sense of carrying a burden. Shoulder injuries form a protective armoring, and we must remember to ask about them in our history-taking. This is an emotion-laden area and mustn't be forgotten.

The heart. Many complications of the circulatory system, especially the heart, have psychological significance. When people suffer emotional injuries, symptoms sometimes show up in the circulatory system. Our questioning here covers blood pressure, history of heart attack, angina, tachycardia, heart murmur, irregular heart beat, and pains in the extremities. Extremes in blood pressure— either high or low— can indicate emotional problems related to stress, poor diet, and lack of exercise. The breathing work can balance the autonomic nervous system (ANS). By stimulating one part of it— the sympathetic nervous system— we can raise the blood pressure and by stimulating the other part— the parasympathetic nervous system— we can lower the blood pressure. However, severe heart problems or extreme blood pressure levels could contraindicate the work. Timing of the onset of heart problems is important. Also, the correlation of Type A behavior and heart disease must be considered.

Figure 4: Characteristics of the Type A Person

Do you:

☐ Have a habit of explosively accentuating various key words in ordinary speech even when there is no need for such accentuation?

Shortened and adapted from Meyer Friedman and Ray H. Rosenman, *Type A Behavior and Your Heart*, copyrighted by Meyer Friedman, 1974, and reprinted by permission from Alfred A. Knopf, Inc., New York.

- ☐ Finish other persons' sentences for them?
- ☐ *Always* move, walk, and eat rapidly?
- ☐ Become easily angered by slow-moving lines or traffic?
- ☐ Quickly skim reading material and prefer summaries or condensations of books?
- ☐ Feel an impatience with the rate at which most events take place?
- ☐ Tend to be unaware of the details or beauty of your surroundings?
- ☐ Frequently strive to think of or do two or more things simultaneously?
- ☐ Almost always feel vaguely guilty when you relax, vacation, or do absolutely nothing for several days?
- ☐ Tend to evaluate your worth in quantitave terms (number of A's earned, amount of income, number of games won, etc.)?
- ☐ Have nervous gestures or muscle twitches such as grinding your teeth, clenching your fists, or drumming your fingers?
- ☐ Attempt to schedule more and more activities into less time, and in doing so make fewer allowances for unforeseen problems?
- ☐ Frequently think about other things while talking to someone?
- ☐ Repeatedly take on more responsibilities than you can comfortably handle?

The lungs, ribs, breasts, and diaphragm. Any questions about the respiratory system that weren't covered earlier should be asked now. Any chest surgery, even the removal of benign cysts or moles, is important. So is the breaking of ribs or clavicle, because trauma to this area can cause restricted breathing patterns. Milk secretion in a woman's breast when she is not nursing could be related to prolactin levels, which can decrease sexual desire. This is an example of an apparent sexual problem that can have a purely physical cause. However, unexplained milk secretion could also mean that a tumor in the pituitary gland is causing a rise in prolactin levels; this condition may indicate the need for an examination by a physician. Mammary cysts could be caused by nutritional imbalances, especially too much caffeine and sugar.

The thoracic segment includes the back, so we ask if there are chronic back pains, muscle spasms, or lumps. Any of these may be associated with emotional holding in this segment. When a person controls his emotions by holding his breath, he will develop a tight diaphragm and rib cage. A diaphragmatic block can also be caused by excessive use, as with people who sing professionally or who play wind instruments, dive, or practice advanced yoga techniques.

Cynthia, a professional singer, was in IBP therapy. She was particularly interested in anything to do with breathing techniques, and she practiced breathing exercises at home. One night she was practicing kundalini breathing, which involved very rapid, shallow breaths. Suddenly her chest was filled with pain. Certain it was a heart attack, her husband called the paramedics and she was rushed to the hospital. Once there, she was a mystery, with no evidence but pain for a heart problem. She had test after test for two days, with no conclusion. On the third day her IBP therapist visited her. She told him the story — how she had been breathing fast when the pain hit. The therapist suggested that her diaphragm had gone into spasm because of the rapid breathing. After treatment with massage, the contractions relaxed, the muscles released, and the pain subsided. Since breathing is central to our work, blockages in the diaphragm are important and of great emotional significance. They are also very common, along with a corresponding tightness in the spine. The diaphragm is unique in that it is the only place in the body where we have access to the autonomic nervous system through the central nervous system. That's why it's so important in IBP— we use the breathing techniques to influence and balance the autonomic nervous system.

A blocked diaphragm may also be related to digestive problems, ulcers, gastritis, inflammation of the intestines, or other problems. Stasis/stagnation can result from a rigid diaphragm because the movement of the normal diaphragm presses and releases constantly upon the stomach and intestines, massaging them gently.

The abdominal cavity. The digestive system is another area of emotional significance because it is so susceptible to psychosomatic disorders. We need to ask many questions about digestion, elimination, pain, and discomfort, as well as the history of any liver, gallbladder, and kidney problems because so many of them can be related to emotional reactions. Stress, for instance, creates havoc with digestion and many a bellyache can be traced directly to an emotional upset. Almost every symptom of the bowel has an emotional component, and many have a nutritional one as well. One of our clients had a severely spastic colon, giving him diarrhea every single day of his life since his youth. When we met him, he was in his late forties and still suffering. His controlling, rigid father died suddenly, thereby releasing him from the tyranny of nearly five decades. His symptoms ceased entirely, far too early in therapy for us to take any credit.

The pelvis. The pelvis is so important that it is featured in a separate chapter on sexuality. In taking a history, it is necessary to cover any possible trauma that has occurred in the pelvic area because of the likelihood of blockages. We routinely ask about catheterization, which is related to bladder and urinary problems. We ask women if they have had hysterectomies, pregnancies, miscarriages, abortions, D & Cs (dilation and curettage), and cystitis. We also ask about gynecological examinations in case there have been any traumatic ones, and, of course, about their experiences giving birth. The process of giving birth can be as traumatic to the mother as it is to the infant and may have lasting effects on both. We want to know, additionally, about any chronic menstrual and gynecological difficulties and about when menstruation began, as these can affect emotional attitudes about genitals and the pelvic area.

We ask men a different set of questions, including ones about nocturnal emissions. These can frighten a boy, especially if he had a history of bed wetting in his childhood. Then the sudden wet spot in the bed can rouse in him feelings of shame and embarrassment. We ask if he was circumsised and, if so, when (the later it was done, the more traumatic it would have been). Vasectomies and prostatitis are other traumatic events that can cause holding and tightening in the genital area.

Toilet training is a much more notorious source of later difficulties than other traumatic occurrences. Studies show that there is no completed neurological connection between the cortex and the anal sphincter muscle until the child is about eighteen months old. A child who is pressured earlier than that to control himself would have to do so by holding his breath and tightening the striated muscles of the pelvic floor, thereby tightening the whole area. This would be uncomfortable and the child would learn to shut off the discomfort. By doing so, the child would also shut off all feelings, and the resultant blockage could last throughout life. Another important emotional and physical memory connected with toilet training is found in people who suffered from enuresis (bed wetting) when they were children.

It is difficult to ask questions about a client's sexual history without seeming intrusive. Information about traumatic sexual experiences is seldom volunteered, though, so proceeding with caution and sensitivity, raising as little anxiety as possible, we ask. People are often reluctant to bring up things that have caused them anxiety, and sometimes they bury them so deeply that they forget what happened, unless they are reminded. Our credo is: *If you don't ask for the information, you won't get it.*

Shirley's case illustrates the truth of this credo. She had been in analytical therapy for three years prior to IBP. Among her other problems, she had trouble defecating. In thirteen years she had never had a bowel movement without an enema. During the routine questioning she was asked if she'd ever had an abortion. She looked puzzled for a moment, then said, "Oh yeah! I forgot about that." She went on:

"When I was eighteen I was a 'good' girl. I'd been going with my boyfriend for a year and we were both so good that we'd never really had sex, just fooled around. But finally one summer night we were making out in the back of his '54 Chevy and went all the way. Worst time of the month, too, and I got pregnant. I thought it was the end of the world. Abortions were illegal in those days. You could go risk your life in Tijuana or creep into some shady back office after hours. We knew all about it from the "True Confessions" magazines and I was scared to death.

"I went to a strange doctor who said, of course, that he couldn't do an abortion, but, if I happened to be bleeding already, he *could* do a dilation and curettage. He gave us the number of an old woman who met us in a warehouse down where all the fish canneries are and she used a crochet hook, just like they did in the magazines where the heroine always died or became sterile.

"It worked, sort of. I started bleeding after she worked the hook around in my uterus for a while. The next day I had a fever and was bleeding badly, I sneaked out of the house and went to the emergency hospital where they delivered a tiny fetus.

"I went home and went to bed, hoping the bleeding would stop, but it didn't. My mother kept pestering me with soup and tea and I was so scared I wanted to tell her all about it but didn't dare. Finally I had to. I was having terrible cramps and went to the bathroom in the middle of the night. When I bore down, instead of having a bowel movement as I expected, I pushed out a second fetus. It must have been dead since the old lady dug around with the crochet hook because it smelled bad and there was blood everywhere. I'd never seen so much blood. I screamed for my mother and she came in and helped me deliver the placenta, but she was screaming more than I was. It seemed that the volume of blood all over the toilet, the floor, the rug, the walls, and me was just exactly as reprehensible as her daughter having to have an abortion. *Her* daughter! She wrapped the fetus in a paper sack and threw it into the trash can. Then she cleaned up the bathroom. And, finally, she took me back to the hospital where they made sure I was cleaned out this time, but she didn' t speak to me for three weeks. She never mentioned it again and I' ve never told anybody till just now."

"Why not?" asked the therapist.

"Nobody ever asked." she replied.

"How long ago did it happen?" asked the therapist, having already figured it out.

"Well," she figured, "if I was eighteen then and I' m thirty-one now, it must have been thirteen years."

Suddenly her eyes widened slightly. "Thirteen years" she repeated. "Could that be it?" she asked, half to herself, half to the therapist.

With the association made, a little breathing work started releasing the holding pattern in her pelvis, and she began to have bowel movements without an enema. It was a simple connection, one that might have been made much earlier in her life had anybody thought to ask her if and when she had ever had an abortion. We try not to overlook obvious connections between symptoms and emotional events, and the best way is to make sure we get as much information as possible by asking pertinent questions.

The skin. Like the back, the skin also is of great physical and emotional importance and is often overlooked. The skin is the largest organ of the body and is often closely associated with allergies. Because the skin is our prime exposure to the world, its appearance affects our feelings about ourselves as well as people' s initial reactions towards us. Therefore, our questioning covers such potentially traumatic problems as skin allergies, eczema, sensitivities, rashes, and acne, which can have a profound effect upon social and psychological development.

In general. We ask about other traumatic life events: surgery, illness, accidents. We ask about a person' s birth, since the trauma of birth itself is an important factor in his later development. An infant emerges from the totally supportive, warm, nourishing environment of the womb into the noisy, bright atmosphere of the delivery room. Even before he takes his first breath, the separation from his mother and the assault on his senses can create negative imprints on the infant. Trauma can precede birth, for maternal trauma will affect the fetus, causing its body to adapt and to construct defensive behavior in response to harsh stimuli or threatening situations. Our work often deals with the early traumas that are re-lived when the breathing work stimulates them.

We always watch for the timing of illnesses and accidents. We ask the client what else was going on at the time, how he coped with the situation, what it meant to him, and what he thought his body was telling him with an illness. Conditions such as rheumatic fever, measles, scarlet fever, mumps, arthritis, diabetes, and hypoglycemia may bear directly on body chemistry or the autonomic nervous system imbalances and should be noted.

When we take the physical history, we store the information away for later use. Often, though, simply the asking of certain questions elicits emotional responses and we work with them superficially at the time (by acknowledging the emotions, for instance). We prefer to note the response and return to it during the actual body work when a person has a heightened awareness of his body and is feeling strong emotions. At that time we can make powerful connections for him between the emotions and the historical information gleaned during the earlier sessions. Often just making the connection causes a person to consciously give up his symptom or behavior. That was the case with Shirley, whose gruesome experience with an abortion had left her unable to have normal bowel movements. Later on, during body work, she was able to tie the feelings in her pelvis directly to her feelings about the abortion.

With another client, we might sense emptiness or loss while working in the pelvic area, which would remind us that she had once had an abortion. If we mention the abortion and ask her feelings about it, she might become aware of the feelings in her pelvis and associate them with the abortion. She may realize that she closed off her pelvis at the time of the abortion and, if she were willing to work through the feelings of loss during the therapy, she would be able to allow her pelvis to open again.

The history is important because it provides the therapist with a map showing him how to proceed. Any conditions that turn up that would contraindicate body therapy would simply be treated by other, less stressful methods such as sensory awareness, gentle movements, guided fantasy trips through the body, and verbal psychotherapeutic techniques, which can be used both with or without the body work.

During the physical history and the gathering of nutritional information, we make a general assessment of the client. Because everyone is so different, we have to decide on the direction and focus of therapy on an individual basis. In some cases we might refer him to a medical doctor, psychiatrist, or another psychotherapist with expertise in an appropriate area.

While we ask the client questions directly, we ask ourselves questions about him: What does he want from therapy? What does he think he's coming for? Why is he here? Does she have a strong sense of reality? Does he have delusions or hallucinations? The degree to which a person seems confused determines how cautiously we must proceed with the breathing work, as body work can increase confusion. Taking away the character structure, the support of the body and the identity it lends can be very disturbing to someone whose sense of reality and Self is already tenuous.

Is he split off (not "there")? Unable to look at you when he speaks? If you cannot maintain contact with a person, the breathing work will only cause panic, so the issue of contact must be worked with first ("Look at me," "Focus on the lamp, the clock, the table. . .," and so on).

How does he see the possibilities of body work? Is he convinced it will solve all his problems or does he doubt that it will help at all? It's important that a client understand that therapy leads, not to a miracle cure, but to his learning to take responsibility for his own life, his own cures. Only then will the body work begin to help, for body work is something a person must be ready for. If he isn't ready, the body work not only will not assist in the growth process but may actually hinder it.

We need to ask these questions as we go along. The answers we find by questioning and observing the client help us know how fast therapy can proceed, which techniques to use and which to avoid, and how cautious we must be in dealing with a person's character structure and his sense of identity.

Nutrition and Emotions

The only aspect of nutrition that we as therapists are interested in is how it affects the emotional well-being of our clients. We never intended, at the beginning, to involve ourselves in the nutrition of our clients but we found almost immediately that what they ate was sometimes as important as their early experiences. Even well-educated adults abuse their bodies. Although they read studies about students who learn better after well-balanced, protein-packed breakfasts and conscientiously feed their own children accordingly, they, themselves, come in with symptoms of nutritional deficiencies and imbalances. After some startling examples, we began questioning our clients about nutritional habits early in treatment, often before psychotherapy begins.

Sonia was one of these examples. She was a svelte lady in her late forties, elegantly dressed, well-coiffed, and delicately perfumed, but her hands shook and her eyes were frantic. She was terrified. Her moods ranged from nervous to hysterical, swinging back and forth so unpredictably that she thought she was going crazy.

Tipped off by her slim figure as much as by her symptoms, the therapist asked about her eating habits. As he had suspected, she was perennially on a diet. She had coffee and a doughnut in the morning followed by little more than fruit juices, diet soft drinks, and coffee throughout the day, until a light supper late in the evening. She consumed almost nothing each day but stimulants and refined carbohydrates. At our suggestion, she changed her diet, eliminating sugars and adding proteins and complex carbohydrates, and was soon able to report that her mood swings were much less violent and that she felt full of energy and alive again.

Changing her diet didn't solve all her problems, but it was a start. Her mood swings continued, though greatly reduced, so we sent her to a physician for hormonal and thyroid tests. Her progesterone level was very low, indicating that she'd begun to go into menopause, and her thyroid was low too. With minimal doses of the proper hormone supplements she was much improved within two weeks and her mood swings disappeared. By then it made sense to tackle the emotional problems concerning her divorce and her son's leaving home, but it wasn't these problems that had brought her into therapy. She had been driven in by such violent symptoms that her previous therapist had considered hospitalizing her, symptoms that proved to be physical and not psychological.

Occasionally we get a client who quickly grows impatient with our questions about his diet. Following our intuition, we often quiz these people the most. Many times their symptoms indicate immediately that their problems are partly nutritional (see list of hypoglycemia symptoms, for instance). Our prime concern is for our client's sense of well-being. The best therapy in the world won't make him feel better about himself if he habitually consumes food or drugs that affect his emotional well-being. Besides some of the universal relationships between diet and health, such as in hypoglycemia,

Figure 5:

Hypoglycemia: What Are the Facts

Do you experience several of these symptoms on a *regular* basis?

Exhaustion	Depression
Insomnia	Anxiety
Irritability	Headaches
Vertigo	Sweating
Crying spells	Tachycardia (palpitation of heart)
Muscle pain/ backache	Anorexia (significant lack of appetite)
Tremor (internal trembling)	Phobias (unjustified fears)
Difficulty in concentration	Numbness
Chronic indigestion	Mental confusion
Cold hands or feet	Blurred vision
Muscular twitching or cramps	Joint pain
Unsocial or antisocial behavior	Restlessness
Obesity	Staggering
Abdominal spasms	Fainting or blackouts
Convulsions	Suicidal tendencies

How many times have you been diagnosed as having nervous tension, having hypochondria, or worrying too much? You may be one of the thousands of people suffering from one of the most common yet most missed or misdiagnosed conditions in existence.

Hypoglycemia (low blood sugar, or hyperinsulinism) is a condition caused by the body's inability to properly metabolize sugar. It is the opposite of diabetes, which is high blood sugar or too much sugar remaining in the blood. Its symptoms are so varied and changeable that it mimics other disorders; thus it is often misdiagnosed. It often results from a combination of living in the stressful environment to which most of us are subjected and the overconsumption of sugar, which has become the American way of life (as a look at the ingredients of almost every package and can in the supermarket will show).

A correlation has been shown to exist betwen hypoglycemia and hyperactivity in children, emotional and mental disorders, asthma, hay fever, alcoholism, ulcers, violent crime, and car accidents, and it is suspected in drug abuse.

Reprinted by permission of the publisher, from *Hypolgycemia: A Better Approach*, Paavo Airola, Ph. D., Health Plus Publishers, Phoenix, Arizona 85028.

there are individual reactions to foods, sometimes amounting to definite allergies. Vitamin or mineral deficiencies can have pronounced effects. Certain heavy metal toxins known to be present in our bodies can inhibit certain metabolic functions, giving rise to an inefficient utilization of energy. A nutritional consultation may be indicated to help re- balance and stabilize the body chemistry.

In the meantime, we give each client Food Intake and Mood Cycle

Charts (Figure 6) and ask him to record everything he consumes for six days and to keep track of his moods and any exercise he does. It's very important to track the sequence of food-intake and mood. We want to know what happens when a person feels low: Does he eat? Smoke? Take aspirin? Sniff cocaine? Lose his appetite entirely? And then we want to know what happens after he does any of these things. Do they make him feel good? Bad? Worse? Better? And it's not just the *fact* of eating that needs to be correlated with his moods, but the *content* — what was eaten. What sorts of moods follow high protein meals? Sugary snacks? High fat foods? The correlations are fairly predictable, but carrying out this exercise for six days and seeing for himself the correspondence between mood and food is very convincing to the client.

The chart also asks for "place eaten." The situation in which one eats is significant. Many people eat on the run. They snatch at food in the kitchen and eat as they go out the front door, or they buy fast foods and eat in their cars. Sometimes they eat standing up and sometimes they eat while reading, oblivious to the food they're consuming. We know one lady who does both. She props the newspaper on the breadboard, sets her food in front of it, and digs in. If the food disappears before she finishes the paper, she replenishes it, but if she finishes the paper before her food, she's surprised at how full she feels and throws the rest of the food away. She is scarcely aware of what she is doing and confesses to occasional phantom hunger pangs when she forgets that she has already eaten. People who eat without much attention are so "split off" that they have little awareness of their food and are often not eating for nutritional needs but to fill an emotional hunger. The client who fills in the Food Intake and Mood Cycle Chart develops an awareness of the relationship of food and mood. When a client can *see* on a chart that he habitually eats sweet foods when he feels down and then always feels worse within two hours, he can begin to change the pattern. There is also the reassurance that comes from finding that what one supposes to be serious psychological disturbance is easily correctable. We often save months of psychotherapy through the use of this simple chart.

A physician who came into IBP treatment dramatically illustrated this. When asked about his nutrition, he said, "I'm not here for nutrition, I'm here for psychotherapy. I eat well and I take care of myself physically." The therapist, not wanting to push the client, and naively believing that he knew about nutrition, didn't pursue the matter at that time. The client's main symptom was depression. One day he came into his session, which happened to be at 4 PM, feeling in despair — everything was wrong with his life, there was no hope, there had never been any hope, he might just as well kill himself and get it over with. On this particular day, the therapist asked him what he had eaten for breakfast. Since he had worked a night shift the night before, he answered, "I just had coffee in the morning, and a salad at lunch," so the therapist got an apple, cut it into slices, and as the session progressed, he handed slices to the client. By the time the apple was finished the client felt much better. His expression and tone had radically changed. "You must think I'm crazy," he said, "but I can't remember what I was feeling so rotten about." He had refused to consider his nutrition as a factor in his emotional health until the dramatic results of this session.

Although he was an M. D. and perhaps should have known better, he had a typical emotional response to low blood sugar. Most people do not react as severely, but it is still a common pattern, caused by the reactions of the pancreas, which is over-reactive in many people. What happens is this: someone eats a breakfast of refined carbohydrates such as pastries or fruit juice. This puts a shot of sugar almost directly into his bloodstream. The pancreas reacts to the high blood sugar level by introducing insulin to lower the sugar level. It drops to normal then, but it keeps on dropping. You saw the list of symptoms of hypoglycemia — the person whose blood sugar continues to drop probably feels some combination of some of these symptoms. Then he gets some lunch. Even if he refrains from eating sweets, he's likely to consume more refined carbohydrates and fats in the form of fast foods, which raises the blood sugar level. Again, the pancreas supplies more insulin to reduce the blood sugar level and, again, it drops too much. The emotional symptoms reappear. This accounts for the afternoon fatigue, depression, or the "blahs" that many people feel even when not diagnosed as hypoglycemic.

To prevent these excessive highs and lows, one should eat proteins and complex carbohydrates. Instead of fruit juices, one should eat the whole fruit. Not only does a glass of orange juice contain the sugar content of several oranges — more than most people would eat comfortably at one time — but it lacks the pulp surrounding each droplet of juice. It is the work that the digestive system does on the packaging material of our foods that makes the difference. When we eat whole grains and the whole fruit instead of fruit juice we are getting complex carbohydrates instead of refined ones. Refined carbohydrates such as sugar enter the blood stream almost immediately upon ingestion, but the complex ones have to be processed for

Figure 6: Food Intake and Mood Cycle Chart

Day's Intake Considered:

Typical _____
More than usual _____
Less than usual _____

DIETARY INTAKE, DAY _____

NAME: _____
DATE: _____
DAY OF WEEK: _____

Time of day	AM/PM	MOOD 1 – 10	FOOD, DRINK, MEDICATION, DRUG		Place Eaten	Amount Eaten	Amt./type Exercise	Record Heart Rate	Don't Write In This Space
			Item	Description					

1985 Jack L. Rosenberg, Marjorie L. Rand, Diane Asay

a while. This prevents the sudden dumping of lots of sugar into the bloodstream that induces the pancreas to send in its insulin. Instead, the sugars are introduced slowly as they are broken down. The pancreas supplies just enough insulin to deal with the sugar that's there. A little more sugar enters and a little more insulin goes in to take care of it. This is a simplified description; you can read about metabolism of foodstuffs in any good nutrition book. We use Covert Bailey's *Fit or Fat?* for a highly readable and convincing guide to nutrition and exercise.[1]

We have focused on refined carbohydrate intake because this practice induces symptoms and this is what we are looking for. We do not attempt to be experts in nutrition, but are interested in specific imbalances which, when corrected, can support the IBP work.

When we work *with* our body, we generally feel and function much better. Simply understanding what happens when we dump in a lot of sugar helps us plan a better diet. Figure 7 shows the difference between a diet high in refined carbohydrates and one high in protein and complex (unrefined) carbohydrates.

Figure 7: Carbohydrates and Blood Sugar Levels

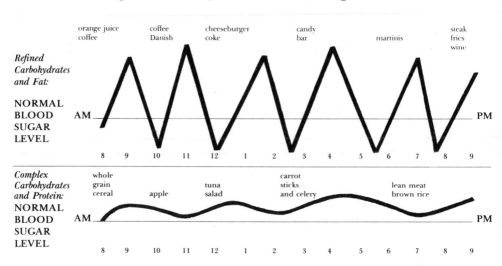

Notice that it is not just the quality of food eaten that differs between the person with the wide fluctuation in blood sugar level and the person with the steadier pattern. The one who maintains a more or less even level has snacks between meals — an apple or carrot sticks and celery or some light snack of complex carbohydrates.

Drugs

We include drugs in the section on nutrition because we are interested in any substance that enters our clients' bodies, whether it is introduced by a fork, a glass, a sniff, a cigarette, a syringe, or a suppository. As with our emphasis on food, it is not our intention to bring about great reforms in diet or drug use. Rather, we are concerned with the effects of foods and drugs on our clients' emotions and their sense of well- being. As we have shown, food intake can have an enormous effect on people. Drugs have a powerful effect, too, often far more devastating.

First we must know of any prescription drugs a client is taking and note any side effects as well as how long he has been taking it. Use of any non- prescription drugs (even vitamins and aspirin), marijuana, and the various psychoactive drugs must be indicated, as well as any history of drug or alcohol abuse. If the food chart is used correctly (and honestly), regular use of anything will show up on it.

Long term use or misuse of drugs can substantially alter body chemistry and emotional balance. Many people become virtually addicted to such non- prescription drugs as aspirin and coffee, not to mention alcohol, which is a depressant high in carbohydrates. These carbohydrates enter the bloodstream almost immediately upon ingestion and the pancreas responds as it does with fruit juice, by introducing insulin to lower the blood sugar level. Caffeine, found in large amounts in Anacin, No- Doz, black teas, coffee, and cola drinks, is a stimulant that must be repeatedly ingested for its effects to be maintained. When the stimulant stops, the body reacts by feeling even more depressed than it actually is. "Anxiety symptoms can be brought about by coffee drinking generally not considered excessive. One to three cups can produce an emotional reaction: even one cup of coffee contains ninety milligrams of caffeine," E. Cheraskin said in *Psychodietetics: Food As the Key to Emotional Health.*[2]

After doing the breathing work, our clients may have decreased tolerance for alcohol, sugars, and caffeine. The effects of these and other depressants and stimulants will be far greater than before the breathing work for two reasons. One is that the breathing work helps the body cleanse itself of toxins, making their effect more obvious. Another is that, as the person's awareness of his body increases, he notices imbalances more easily and will be less willing to tolerate them.

Other, more dangerous drugs are in common use. There are the "uppers" such as amphetamines, and cocaine. Most prescription diet pills contain amphetamines and are addictive. Cocaine is psychologically addictive and it anesthetizes and eventually causes necrosis of the nasal mucous membranes when sniffed. Many people use it for a sense of euphoria and omnipotence. It can give a powerful sense of well-being but, when it wears off, it may bring a shattering loss of that sense. It takes more with each use to get the same sense of power and feeling good, and paranoia and extreme depression often follow the wearing-off of cocaine's high. Even people who aren't addicted to cocaine but use it recreationally— at parties or only on Saturday nights— may find that their sense of well-being becomes more elusive between highs. The sense of Self is such a delicate awareness in the body that its gross exaggeration by the cocaine seems to dull a user's sensitivity to it.

Nitrous oxide (laughing gas) is another common but dangerous drug. It produces a pleasant euphoria by inhibiting delivery of oxygen to the brain. Unless this is monitored carefully and the nitrous oxide is combined correctly with oxygen, it can cause brain damage and even death. A certain dentist, for instance, had a bad day and decided to soothe his battered nerves after his nurses had left. He relaxed happily into euphoria and failed to notice that the combination of nitrous oxide and oxygen was out of balance. The equipment was supposed to shut off automatically if that happened, but it was faulty. The dentist, physically capable of monitoring the process, was too blissful to care. He died.

We cannot emphasize enough how important it is to be aware of a person's drug intake in order to understand the reactions of his body to the breathing work. As the sense of identity (Self) emerges through the breathing, people will often decrease or stop entirely their dependence on drugs for a sense of well-being. They do this on their own, without the therapist taking the role of a disciplinary parent.

Phenobarbitol, Seconal, Amitol, Quaaludes, and other "downers" inhibit the body's ability to develop an energy charge. Therapy can be frustrating and discouraging when a client uses these drugs. Marijuana has the same effect, and it takes from eighteen to thirty-six hours for its effects to be cycled out of the body. Some over-the-counter cold tablets have antihistamines, which are depressants with a similar long-lasting effect. Likewise, cigarettes are a depressant, adversely affecting the lungs and the ability of the adrenal glands to maintain proper blood sugar levels; at the same time they cause a nicotine addiction. E. Cheraskin described the ill effects of nicotine in *Psychodietetics: Food As the Key to Emotional Health:*[3]

"Nicotine disturbs the digestive system by impairing vitamin C absorption, and interferes with blood circulation. By constricting the blood vessels, nicotine robs the brain of its supply of essential nutrients, particularly its major fuel, blood glucose. . . Nicotine also encourages hypoglycemia by causing an increased release of adrenal hormones."

While we don't deal with hard-core drug cases in IBP (we think they are better handled by de-toxification programs), we turn up many cases where people actually have drug problems of some sort without their having realized it.

Scott, for example, was a thirty-five-year-old professional man, involved with only limited success in his career, his marriage, his children. He wasn't even successful in the various affairs he pursued to take his mind off his other difficulties. Year after year he had sworn to change, but he never got any better. When he came to IBP he denied more than occasional use of marijuana, but his therapist grew suspicious because Scott had difficulty building a charge and he never seemed to be quite present at their sessions. Upon close questioning, he admitted that he not only smoked marijuana every day and had done so for fifteen years, but he made it a point to smoke before his therapy sessions. It was obvious that he couldn't deal with his problems because he was always stoned instead of grounded in reality. He agreed to stop smoking dope temporarily and, when he had done so, his problems came into sharp focus. "I've hated my profession since before I graduated," he moaned, "and my wife almost as long. The only way I could tolerate either was to blur them out with grass." Although his therapist advised moderation, Scott quit his job immediately and went back to school. He stayed off drugs, despite the pain and disruption clarity had brought, and remained in therapy where he began working seriously on his problems with relationships and establishing his boundaries.

Sandra had a drinking problem, although she would have denied it. At thirty-four she was a business woman, hard-driving and very successful. Her primary complaint was that she felt great fatigue and a sense of emptiness, which she couldn't understand in light of her business success. The nutritional intake showed that she normally drank two glasses of wine at lunch and started drinking hard liquor at Happy Hour. By the end of the evening, whether she was out dining with clients or home preparing for the next day, she had consumed a considerable amount of alcohol. In the morning she jostled herself back into action with several cups of coffee and started the cycle again. "How could I be alcoholic?" she asked. "I go to work every day and have a responsible job. Alcoholics call in sick and sleep on park benches." Nevertheless, Sandra had compounded her emotional problems for years by excessive drinking. Had she not been asked in detail what she ate and drank, she might have gone on for more years attributing all her problems to emotional causes. Most therapists don't ask such detailed questions, but with those of us who work with the body as well as the emotions, it is routine to do so.

We discovered another drug problem — again with alcohol — in a roundabout way. It was before we systematically used food charts and took thorough physical histories. Kirk was a high school football coach, a big, handsome twenty-eight year old who was the picture of health. Yet he complained of frequent stomach aches. When asked what he ate and what medications he took, he said he took several aspirin every morning. "Why?" asked the therapist, puzzled by the absolute regularity. "For my headaches," answered Kirk, as though it were as normal as brushing his teeth. With more questioning the story emerged. Every day after work, Kirk stopped off for a couple of beers with the baseball coach. Then he went home to his apartment and had a few more beers while he cooked his dinner. Sometimes he called girlfriends or his ex-wife, but usually by the time he had finished his dinner and a couple more beers, he was tired, passing out around ten o'clock. By drinking himself into a stupor every night, he avoided dealing with his emotional and relationship difficulties, but he had never considered it a problem. Indeed, we might never have discovered the problem had it not been for his stomach aches, which went away as soon as he quit taking aspirin.

Exercise and Emotions

It is not only *what* goes into a person's body that affects the course of therapy, but also *how* that food is utilized. The condition of the body, the amount of exercise it gets, and the tone of the muscles help determine the efficiency with which the body uses its fuel.

Besides relieving stress and contributing to a general sense of well-being, exercise is essential to optimal body maintenance. The most efficient exercises are aerobic exercises, especially those that use the long muscles of the body, such as walking, running, bicycling, and swimming. The efficiency of exercise is measured by how fast the heart goes. Heart rate varies with age and with individuals. For regular everyday efficient exercise, we need only work hard enough to make our hearts go at 80 percent of the maximum rate (under stress) for our age for a minimum period of twelve minutes, four times a week. You can use a simple formula to figure it out.

Subtract from	220	
your age	- 46	
Multiply the result	174	
by 80 percent	x .80	
So the optimal heart rate is	139.2	beats per minute.

As a person gets stronger, he can increase the twelve-minute period of exercise at his efficient heart rate.

Anaerobic exercises such as weight-lifting, yoga, isometrics, and stretching are all good for strengthening and toning the body, but they don't affect the cardio-vascular system nor do they affect the utilization of food.

Aerobic exercise enhances our breathing work because, with the extra work we breathe more, increasing the efficiency with which oxygen is used in our bodies. Some anaerobic exercises inhibit the de-armoring process by adding to the rigidity of the musculature rather than to its flexibility. Yoga, though an anaerobic exercise, does work with the breath and the autonomic nervous system to facilitate muscular flexibility as it strengthens the body. The perfect combination of exercise would be an aerobic exercise such as running or swimming plus yoga, for yoga is the best way to stimulate the parasympathetic nervous system, and aerobics are the best way to stimulate the sympathetic nervous system.

Without a healthy body, there can't be a healthy emotional life. That is why we put so much emphasis on nutrition and exercise. There is a column for exercise on the Food Chart, to be filled in whenever it occurs, and to be correlated to the mood levels as well as to food intake. For further reading about the benefits of aerobic exercise, we highly recommend the book *Fit or Fat?*, by Covert Bailey.[4]

The Journal Process

One thing we try to accomplish in the therapy process is to have the client take responsibility for his own therapy. We begin to shift responsibility for change and growth from the therapist to the client by introducing our journal process. This is an integral part of the therapy and the client is totally responsible for it. The journal becomes a tool for working on dreams and rituals, for finishing unfinished business, developing personal imagery, establishing positive introjects, relieving emotionally charged situations, and establishing the objective viewpoint of the observing ego, which provides a bridge between the conscious and unconscious. Often we make assignments for the journal.

We prescribe a book with pages that cannot be removed easily, and the pages should be unlined for drawing, doodling, or whatever comes to mind besides writing. There should be a pen attached to the book, and at night, both book and a flashlight should be beside the bed.

We make no rules about how much to write, other than to suggest that clients write something every day, even if it's only the date. We often find that people don't write on their "good" days, giving a one-sided picture when they re-read their journals. This is akin to people's reluctance to come to a session when they feel good, yet this is exactly when some of the best work can be done, when the perspective is entirely different than usual. The same is true of writing in the journal.

We ask clients to write down dreams immediately after awakening, while their dreams are still clear. And we ask them to write during the times when they're half asleep — just before going to sleep and just when getting up — to observe the contrast in content and mood of the two different states. Dreams, as manifestations of the unconscious, are as important psychologically as what goes on during the day. The relationship between a person's dreams and his daily life is revealing, and the journal, keeping descriptions of both side by side, helps him observe the synchronicity between the waking reality and the dream.

The most important thing about dreams is not their content and meaning. Although we *do* work on dreams, the most important thing for a person to learn is to *live with* his dreams, to let the unconscious become an integral part of his life. As he does this, he begins to honor the unconscious as much as the conscious reality. It is to develop this awareness and acceptance that we have people write their dreams in their journals.

We tell each client to look for his process, his patterns of behavior and feeling in his writing, to watch for central and repeating themes. We say to notice who he is writing to or for; in all likelihood he is writing to *somebody* and he should ask if that somebody is outside or inside of himself.

We explain that the journal is a person's "private poetry," to be kept where other people can't read it— locked, if necessary— for he must feel free to write whatever he wants.

The techniques for using a journal are numerous. A few especially useful ones are: writing dialogues with significant others (present or not), scripts, and letters to people that are never to be sent. For an excellent discussion of journal techniques, read Tristine Rainer's *The New Diary* (1978, Tarcher/Houghton-Mifflin).

Rereading the journal after a few weeks or months is interesting as well as enlightening. The process and patterns become apparent. One's life can be seen in passages or phrases. Single events or reactions that may have been disturbing at the time can often be seen as parts of sensible patterns. Sensible, that is, meaning coherent. One man, for instance, felt ashamed and mystified at some of his behavior. He was fifty years old with a wife and children and was disturbed by his outbursts of childish behavior and irresponsible actions, like spending too much money on gadgets, taking the afternoon off to walk on the beach, and petulantly talking back to the cafeteria lady at his company. When he re-read his journal he saw the pattern that, as his responsibilities weighed more and more heavily upon him, he would burst out and re-live his own teenage behavior. He still didn't admire himself much, but he could understand it once he saw it in context.

The journal is also an indicator of growth and change. A young woman who was being treated for depression, a reaction to the loss of her mate, said she went back to the beginning of her journal and noticed that she'd mentioned her ex-husband's name on every page. This went on for months. Gradually, his name stopped appearing, until it disappeared altogether. She was able to chart the lifting of her depression accurately by that alone and the realization that she was getting over it gave her an added surge of good feeling.

The journal is an excellent way to get in touch with one's repetitive patterns. When a client gets upset in a current event situation, we suggest that he write about it in his journal. When he has the event down on paper, we ask him to assess its emotional impact on a scale of one to ten, one being little impact and ten being great impact. Then he is to write about another event on the opposite page, an earlier event that evoked the same emotion. When he has both events written down, he is to take the value he assigned to the current event and split it between the past situation and the current one. That is, if he assigned a seven to the current situation, he might rate the past event a five and the current one a two.

CURRENT EVENT	PAST EVENT
I am so angry! My room-mate is getting married! She's only trying to get someone to take care of her, and *she* calls herself a feminist! What a hypo-crite! Total Impact: 10 Impact of Current Event: 2	When I think about that kind of rage, I realize that it really has more to do with my jealous feelings of never having been taken care of myself. I guess my roommate has a right to live her life the way she wants to. I can see that I am still angry with my mother for leaving. Impact of past event: 8

The point of this, of course, is to guide the client into the realiza-tion that he brings a great deal of the past into the present — that the past, in fact, determines how he will react to the present.

Chapter 3
The Source:
The Primary Scenario

The Primary Scenario is both the beginning and the end of therapy. The process of therapy is an adventure, an exciting search for the source of the personality, the Self, the very beginnings of a person's behavior patterns — and the Primary Scenario is this source.

We call it a scenario — originally the outline of a play and, more recently, a screenplay — because of the many analogies between our lives and the world of the theater. "All the world's a stage, and all the men and women merely players," Shakespeare said. We speak of roles that we assume at different times and in different situations, and we occasionally have flashes of insight in which we speak of performing our lives instead of living them, of doing things in ways that seem foreordained. "Where is it written that I must always pick up after you?" questions the irate wife. Most of us recognize that we have a great deal of pattern in our lives — we are reliable, flaky, depressing, lots of fun, fussy, easy-going, or productive. When we do things the way our parents and our grandparents did them, we call it tradition. The only time we bemoan this consistency and predictability is when things go wrong — again! "Why does this always happen to me?" we ask. "Why does she always drag home the same kind of man?" "Why can't I ever get a decent boss?"

Good or bad, such consistency comes from the same source, the period of our lives in which the stage is set, our lifelong patterns established, and our traditions re-affirmed. This is the period we call the Primary Scenario. It is essentially completed for most of us by the time we are about six years old, but the first three years are the most important.

During this time the first bonding takes place, as a person's first relationship develops with the mother (or other significant person who takes care of him all the time). The Primary Scenario is the history of that first relationship as well as the blueprint for all relationships to come. Ideally, during this time a person develops an increasing confidence in himself and learns to have warm, fulfilling relationships with his parents, siblings, and eventually, the outside world.

As therapists, however, we usually see less ideal versions of the Primary Scenario and know that it's just as apt to lead to a lifetime of compulsive behavior patterns adopted by the baby as protection against pain of having his needs un- met. It can be the scene in which the Self, unable to develop fully, withdraws, puts up barriers, and remains inside, stunted and fearful of annihilation.

The paradoxical thing is that, while it takes place over a relatively short period, it affects a person's entire life. *Most of us continue to unconsciously and compulsively re- enact our Primary Scenario all of our lives in an attempt to meet the needs that weren't met at the time, to complete the task of the time — the development of the Self.*

The Primary Scenario is the sum of emotional and physiological experiences of a person's earliest months and years. It is the cultural, social, political, and family setting into which he is born and by which his character will be molded. A newborn baby is a mass of neuro- logical responses and is almost infinitely malleable. He has no language or culture to help him analyze the situation he is born into, nor has he the experience with which to resist or exploit it. Thus a child raised from infancy in an urban New York environment is largely a product of his environment, and is a very different product than a child raised in an aboriginal Australian culture.

In a less global sense, the Primary Scenario is nothing more than the family system a person is born into: mother and father, grand- parents and great- grandparents. It includes the family wisdom and folly, its prejudices and its values. It includes all its personal tragedies as well as its reactions to global ones. It includes, especially, its reactions to the new baby. Everything a baby learns about relation- ships, love and hate, pain and pleasure, and fear and security comes from the people of his Primary Scenario. His character structure grows in direct response to it.

So powerful is the Primary Scenario that everybody carries its lessons around forevermore, inextricably locked in the body and manifested in patterns of behavior. The child whose physiological and emotional needs aren't satisfied in timely and loving ways learns to tighten his muscles to seal off the pain of hunger and neglect. He "steels himself against it" because it is intolerable.

The process is simple, whether it's the sealing off of physical pains such as hunger or emotional pains. A baby, bonding to its mother, is very sensitive to her feelings, which she expresses in her body just as he does. If she is nervous about feeding or holding him, that nervousness is transmitted by body contact and the energy he receives from her is not the warm, satisfying energy he needs. If she doesn't pick him up much just to cuddle him, or if she feeds him efficiently and puts him back down quickly, then he doesn't get the loving he needs. The pain of the insufficient loving is too much to bear and he seals it off the same way he seals off the pain of hunger. He might not cry much and might appear to be a "good" baby, but his silence is a defeated silence. His body has encapsulated the pain to prevent his feeling it, and, after a while, not many feelings penetrate at all, for the muscular blocks don't discriminate between positive and negative feelings.

Since a baby needs a sense of well-being from his mother for his Self to develop properly, the less his positive feelings are hindered, the better. Fortunately, most mothers are capable of giving whatever it takes for adequate bonding, for the bonding phase sets the stage for later developmental phases. It establishes the vulnerability of the child within that relationship, making further growth possible and determining the quality of that growth.

The tension or muscular holding patterns (or *blocks*, as we call them in terms of the energy flow within the body) form the child's structure. We commonly describe character in physical terms:

> She keeps a stiff upper lip.
> He's walking on eggs.
> He's got a chip in his shoulder.
> Butter wouldn't melt in her mouth.

Some people characteristically walk as if they're being chased, look down their noses at other people, and stand rigidly lest they touch those next to them. They are the obvious ones, but everyone has fixed muscular patterns indelibly stamped on his body. They formed initially as protection against pain but they remain, vestigial lines of defense that simultaneously cut off painful feelings and set the person off in predictable behavior patterns.

A sociologist in our ranks did a casual and (she thought at the time) humorous study of cleanliness in the families of her cooperative baby-sitting group.

"From the moment the first mother began feeding her baby semi- solid food, it was obvious there were going to be differences, and I was curious how they would show up as the children grew.

"I studied only the extremes — the Cleans and the Messies. The Clean mothers always had an extra diaper handy to wipe vigorously at their babies' cheeks whenever a drop of pureed prune went astray. It made me marvel at the resiliency of babies' skins.

"I surreptitiously placed myself behind high chairs and was soon able to predict that the diaper would be applied immediately after the mother's face changed from pride to disgust.

"The Messy moms gave their kids spoons early and only interfered with the feeding process when the babies got frustrated and hungry. Watching from behind, I could predict only one thing: when Mom's expression showed amusement or fond resignation, I could be sure that Baby's face was smeared to the eyebrows with Gerbers!

"I was able to follow many of these children through kindergarten. The Cleans stayed clean, but it seemed hard on them. It was on me, certainly, to watch a three year old trying to eat a tangerine without dripping on her dress, then crying because she had. Of course, one had to be careful making physical contact with a Messy because you'd likely stick to him, but they were a joy to watch at fingerpainting. They literally threw themselves into it.

"Even when new kids came into the groups I could tell whether they were Cleans or Messies by the way they approached the paints. The Cleans were tied up in knots, their little shoulders raised and their arms folded across their fronts, one hand holding the other arm. They really *finger*- painted, too, extending one thin finger as far out as possible, inscribing neat, clean lines. You know what the Messies did — you've seen kids like that.

"After a painting session I'd wait at the door with kids and watch the mothers come to collect them. I could always tell when a Clean mother caught sight of her kid by the way her face changed, and I'd swear there wasn't ever a drop of paint on him. And the child's little shoulders would shoot up again when he saw his mom and his arms wrap in front of him. Messy moms either didn't notice anything or they would laugh and ask if they could see the paintings. The kids never caught on. They always asked 'How did you know we painted today?' convinced their mothers were magic."

Other vignettes from the Primary Scenario that emerge in therapy testify to the body's retention of its early physical reactions:

"My husband can't hear requests made by women in the same

pitch as his mother's voice," said one woman. "If I want something, I have to speak much higher or lower than my normal voice, which is much like hers."

"I know it's impossible, but I have this feeling that I never really digested a meal until I left home."

Just as the family transmits culture and language, it transmits the compound neuroses of past generations, passing on all the gaps in learning and feeling it has accumulated. It's no accident that a sour person has a sour family in his background while a happy person has a jolly one. Whatever bit of loving was left out of our parents, whatever bit of hatred was instilled in our grandparents, you can be sure of finding it somewhere down the line in our own behavior.

In gathering the Primary Scenario, therefore, the therapist must watch for the family process through several generations. It is a history of relationships that he is gathering, patterns of relationships impressed upon a child that he will probably follow unquestioningly throughout his life. We may resist the idea that a grandparent's childhood could determine what we do with our lives, but the evidence that it does is compelling.

It is the consistency in a relationship that affects a child. Occasional bursts of anger or expressions of disgust from his mother won't have a permanent effect on a child, but regular ones will provoke patterns of reacting, or coping. As the sociologist noted with the Clean and Messy families, the children were responding to consistent, predictable early training. Unless something happens to break the individual patterns, the children will raise their children the same way. As one mother said, "I thought I'd learned so much and come such a long way from my mother, but when my son emptied the cupboard yesterday, the shriek I emitted was precisely the same as the one I used to hear from *my* mom."

A dentist named Alan jokingly tells a story that illustrates the multi-generational quality of the Primary Scenario. He states, "I hate the Sioux Indians," then waits for someone to call him a bigot so he can explain: "They made me what I am today, eternally seeking strong women who become helpless and then despise me."

"In the mid 1800s, my great-great grandmother was born in a covered wagon traveling from Missouri to Montana. In South Dakota the wagon train was attacked by the Sioux, with everyone left for dead. A day or so later another wagon train came by and found my three-month-old great-great grandmother, hungry and worn out from crying. Out of pity, they adopted her. Out of necessity, they rotated her amongst the families with nursing mothers, but she seldom had the same "mother" two days in a row. When the wagon train reached Montana, they found someone willing to adopt her, a stern, uncommunicative woman whose idea of raising a baby was no different from her idea of raising livestock. Accordingly, my great-great grandmother was well fed and kept clean and clothed, but got no unnecessary frivolities, like love and affection. Needless to say, she grew up strange and uncommunicative.

"Oddly enough, she married and had a daughter of her own. Do you think she profited from her experience? Nothing doing! She had learned the mothering act cold (literally!) and repeated it perfectly with her daughter, my grandmother.

"Time came and Granny married. Same thing. She had my mother and kept her at arm's length. We've always been a 'reserved' family," parodies Alan, mimicking the haughty expression and cold demeanor of his mother and grandmother. "Then my mother had me and did it again. Kept me at arm's length while assuring me she was hugging me to her breast.

"Now," he sums up triumphantly, "can't you see why I hate the Sioux?"

Alan uses humor to help him bear the discomfort inherited from his great-great grandmother's tragedy, but there are family histories about which no one laughs. The horror stories of people who saw the Holocaust and survived concentration camps didn't end when the war was over. The damage done to young people then has been passed onto the second generation who are now coming to therapy in large numbers. Without a great deal of help, this damage will be perpetuated in succeeding generations. The tendency for an abused child to grow up and abuse his own children is a monstrous testimony to our thesis—that we learn our patterns of behavior within our earliest relationships, then compulsively and unconsciously repeat them within all subsequent relationships.

Gathering the Primary Scenario

Because of the importance of the Primary Scenario, the IBP therapist begins gathering it as soon as the medical and nutritional intake are complete. We say "gathering it," but we could as well say "pursuing it" or "ferreting it out" or even call the process "the quest for the Primary Scenario," because all these fit as well. Gathering implies the simplicity of picking berries, but also the painstaking collection of discrete bits and pieces over a period of time, which is exactly what happens. Although we get the major outline of the Primary Scenario in one or two sessions, we continue to gather essential bits— forgotten, repressed, or considered irrelevant at the time— throughout the process of therapy.

The idea of "ferreting it out" and "pursuing it" fit all the detective work involved in finding the source of a person's identity and character structure. We find clues where we can: in his peculiar body characteristics, muscular holding patterns, his physiological problems, his patterns of relationships, his anecdotes about his family, his prejudices, his passions, and even the old family picture album.

And sometimes we like the phrase "the quest for the Primary Scenario," for it is no less an adventure story than that of an explorer braving jungles, precipices, and hostile savages to find the source of a major river. The trickle of water seeping from a rift in a stone and hidden by a fern may seem anti-climactic, but the explorer isn't disappointed. On the contrary, he feels the thrill of discovery and a respect for the humble origins of his mighty river.

Similarly, a client going through the process of therapy, closing in on *his* sources— his Primary Scenario— has the same thrill of discovery. An early image of his mother glowering at his dirty face, grim though it may be, can provide the same thrill the explorer felt finding his ferny seep.

There are many ways to gather the Primary Scenario. The best method will depend on the preferences of the therapist and the different ways each client sees and remembers his past. We usually use a white board or chalk board to make a rough family tree as the client talks, filling it in with brief comments or notes. Diagramming the Primary Scenario is of particular importance because the visual aspect seems to make a much stronger impression on the client than merely talking about his history. On the diagram, we indicate the most relevant relationships. We take notes about details to explore later on. An example of Alan's family tree copied from the white board and a brief account of his Primary Scenario are on pages 84 and 85.

One good method uses as a guideline a list of questions compiled by IBP therapist Jodi T. Samuels, Ph. D. We don't ask *all* clients *all* the questions. We ask the basic questions and then, if offered any clues in the answer, we'll delve a little further. For instance, if we ask, "Were there any problems when you were born?" and the client says, "Yes, I had jaundice," we ask about things such as the length of his hospital stay.

The answers to many of the questions aren't especially important in content but they are important in how they reflect the quality of the person's early relationships. That is, we are not interested in the fact that someone had jaundice at birth so much as that he was left in the hospital for a week without his mother at a critical time in the bonding of mother and baby.

This is similar to our nutritional intake in that we care about a person's eating habits only insofar as they affect his emotional health.

Questions 1 through 19 look for any injuries done to the child; the rest look for the repetitive patterns determined by those injuries.

1. Imagine your early life as a movie.

This is a useful technique in several ways. So many patterns of behavior are set up in the Primary Scenario that we sometimes see a person's life as a one-reel movie, playing over and over again. He projects this movie onto the world and then participates in it. In projecting his expectations onto the world, he generally makes the people in his relationships conform to the patterns established when the movie was first filmed. He acts out his roles, they act out theirs. Another reason this works is that many of us have old family photographs depicting our parents and grandparents as children and as young married people. This helps us imagine more what they were like at ages significant to the Scenario, rather than going by our personal memories of them as much older people.

2. Start with your mother and father. What actors that remind you of your mother and father would you pick to play them in your movie?

This is your first good clue. Does the client choose Ruth Gordon, Olivia Newton-John, or Cloris Leachman to play his mother? Does he choose Clark Gable, Dustin Hoffman, or Darth Vader to play his father?

It is important that the therapist refrain from interpretation during the gathering, and simply note down information for later reference. For one thing, he doesn't want to get sidetracked. The prime reason though, is that it is only further into therapy that a trusting relationship develops, and only then will a client be able to accept interpretation, to "own" unpleasant connections that the therapist may have guessed immediately.

3. What were your mother and father like when they met? How

old were they? What person was your mother closest to? Who was your father closest to? Were they happy? Were they eagerly looking for marriage partners or happily pursuing independence (not necessarily the same for both parents). Were they healthy? What were their values? Their goals? What did they look like?

4. What were they doing at the time? Were they in school? Working? In the Peace Corps? In jail? In the hospital? Were they yachting around the world, ardently pursuing careers, caring for elderly parents, fleeing the draft?

5. Tell me about your grandparents. What were your parents' relationships with them like? What were their relationships like with each other? Tell me also what they were like when they were older, when you knew them, if you did.

The grandparents are very important. If the therapist knows something about the Primary Scenario of his client's mother, for instance, he can get an idea about what injuries she received and, therefore, what injuries she passed on to the client. People tend to raise their children either just as they were raised, or just the opposite, in an effort to make up for what they didn't get.

Thus, there is sometimes an alternation of generations in the family patterns. For instance, one family raised its children in very poor circumstances. The kids all had to work and they had very few comforts. When they grew up they worked very hard and gave their children everything. When those kids grew up, they concluded that they'd had it too easy and proceeded to raise their children in a spartan manner, insisting that they work for their allowances and get summer jobs.

People often identify more with their grandparents than with their parents. Maybe the relationship is more pleasant and easier. Maybe family stories excite the child's imagination or his sympathies, making him want to be like a grandparent rather than like a parent. Whatever the dynamics in any particular family, the grandparents are influential characters in the Primary Scenario.

6. Who is the father to the mother and vice versa?

This is one of the questions that may be modified and augmented as therapy goes on. At the first gathering of the Primary Scenario, it may be pretty much of a guess. On the other hand, it may be clear immediately. Lots of families have stories about this, often unflattering. "He thought he was marrying somebody just like his mother," said one woman frequently. "Was he ever surprised when he found out that I expected to *get* breakfast in bed instead of *serving* it." Often they're in the form of family jokes, like the one man who always told his children with rueful pride, "I thought your mom was a sweet little lamb like my mother, but she turned out to be a tiger!"

The client may be encouraged to guess at the possible relationships if he doesn't know right off. Their relative ages may be a clue, with a wide difference suggesting a search for another parent, perhaps. Their jobs might suggest whether one was obviously more dominant or successful or stable than the other. Such clues might also be misleading so, again, the therapist should only try to jostle the client's memory and imagination, not interpret.

7. What did they bring to the relationship?

Had they been married or deeply involved before? Did they already have children? Had they lost loved ones or had severe illnesses? Were they very religious? Did they get along with parents? What were their expectations of marriage?

8. How long were they together before they married? Did they live together? Had they known each other long?

9. Did they have money problems in the beginning?

Did either of them have to make any job or school changes because of the financial impact of their marriage? How did they feel about that?

A lot of people in therapy now and in the last twenty years were born of parents married during the Depression. One such man grew up poor, with everything bought at thrift shops or scavenged. Even thinking of spending money on non-essentials was frowned upon. It was a great shock for him when his parents visited him at college, took him out to dinner, and ordered steak and lobster tails. "I felt betrayed," he said, "and began questioning everything they'd taught me." He had grown up knowing that he must be exceedingly careful about how he spent money but he had learned this morality and made it a part of his character structure from parents who'd learned it as young adults. To them it was a survival technique and not part of their character structures, so, when times were better, they were able to spend money comfortably. Not so their son who, to this day, has stomach cramps when paying his bills.

10. How long was it until they had their first child?

Why so soon or why did they wait so long? Did your mother have any difficulty getting pregnant? Did pregnancy precipitate their marriage? What kind of lifestyle did they have and how did having a child affect it?

11. Were you a wanted child?
Who wanted you and why or what for; that is, were you to provide meaning in life for mother? To carry on your father's name? What kind of messages do you think you got being born into this family?

12. If you had to do it all over again and you couldn't change anything, would you want to be born?
In continuing the movie metaphor, we ask the client to picture the scene of his birth and then ask him this question. People who answer "no" often show chronic depression or psychosomatic illness. Those who hesitate and then say "Oh well, I might as well be born," have never quite decided to live, to embrace life fully. They hover in a victimized role throughout their lives, never taking responsibility for what happens to them. Many people were angry at having to be born, to be thrust from the warmth of the womb, and they spend their lives in a continual tantrum protesting the fact. And, a lot of people answer "Yes, of course!" and they're the eager ones who embrace life enthusiastically.

13. Were you premature?
Did anything in particular precipitate it, like premature separation of the placenta or maternal illness or a car accident?

14. Were you in an incubator?
Why? For how long? Could your mother come and hold you? Was there any one person who was able to give you consistent care?

15. Were there any problems when you were born?
Was your mother healthy during her pregnancy? Were there any fears that you'd have inherited or developed drug-induced defects? Was it a normal or Caesarian delivery? If a person was adopted, he probably only knows the details of his birth if they were highly unusual. He may know any problems connected with his adoption. Was he adopted immediately or did he spend time in the hospital, an orphanage, or with foster parents? It's important to know how old he was when he was adopted. If he was adopted at birth, all the

rest of the questions about his parents and grandparents (the adoptive ones) are as significant as they are for children raised by natural parents.

16. Was it a difficult labor?

Was it natural or induced? Did your mother have any medication for pain or any anesthetic for the delivery? Was your father with her during labor and/or delivery? Where were you born?

17. Were there any feeding problems? Were you breast or bottle fed? If bottle fed, did you have any trouble tolerating formulas? Did your mother have any fears about not having enough milk for you? Were your father's mother and your mother's mother supportive of her way of feeding you?

It's often surprising what people know about their early eating habits, when they know almost nothing about any other details of their lives. It's symptomatic of the importance we attach to food. As providers, we are concerned that we won't do well, and new mothers are vulnerable to fears that are ridiculous in light of the mammalian success story. Ridiculous or not, the fears are transmitted to the infant, and he may react in such a way as to make his mother's fears worse. Imagine a scared mother, nervously holding her newborn, so tense that her milk won't let down. The baby sucks at the nipple, gets nothing, tries again, then cries. The grandmother says "Last time I heard a baby cry like that, he didn't live through the night." This happened to one lady we know. "My mother's milk dried up on the spot and she started giving me formula, but she never got over her guilt and resentment at not being able to feed me herself."

18. Do you have brothers and sisters? Who was born after you and how did the birth of a younger sibling affect you? What was his/her relationship with you? With your mother? With your father? How long was your mother away having the baby and where were you? Who was taking care of you?

The birth of a younger brother or sister can be one of the major emotional traumas to a child. For a year or so, at least, he has enjoyed the single-minded attention of the parents, especially the mother. Even when there are older children, the youngest, necessarily gets the most constant attention. When this attention is suddenly withdrawn the child loses his sense of total importance, his place in the sun, his eminence. The quality of the relationship with his parents and the way in which they help him minimize his loss affect his developing sense of Self and the formation of his character. The father's support at this time is important in helping him bridge the transition between being Number One and *not* being Number One. Alan, the man who hates the Sioux, described the birth of his sister: "I was the first child, the apple of my mother's eye. I conducted my little family like a symphony orchestra— I told my mother what to do; I told my father what to do. The whole world was at my command. Things burst into motion at the flick of a finger. Then my sister was born and I couldn't even play the radio."

Children react in different ways to their loss of the limelight. Some will rebel and do anything to get the parents' attention. Some will become extra good little boys and girls and help take care of the infant in an attempt to get the love of the mother back. There is a magical (and generally erroneous) belief that, if you take care of someone, you yourself will be taken care of.

Sometimes children are sent away to friends or relatives while the new baby is born. This may be more or less traumatic depending, as always, on the developing Self of the child, on his relationship with his mother and father, and on the person who takes care of him.

For example, one woman was sent away to her stern grandmother for six weeks. She was only two years old and felt not only abandoned but punished, as well. This may be the first real separation issue, although most of the related questions are asked under the question about how the child did in school.

19. How many years apart are the siblings?

Were the intervals planned or accidental? Strange logics are reflected in birth patterns and may reveal a lot about the family dynamics. A common one is two children close together, a gap of six or seven years, then two more children close together. Often the third child was an accident and the fourth planned as a companion as well as to get the family's money's worth out of the new stroller and crib. An unusual spacing was in Siegfried's family. The custom in his native Germany was to send kids away to boarding school when they were six. He was born eleven months after his brother left for boarding school, and his sister was born ten months after *he* went away. When she went to school, the youngest brother was born within the year. "My father never wanted any children," said Siegfried, "then agreed to let Mother have one. When she felt she'd lost that one, he let her have another, and so on." Although he told the story as an amusing anecdote, he speculated during therapy about what it meant in a relationship when a man "let" his wife have a child. Also, what must those children have meant to the mother that she needed to replace them, and what did that imply about her relationship with her husband?

20. Tell me about going to school. Starting with your first school experience (nursery school, day care, or kindergarten) what was it like leaving your mother?

Now answer the same questions for other separations. Did you go to boarding school, to camp, or to visit relatives for fun or while a younger sibling was being born? How did you and your mother handle that separation? How did you handle the separations when you went to high school? To college? To the Army? When you got married?

Separations are important. A child with a well-developing sense of Self, who is confident that his mother is always available to him, will be less affected than a child who feels his mother is only "there" part-time, an unpredictable presence at best. Sandy, for example, went to kindergarten but couldn't stop crying long enough to enjoy it, she was so afraid that her mother would die while she was gone. Such an unreasonable fear shows a lack of healthy narcissism; that is, the mother isn't sufficiently real to the child that he can "take her with him" when he goes away. He needs to check on her presence constantly to make sure she is there.

21. How did you do in school?

What was your socialization like? What were your grades like? Who were your friends? Did you belong to clubs? Participate in school activities? Go to dances?

22. Tell me about important relationships, both male and female, that you have had up to the present.

Here the therapist can often begin to see the repetitions as the client describes relationships in which he was seeking to satisfy needs that weren't met earlier.

23. Have there been any divorces in your family? Any suicides?

Both are important. They set patterns to follow and give tacit permission for problems to be solved in the same ways.

24. Tell me about your current relationship(s). How is this like any of your past relationships? (Include your famiy relationships —

parents and grandparents — as well as your own same-sex relationships).

The repetitive patterns are often quite obvious here.

For one last question, ask the client what title he would like to give his movie. Peyton Place? Ship of Fools? Fantasy Island? The Decline and Fall of the Roman Empire? War and Peace?

The first three years are the most important in the Primary Scenario because it is during that time that the sense of Self and the character structure undergo most of their development. The rest of the history usually illustrates repetitions of the first three years.

We continue gathering the Primary Scenario up to about age six, then jump to the first long-term adult relationship to look for repeating patterns of the Primary Scenario. The period of development not covered here (adolescence and teen years) will be discussed in Chapter 8.

The following is an excerpt from the journal of a client who is just beginning to discover the relationship between her current life and her Primary Scenario.

The level of hurt and anger I was experiencing before my session was very intense and I was dealing with it by avoidance; ignoring it and at the same time holding on to it.

Much to my surprise, in the therapy session, the focus was on the anger I felt towards my father, which I have paid no attention to in the past ten years. I'm thirty-two now, but when I was seventeen years old, I hated my father intensely — this feeling continued for about five years.

What I just realized is that I was married that fith year at twenty-two. It was then that my anger at my father seemed to subside.

A couple of days following the session I wrote in my journal my negative feelings regarding my lover. Comparing the two entries was very shocking — my feelings toward my father and my lover are the same!"

This is a realization of the relationship with her father when she was seventeen, but the relationship had started much earlier. People commonly make connections between their adult patterns and adolescent events, but the adolescent ones are themselves repetitions of early life events. This young woman is returning, in memory, to a period of life that is actually a re-enactment of an earlier period.

Alan's Primary Scenario

Alan's parents met when David was twenty-two and Grace was twenty-one. He would choose Robert Young to play David and Marilyn Monroe to play Grace. David managed a movie theatre and Grace was an usherette at the same theatre. They didn't have much money then nor did they ever. Grace's mother had been stern and un-caring and her father left when she was four; thus Grace never had much of a relationship with either parent. When she married David, she was looking for someone to take care of her, especially a substitute father. David, reared by a strong, domineering mother, was a "good boy," really looking for another mother in his wife. Naturally he didn't acknowledge this and strove to be the hero that Grace wanted to take care of her. Grace, however, was third-generation strange and uncommunicative and was eternally critical of David's good intentions, even though he managed to support her and their children and his mother, who lived with them.

Alan's earliest memories of his father were warm and happy, but David was away from home a lot, trying in vain to earn enough money to please Grace. Grace had had an earlier, brief marriage in which she had a miscarriage. This made her anxious about having Alan. Even when she had a perfect baby boy, her anxiety and a profound sense of inadequacy made her certain that she would lose him by not being able to feed him. This insecurity communicated itself to Alan, who made her more nervous by crying, with the result that she switched to a formula. When he proved allergic to cow's milk, her fears ran rampant till she found that he could tolerate goat's milk.

Her fears caused her to over-protect Alan but, at the same time, she was split-off, never being truly available for him. Returning sporadically to her concerns, she would over-nurture him for a while before splitting-off again. Realizing in the uncanny way of children, her sense of inadequacy, Alan began early to feel responsible for it and to try to take care of his mother. (This is another magical belief of children — that they are to blame for a parent's inadequacy. They respond by taking care of the parent so *they* can get taken care of. Later they respond by *remembering* the parent as ideal as if, by re-writing their histories, they can retroactively be taken care of.)

Alan went through an over-extended bonding period with his mother. She assured him always that she loved him. After his sister was born when he was four, she said she loved him the best, but he never did feel secure. Because his father was traveling so much and his grandmother lived with them, Alan learned to relate to women but not to men.

When his sister was born he was horribly conscious of having lost his place in the sun. The sister never formed much of a relationship with her mother but eventually formed one with her father. Alan quickly learned that taking care of his little sister was the best and maybe the only way to get attention and approval from his mother.

Alan never went to nursery school because of the strong attachment between him and his mother. He didn't go to kindergarten, either, not entering school till the first grade. At parting from his mother, he wept and wailed loudly, racing home afterwards to see if she were still home. She wasn't; she was out having lunch with a friend.

In truth, he realized through therapy, Alan never had separated from his mother, even years after she'd died. He simply had replaced her with a series of wives to whom he was attracted because of their strength, then repelled by their sudden dependence, so much like his mother's. He tells a story on himself: "Every day I walk past a dress shop on the way to my office. Every day the same mannequin is out front, dressed in a different dress. Every time I see this mannequin, I have a surge of desire, of love, and only realize as I move in, that she's just a mannequin, hard and cold and unfeeling as my mother always was, and just like all the women I choose as mates."

Alan's injury, as he learned in therapy, was in what is called the "mirroring" stage, the stage in which a child begins to develop a sense of who he is. Alan was unable to see himself except in relationship with women.

Figure 8: Alan's Primary Scenario Diagram

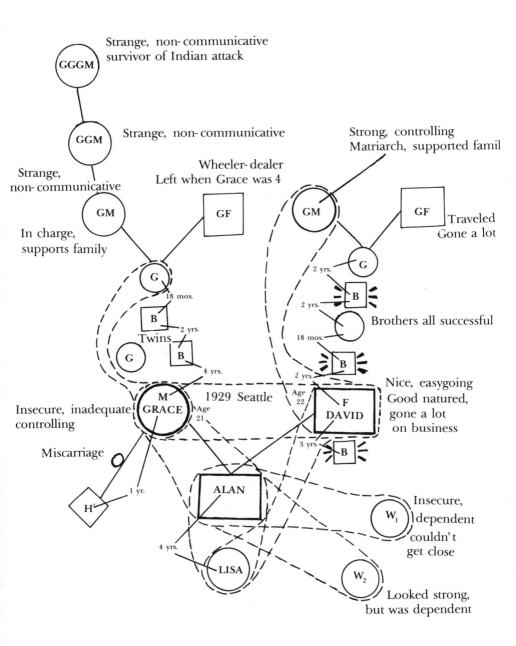

Eventually she will go back further, but as yet, she has no conscious memories of events before she was thirteen. This indicates that she was "split-off" even then, a pattern she continues in therapy today. Tracking her patterns, working with her body, and allowing her unconscious memories to emerge will continue until she detaches from her Primary Scenario. Success in this endeavor will depend on keeping her present in therapy— that is, not allowing her to split off and avoid facing the feelings that her memories evoke.

The Necessity of the Primary Scenario

Before they are aware of the compulsive nature of the Primary Scenario, most people operate under a magical assumptive system. They follow the cliche, "If at first you don't succeed, try, try again," but they pervert it slightly to "If I keep doing the *same thing* over and over again, it will turn out differently." Unfortunately, it doesn't work and all they get for their diligence is despair, discouragement, and feelings of powerlessness. Once a person becomes cognizant of his Scenario, he can stop making this magical assumption. Now he can see the patterns in his own life that haven't worked. He can even go back and see similar patterns in this parents' and grandparents' lives that didn't work either. Seeing this, he can begin to take responsibility for the senseless repetitions.

Once the Scenario becomes conscious, the therapist and his client work to make connections between the Scenario, the holding patterns in the body, and the current life situation of the client. Gradually he may consider the possibility of making changes.

Before the client's awareness there is no choice about his behavior, and after awareness there is, but change does not occur with insight alone. There may be a considerable length of time in which a person is aware of what he is doing and still doesn't change it. This is a crucial time in the growing process and the therapist must allow the client to remain just as he is, assimiliating his awareness at his own pace. It mustn't become another source of guilt or discomfort, self-abnegation or despair for those who already tend to castigate themselves for running their lives badly. They shouldn't use their awareness to punish themselves for not changing immediately. Rather, they should direct their energies toward deeper understanding of the needs that weren't satisfied when they were children, how to break the defensive habits they developed, and how to satisfy their needs in productive, adult ways.

This is the phase in therapy when a person observes himself for a while in the Scenario before choosing to detach himself from it. Taking time for reflection fosters the development of the observing ego. While awareness is the key ingredient in a person's being able to decide to change, it can take time— sometimes years— for him to actually change. To borrow an illustration from a later chapter: "The process of change is like being on great ocean liner in which the captain is standing at the helm and changes course very quickly with a flick of a switch, a spin of the wheel. The ocean liner doesn't appear to move at all; it does not, cannot whip through the water to point in a new direction. It takes a long time for it to move to the new setting, and when it does, the horizon may appear as before. It takes a very seasoned captain to feel that the course is correct."

The therapist's acceptance can help the client understand that it's all right for him to wait and to accept his own reasons for staying where he is. He must realize that, while he may have some bad patterns running his life, he may have other patterns and values that he cherishes and that do consistently bring him safisfaction. He must time his change to bring his life into a happy balance, and not risk losing the good for the sake of exorcising the bad. As Perls said, "Right now, I can be no other than I am right now."

Marilyn, for example, was the first child of alcoholic parents. She spent her youth excelling at everything her parents expected of her. She took care of her younger brothers, the house, and when necessary, her parents, She did well in school and got a teaching credential. When she was twenty-five she married a handsome paraplegic veteran. They bought a house, adopted two children, and lived happily until the pain of his old wounds forced him to quit work. Marilyn went back to teaching while he babysat and began drinking. The sicker he got, the more he drank and the more he complained about her being away from home. In her sorrow and her love for him, she curtailed her outside activities in an effort to make him happy. When she finally entered therapy, she was gaunt and pale, unable to eat or sleep and miserably torn.

When she saw how she had become a caretaker of her husband as a repetition of her childhood role with her parents, she realized that she *could* break the patterns, divorce her husband, and start a new life.

"But I can't leave him," she cried, "he's dying," and that was that. The best she could do was to understand the mechanisms in her life, take responsibility for what she could control, and reject responsibility for what thing she couldn't, such as her husband's pain and his alcoholism. She began seeing friends again, folk dancing, and skiing occasionally— all things she'd given up because her husband couldn't or wouldn't participate.

For Marilyn, awareness didn't lead to life changes but let her observe herself in action. This helped her make choices within the situation, and these choices saved her from resentment, guilt, anger, and self-pity.

The Primary Scenario is one of the most important things in Integrative Body Psychotherapy. We start here and end here, continually referring back to it throughout therapy. Although we can describe the Scenario in simple terms, any one in particular has many more facets than are first apparent. New subtleties of the relationships unfold as the Scenario is repeated over and over in life and again when it is re-enacted in the therapeutic process. New clues emerge in the body work that expand our knowledge of the Primary Scenario. The more we know about the source of the holding patterns in a person's body, the more able we are to help him give them up.

The work goes on, always playing the patterns in a person's current life against the source of those patterns. Therapy is a healing process, but healing is easier and quicker when we know what is to be healed and how. Knowing a client's Primary Scenario and his character structure, we can diagnose what type of body work would be most effective for him and how best to proceed. The Primary Scenario is a powerful diagnostic tool, one that is continually validated by our work with clients.

Chapter 4
Looking In:
Contraction and Expansion

We described the Primary Scenario as, among other things, a diagnostic map that guides us in the therapeutic process. From it we have some clues as to the sorts of injuries a person may have suffered in his childhood. By putting these clues together with what he tells us about his current relationships, we can make a preliminary diagnosis about the type of body work that will be the most effective and acceptable. Then we go to the body to learn more and to begin to heal the old injuries.

To illustrate how we use the materials from the Primary Scenario to get the most out of the body work and how we use the body work to alleviate problems that arose in the Primary Scenario, we start with Sara's description.

Sara was an agreeable free-lance artist in her forties. She was strong, healthy, cheerful, capable, motherly, and above all, agreeable. In fact, it was her very agreeableness that brought her into therapy.

"First I agreed to do this little task," she said, "and then I agreed to do that. Then I admitted I might have time for the third job, and finally, just before I collapsed, I sandwiched in a three-week vacation with my boyfriend. All I need is a three-ply week and I'll do fine. Imagine — three days running simultaneously. I ought to be able to take care of everybody then."

She went through the beginning sessions of therapy doing the nutritional intake, physical history, and gathering the Primary Scenario. Then she had her first body session and described it thusly:

"I had seen Helen, my therapist, for a few months and gotten to know and trust her while she took my physical history and found out about my terrible eating habits. When she gathered my Primary Scenario, I told her the usual tale of my life. I've always been proud of what a happy, untroubled childhood and adolescence I had. My mother and I had always been good friends, even through my teens. I did well in school and have always had good, responsible men around me. Amazing, considering that my handsome father had been a womanizer, breaking my mother's heart and then bruising her body when she complained. I told Helen how happy my mother was to have me because I was such a good baby. I slept a lot, woke up smiling, and never cried. My brother, on the other hand, was a hellion, a hyperkinetic kid born before they had any idea of what to do with his symptoms. He had cried twenty out of every twenty-four hours and my mother followed the belief of the day and didn't pick him up except at four-hour intervals, so he cried a lot, and then scowled all his life, and finally drank himself to death. But lucky me. Mother had decided to feed her next baby when she felt like it, so I never needed to cry. No wonder I turned out so well.

"I felt that I had 'accomplished' my Primary Scenario quite well. I'd been through conventional therapy before and had my history down pat. I blamed any little problems I did have on my father and knew there was nothing my mother ever did wrong. From the time I was small she gave me the respect one would give an adult. She trusted my judgment, admired my intellect, and built up my self-confidence. I was reluctant to explore anything too deeply, though, because I didn't want to find that she wasn't the wonderfully charming, humorous, considerate person I had always thought. What if I dug up something awful, like she beat me daily and locked me in the closet— such a discovery would undermine my foundations. But I wasn't too afraid this would happen. My other therapist had dug and poked around a lot and my mother's image remained unscathed.

"Nevertheless, I came to the session with considerable trepidation and determination. I wasn't used to expressing anything but my pleasant emotions and I didn't want to. I never had, how could I start now? I'd heard about body work and releasing emotions and it scared and disgusted me, just the thought of crying or gagging in front of anyone. God forbid, what if I regressed and sucked my thumb— I'd never be comfortable with the therapist again. But in the midst of this fear, I reassured myself that it probably wouldn't happen anyway. For one thing, I thought I had enough control so that I could face up to a submerged emotion with dignity, without funny noises or unpleasant scenes. For another thing— and I really comforted myself with this thought— I didn't think I had very many nasty emotions, at least not repressed ones. I habitually swore at bad drivers and kicked machines that didn't work, but those were open and unrepressed, so maybe I had nothing to fear at all. God knows I was considered cheerful, happy, serene, calm, and confident by the people who knew me. 'So maybe nothing lurks underneath,' I told myself. 'Won't Helen be surprised,' and I went to that fateful session with the same smug confidence I had always taken to examinations in school.

"I had worn a snug fitting tank top and tights because Helen had said it was important for her to see as much of my body's movements and coloring as she could. I was used to very light clothing but this morning, sitting in the waiting room that was always too warm, I was chilly. I was even colder in Helen's office where it was probably five degrees warmer, but I refused to admit that I might be tense. 'Not me, I'm easy; I'll do just as I'm told,' I thought, as she told me to lie down on the massage table.

"'Lie on your back,' she told me, ' and bring your knees up. Now place your feet about as far apart as your hips and put your arms at your side.' I complied, 'Now put your legs a little farther apart,' she said. I squirmed my feet over a bit. 'And now your knees,' she said patiently. I looked at my knees; they were clamped tight together like a pair of magnets. I pulled them apart and watched them snap back together. 'That's okay,' said Helen, 'just relax a little bit and they'll come around as we work.' 'Now look at me,' she said. Her voice was low and vibrant. There was an aliveness to it that made me constantly aware that she was 'all there' and more attentive to my words and feelings than I was myself. I had learned to trust her, so I obeyed, frightened though I was.

"I looked in her eyes, at her pleasant, friendly expression, and hoped earnestly that I wouldn't disappoint her. 'Are you here?' she asked. 'Are you ready to work?' My affirmative answers sounded like a strangled squeak. 'What do you feel?' she asked. I was uncomfortable because I didn't feel much, but I described the sensation of my arms on the table, the tautness where my knees bent, the hardness of the table against my head. 'That's it?' she asked. 'Yes, that's it,' I apologized.

"'I want you to breathe now,' she told me. 'Breathe through your mouth and breathe into *here* — do you mind if I touch you?' she asked, indicating a spot not much below my collar bone. I didn't know my lungs were up that high, but I did as I was told. Or I thought I did, but she said, 'Now see if you can make your chest move.' I tried again with a big deep breath, pushing my shoulders back as far as I could against the firm table. That time even I could see that nothing much moved. She put her hand on my upper chest, and pressed firmly. 'Now breathe,' she said, 'and push against my hand.' We did that several times until I began to have the feeling that I could, indeed, move her hand. Then she released the pressure suddenly and my chest expanded. 'Good, now keep it moving that much,' she said, and I tried. It was hard work.

"'What do you feel?' she asked. This time I could tell her something. My mouth was dry from the breathing, my chest felt a bit frantic, making me think of coronaries, and my fingers were tingling. Not altogether pleasant, but I was pleased to produce some feelings for her.

"I kept on breathing deeply, watching my chest rise and fall. When Helen said to breathe faster, I did so, although I felt as though I'd had quite enough air for the next month. 'What do you feel now?' she asked again, and I told her that I felt as though I were ready to go, that I was poised for action somehow. My lower arms, my thighs, and my calves seemed to be outlined in tingles and my feet were eager to bear my weight even while they felt completely relaxed. 'Are you warmer now?' she asked. I said I was, but then I began to tremble. My knees, which had finally relaxed to a comfortable distance, were knocking against each other. My ribs were moving sporadically in and out while a convulsive wave sped from my belly to my neck, back down, and then up again. It barely passed through my mind that I might be getting sick, but I was too caught up in trying not to tremble so violently to worry.

"'You can let some sound out as you breathe,' offered Helen. I wondered why she thought I might like to, but decided to try. First I emitted a small squeak, then a faint wheeze, then a timid croak. 'Good,' said Helen, sounding like a mother praising an inept but earnest child. 'Try some more.' I tried, but suddenly I didn't have to try. The trembling in my body, the convulsive wave I was afraid was nausea must have reminded me unconsciously of the noise I needed to make and I began to sob. 'There!' said Helen, sounding so satisfied I didn't even feel apologetic about losing my dignity. It felt so wonderful to cry, to sob like a baby, though why I wanted to just because I'd been breathing hard, I couldn't fathom.

"Helen's voice came through my sobs. 'What do you feel like?' 'Like a little girl,' I sobbed. 'Can you picture that little girl?' she asked. I could. She was that sweet little toddler playing by the lake that I knew so well from our family movies. Around her bald head was tied a blue ribbon and she wore the apple- cheeked smile she always wore. Cute happy little kid.

" 'Now what would you like to do with her?' asked Helen. Dumb question. The kid was perfectly happy picking flowers, so why disturb her, but to my surprise I burst out, 'I want to hold her.'

" 'So hold her,' said Helen, as though it were only reasonable. I scooped her up in my arms and she only struggled a little bit. 'You can hold yourself, too, you know,' offered Helen, and she helped me wrap my arms around my shoulders the way you do when you' re alone and *must* hug yourself in joy or sorrow.

"It was the strangest thing. I had imagined hugging a sweet child who obviously didn' t need a thing, but I knew at the same time that that sunny little girl was the same as the grown- up lady sobbing uncontrollably. And putting my arms around the baby in my imagination was the same as hugging myself and trying to console *me* for whatever sadness was hidden there underneath my ribs.

"Helen had me roll over onto my side and I curled easily into a fetal position. 'You can hold that little girl any time you want to, you know,' she said. 'Your mother had a lot of worries. She must have felt bad when your brother cried and your father hurt her. She counted on you to be her good girl. It must have been awful never to be able to cry or disobey.' I had never thought of myself as being anything but naturally docile, but the continuing sobs, coming straight from my gut, agreed with Helen that it had, indeed, been awful.

" 'Babies cry and get dirty and throw up and break things,' she went on. 'It' s normal. You can help that little girl inside you grow up. Just comfort her whenever she feels bad and let her know *you* love her even when she' s not the perfect, smiling baby her mother loved. Tell her that her bad feelings are just as acceptable as her good ones and you' ll always love her.'

"I cried a while longer, then rolled onto my back. 'Notice the feeling in your body,' said Helen, and this time it was a pleasure to take inventory. I wasn' t tingling, but I could feel my body, every inch of it, even the calloused soles of my feet. At the very same time I felt wondrously relaxed and full of life. I could have slept soundly or gone dancing. 'Look at your face,' said Helen, handing me a mirror. 'See how easy the lines are around your eyes and how open your expression is.' She was right. My jaw looked smoother, too. I looked the way I look when I' m in love or serenely happy, eyes wide open and unguarded."

Sara's experience followed the classical pattern we depict in Figure 9, when we tell about the breathing work and developing a charge. Because she was physically active and had a healthy awareness in her body, she learned more from her first session than would a person who was less aware and more defended.

And she learned a great deal. Her fears that she would find out terrible things about her mother didn't come true. The injury her mother had inflicted was in not seeing or accepting the normal, negative side of Sara's nature. Punishment was in showing her disappointment, and by gently chiding, "Oh Sally, how could you?" The gentleness was insidious, for it made Sara stifle any impulses that might lead to her mother's disappointment.

"To this day," says Sara, "whenever I do something clumsy or forget some dumb thing, I call myself by my baby name in exactly the same patiently irritated voice 'Oh Sally. . . .' "

Yet the injury, inconsequential though it was from a grown-up's vantage point, made Sara grow up afraid of disappointing people. She couldn't stand the disappointment in her mother's eyes, and as she grew older she learned how to avoid provoking disappointment in other relationships. She became eternally agreeable. Her friends liked her and a lot of people took advantage of her, but other people thought she lacked spice and asked, "Don't you ever have opinions or objections?"

"I don't," she said. "I honestly don't usually care where we have lunch or which side of the bed I sleep on." This is consistent with her fear of disappointing people. She learned to suspend strong feelings and wait until she found out what other people wanted. She wasn't, however, totally without opinions and preferences, but she generally kept these to herself. Eventually, it all backfired. She couldn't please everybody, and in trying to do so, she began disappointing them. This was so hard on her that she hunted up a new therapist and began looking at her life.

She was surprised that her feelings came out so quickly, for she had kept them well hidden from her previous therapist. Of course he hadn't taken her Primary Scenario nor thought to look for the repeating patterns in her life. And she had breathed normally in her sessions, which meant that she had barely breathed. She hadn't inveigled her body into giving up its secrets by infusing it with oxygen in a way designed to do just that. She just sat there, talking. *And just talking won't do it.*

Basic Concepts of Body Therapy

We owe a great deal to Wilhelm Reich for his pioneering work in bringing the body into psychotherapy. Freud didn't believe in looking at his clients, let alone touching their bodies, and generations of psychotherapists followed his example. Reich came along and changed that. He believed in contact, so he sat facing his clients, looking into their eyes, and occasionally touching them. In *Character Analysis*, he addressed the issue of "contactlessness":

> Whenever natural, adequate, instinctual impulses are denied direct relationship to objects of the world the result is anxiety, as the expression of a crawling into oneself, and the development of a wall of contactlessness.[1]

He went further than superficial contact, though, and his work with the body is the foundation and core of most "body therapies." His theories deeply influenced Fritz Perls, developer of Gestalt therapy.

Reich believed, as did Freud, that the cause of neurosis was repressed sexual energy. Reich also believed that the ultimate goal of therapy was to restore free, natural energy flow. This would establish "full orgastic potency," the ability to build up and release full energy in orgasm. The way to restore the energy flow was to dissolve the neurotic character structure that restricted it. He said that the energy was restricted by way of "armoring" in the form of fixed muscular attitudes. "It is as if," he states in *Character Analysis*, "the affective personality put on an armor, a rigid shell on which the knocks from the outer world as well as the inner demand rebound. This armor makes the individual less sensitive to unpleasure, but it also reduces his libidinal and aggressive mobility and, with that, his capacity for pleasure and achievement."[2]

Reich's formulation of a muscular theory of repression was a major paradigm shift in psychological circles and has effected much change in therapeutic methods.

When people are in a state of repression— that is, when they try to keep an idea or impulse from consciousness— they experience tension, or muscular contraction. If a waiter, for instance, has to carry out his duties politely no matter how boorish the customers, he must repress any urge he has to spill coffee in their laps. If it's a long night of boorish customers he will probably go home with a headache or a stiff neck or a muscle spasm somewhere. When this contraction is severe and chronic, it becomes armoring; the muscles are fixed into patterns and cannot readily expand. Reich called this armoring "the freezing of emotions." It results in deadness. The body shrinks or contracts to avoid pain and thereby cuts off pleasure as well, since muscular expansion is associated with pleasurable sensations.

The natural diversion of energy to a muscle is functional, but when the work is done, the muscle should relax or expand, and release the energy. If the energy remains bound up in the muscle and the muscle remains contracted and ready for work, the flow of energy is cut off and the natural functioning of the body becomes blocked. If the body remains in this state, sexual excitement and orgasm, among other things, are inhibited. The aim of Reich's therapy was to relieve this inhibition by ridding the body of chronic muscular armoring and allowing the release of repressed emotions until the free flow of energy is re-established in the body.

We don't identify with any current body therapy practices, despite our common foundation in Reichian theory, because of some important differences. The major difference is in the goal of therapy, or the purpose. To Reich, the goal was to dissolve all the armoring in the body to release the bound energy. This would establish "full orgastic potency" or the ability to build up and release full energy in orgasm.

In Integrative Body Psychotherapy we believe that the aliveness in the body, the flow of energy, is the sense of Self. The Self is a non-verbal sense of well-being, continuity, and identity in the body, plus the verbal structure and cognitive process one learns. Our goal in therapy is to find that sense. Although we have built on Reich's theory and methods, we have an expanded theory regarding the energy in the body. That is, we see greater use for the energy of the soul and the Self than simply its full release in orgasm.

Cathartic Release

In many current body therapies, cathartic release occurs without a contact-full relationship between client and therapist, and therein lies their flaw. The value of cathartic release is lost if the client isn't in emotional contact with the therapist during the releasing. It is the contact in the relationship that provides the healing factor, grounds the experience, and makes it real. We've seen many people who have undergone "expressive release" forms of therapy, but they typically don't remember the releases. They feel better afterwards but the sense of well-being doesn't last long. Although many people get hooked on "venting," they are getting only symptom relief. The repeated discharges of emotion, without any deeper awareness, don't contact the underlying injury. The armor is softened only temporarily and re-forms when the person goes out into the world, because the underlying cause of the armor hasn't been touched.

Had Sara done the breathing part of her session alone, she might have broken down into great sobs and felt much better for it, but she would never have known why she was crying. Had Helen not been there, armed with information from the Primary Scenario, to help her see that the tears might belong to herself as a child, Sara might have thought they were caused only by the unusual breathing. After all, our bodies have been hiding secrets from us for many years and won't relinquish them easily. We repressed these secret emotions to spare ourselves pain and will continue to do so. It is only in a situation of trust that we can begin to confront the pain. And in order to make that confrontation a valuable learning experience, we need the therapist to connect the body experience to the emotional one. This is the beginning of the process of integration, of connecting the cognitive, verbal Self to the more primitive physical and emotional Self.

We're reminded of one case in particular in which the client, Stewart, had had several years of release-oriented therapy before he came to IBP. In all those years he had never developed a relationship with the therapist. He would simply lie down and breathe, neither looking at nor speaking with him. When his muscles would begin to contract, he would break through the tension by outbursts of emotion, primarily crying. He had a great sense of relief after each session, and came to IBP expecting a similar process. In the first session it was clear that the previous emotional releases that he had experienced had been of temporary value and had not removed his rigid armoring. His face was mask-like, his neck was extremely rigid, and his body was very thin and tightly muscled. He was a severely armored person, completely unable to maintain contact or to interact with the therapist. His eyes were vacant, and it was difficult to feel his presence. When asked to close his eyes, he was unable to do so completely, and they remained neither closed nor open in a semi-guarded expression. It was clear that therapy could not progress without dealing with the lack of contact. This condition was reflected in his life by his inability to form or maintain relationships. The tragedy was that this client had worked very hard in his previous therapy, enduring gut-wrenching emotional experiences, which were ultimately futile because he was never really touched emotionally.

In IBP the goal isn't release but the discovery of the Self and identity through exploration of the origin of the blocks. Learning to understand the function of the armoring is a major part of the therapy process. Once this awareness develops, release may occur as a conscious choice by the client. In this way, too, he can choose to let go of obsolete behavior patterns and incorporate new responses to the unchanged context of his life. Therefore, our first goal is not to remove defensive character armor, but to use awareness of it and of its function as a base from which to do psychological exploration.

The armor, or block, is a chronic muscular contraction that occured originally as a protective mechanism, and it signifies that a person is holding onto an unfinished situation. In the therapeutic relationship, the client re-enacts this unfinished situation in the present. This lets the therapist see the repetitious nature of the process, relate it to the Primary Scenario, and intervene. Sometimes the therapist will refrain from intervening when the client confronts a block. This can be frustrating for the client, but we use the frustration as a tool to show a person how he interrupts his energy flow and to point out how he does this in his life as well as in a therapy session. We want to show him how he is cutting off his aliveness and his sense of Self.

We want the client to feel safe during the painful process of melting the armor, so we tailor the therapy individually, basing the kind of work we do on our initial assessment and the information we have from the Primary Scenario. Some people tolerate fairly invasive techniques and others must proceed slowly. When the therapist remains in contact with the client and maintains their relationship, the client can eventually take responsibility for participating in the giving up of his defenses. If the therapist does the releasing— that is, if he uses some technique such as massage or movement to release the tension held in a muscle— the client can become dependent upon the therapist. That is why the therapist depends primarily on the relationship to heal the client and give him the strength and courage to drop his defenses. It's similar to the way a parent tries to teach a child how to be responsible because he won't always be there to take care of him.

A person's defenses are important and we respect them. For this reason we seldom use invasive muscular manipulative techniques such as deep tissue massage and stress movement patterns. One danger in doing so is that the client simply withdraws, moving his defenses to a deeper level. It's like pursuing someone with such a fearful weapon that he can only run deeper into the forest.

This door you might not open, and you did;
So enter now, and see for what slight thing
You are betrayed. . . Here is no treasure hid,
No cauldron, no clear crystal mirroring
The sought-for Truth, no heads of women slain
For greed like yours, no writhings of distress;
But only what you see. . . Look yet again:
An empty room, cobwebbed and comfortless.
Yet this alone out of my life I kept
Unto myself, lest any know me quite;
And you did so profane me when you crept
Unto the threshold of this room tonight
That I must never more behold your face.
This now is yours. I seek another place.

Edna St. Vincent Millay

Reprinted with permission from Collected Poems, Edna St. Vincent Millay, 1917, 1945, Harper and Row.

In IBP we find that it is possible and preferable to draw a person out with tenderness and compassion. However, there are situations in which the use of muscular release techniques is of value. For example, when the muscular contractions are so chronic that it is virtually impossible for the person to release himself without outside help, then we may assist with physical releasing techniques.

As the armor is being dissolved, it is important to replace the released painful experiences with "positive introjects." These are not so much images or voices as they are good feelings such as a good parent might instill in a child with a smile, a hug, a look of approval, or some assurance of acceptance and unconditional love. It was the opposite of this that caused the original injuries, and the old injury is healed by the positive introject. This value of the therapeutic transference is that the therapist temporarily provides this ideal parental support until the client has developed a sense of Self in his body and internalized this positive parent. This is what happened to Sara when she wanted to hold the child that was herself. Her therapist let her know that she could give that little child the unconditional loving it needed and she could do it in the present. She helped her replace the chronic tension in her muscles with a positive introject.

The aim is not to eliminate defenses entirely. They will surface when needed in threatening situations, but when the danger has passed, the healthy body can relax, This differs from chronic armoring, which is inflexible and cannot be relaxed. The aim of therapy, then, is to create flexibility and choice. We in IBP see it as replacing defensive, rigid characterological and muscular boundaries with Self boundaries which express the individual's sense of identity and are flexible.

Reich's Notion of Orgastic Potency

Reich came to the conclusion that emotional health was related to the capacity for full surrender in the sexual act, or what he called orgastic potency. Energy bound in chronic muscular tensions prevents that energy from being available for sexual release; thus his concern with dissolving those tensions. It is important to understand that Reich defined orgasm not as an ejaculation or a climax, but as an involuntary response of the total body, manifested in rhythmic, convulsive movements. This same type of movement can occur in a session when the breathing is completely free and a person surrenders to his body.

The release of sexual energy normally comes at the end of the orgastic reflex. Theoretically, a person whose body is free enough to have this reflex during the therapy session would also be able to experience the full orgasm in intercourse and would be considered healthy by Reich's standards.

This is where we depart from Reich, for we believe that therapy continues well beyond the achievement of the full orgastic reflex. The reflex indicates that the body has been opened up to the strong energy currents within, allowing them to pass through it without blocks. With the orgastic release, the person experiences a loss of normal ego awareness, a profound feeling of peace, and a sense of integration and connectedness wth the Self. This altered state of consciouness then becomes the foundation for moving into the transpersonal or spiritual aspects of the therapy. It is as though the orgastic reflex forms the first half of a cycle of energy waves through the body. We now work to move the energy back through the unblocked body in order to achieve a fuller choice of the expression of this energy. While Reich formulated the idea of the life force in the form of orgone energy, he never fully realized the potential of this concept. We will discuss the transpersonal aspects of IBP in Chapter 9.

The Charging Process

Reich's orgasm formula described the cycle of tension, charge, discharge, and relaxation. The Reichian breathing moves a client through this cycle. The reason we devote so much space to the orgasm cycle is that it parallels a typical breathing session in IBP.

Figure 9
Charge/Discharge Cycle*

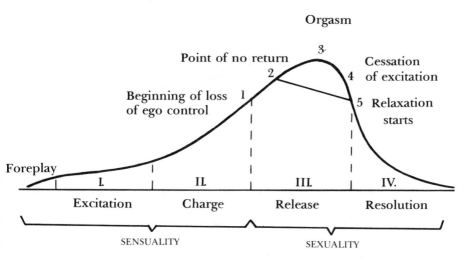

* This diagram closely typifies the male sexual response. See page 240 for the typical female response patterns.

If we look at this graph in terms of a therapy session, we see a build-up of charge that occurs through the breathing process. The person lies on a firm surface such as a hard mattress, knees raised, feet flat (equal amount of pressure on heel and toe), and approximately pelvic width apart. Since we are paying close attention to subtle changes in the body, it is necessary to see as much of it as is comfortable for both the client and therapist. It is more important for the chest and legs to be uncovered, but it rarely is necessary for the client to be completely nude.

Figure 10
Breathing Position

In IBP, intensification and expansion of the excitement in the body are encouraged and are referred to as "charging." A convenient way to look at the level of charge is on a scale of one to ten. We try to work at a charge level of six or seven. One of the first signs of physiological changes is the tingling of the skin, caused by an increase in circulation.

Another sign of charge on the physical level is change in skin coloration. Areas of charge will turn red or mottled because of increased blood flow to the capillaries close to the surface of the skin. Blocked, or uncharged areas will turn white where constriction occurs. The lines of demarcation between the red, charged areas and the white, constricted areas are often as obvious as the bathing suit lines on somebody who is sunburned.

Another indication is change in skin temperature. Even in a cold room, a person doing the breathing work will feel warm as a result of the increased circulation. But where a person's fixed muscular patterns inhibit the increased circulation, the skin will feel cool to the touch.

Think of this expansion and contraction of the body in terms of a balloon responding to pressure from inside. Think, in particular, of a balloon that was partially blown up, then had a picture painted on it. When it's blown up farther, it resists expansion where it was painted because the paint won't allow the rubber to stretch. Similarly, the body (the balloon) expands in response to the charge (the pressure), remaining constricted where it has muscular blocks, corresponding to the paint on the balloon.

Progress in charging seems to be in steps or levels. A person will periodically reach a plateau, and then there will be a sudden breakthrough, and the person will move on from there. The problem is in trying to go too fast. It is important not to go beyond the body's level of tolerance for the increased feelings that come with deep breathing and "letting go." A person's body must be given time to overcome old patterns. Many people "push" themselves in the therapy. The therapist can let them see how they also push themseves in their lives, in their work, in their sexual orgasms. He can connect this pattern to the repetitive patterns in their Primary Scenarios.

In the first part of the charge-building, the excitation phase, we often find that people cannot tolerate the feeling of the charge. We see exactly the same thing on the sexual level. Splitting off is frequently the way in which people avoid their excitement in sex, in everyday activities, and in the therapy session.

During the excitation phase (Phase I), people will interrupt the building of a charge by both physical and psychological means (giggling, for instance, or splitting off). During this phase, we maintain contact to keep the person present so that excitement can build. In the charge phase (Phase II), we see interruptions that are usually more of a psychological nature, such as the client experiencing regressive states which are basically reliving early painful experiences. It is in this phase that healing occurs and the positive introject is introduced. In Phase III we usually see more transpersonal experiences, such as out-of-body states, or in-body states of a very profound nature, such as archetypical experiences (see Chapter 9). In the resolution phase we see relaxation beginning. We ask the person to put his legs down, and a hyperparasympathetic state begins, which is a profound sense of well-being and a sense of Self.

We focus here on the excitation phase by looking at the charge-discharge cycles as a body experience. Now we will describe the breathing process. Ideally, as breathing increases, energy builds in the body, reaches a peak of excitation, and is released or discharged. (See Figure on p. 101). In actuality, each person's process of excitation and release is different. (See figures 11, 12, and 13).

Figure 11
Lack of Tolerance for Excitement
and Rapid Discharge

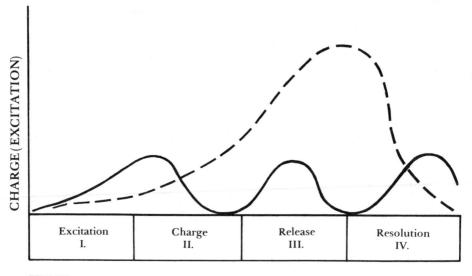

| Excitation
I. | Charge
II. | Release
III. | Resolution
IV. |

TIME

    This person cannot tolerate increased excitement and discharges rapidly. Consequently, low levels of charge are reached and quickly released. On a psychological level, this can be seen as an inability to tolerate pleasurable feelings. On a sexual level, premature ejaculation is an example of this. Focus should be on learning to contain and build a charge (excitement/pleasure).

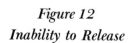

Figure 12
Inability to Release

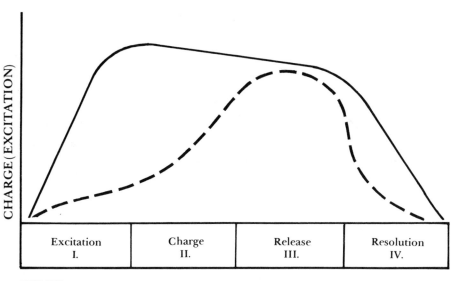

| Excitation I. | Charge II. | Release III. | Resolution IV. |

TIME

This person builds a high charge quickly but cannot release it. May have minimal orgasm but release and resolution stages are protracted. Focus should be on maintaining contact, grounding, and paying attention to release impulses that are being avoided. On a psychological level, this indicates splitting off from the situation so that excitement is not experienced and greater and greater levels of stimulation do not bring release. Sexually, this is very common in pre-orgastic women who seem to need a great deal of stimulation for release, or in retarded ejaculation in men. In life, this can be seen in people who seek constant stimulation, often dangerous, in order to make them feel alive.

Figure 13
Flexible Charge and Release Pattern

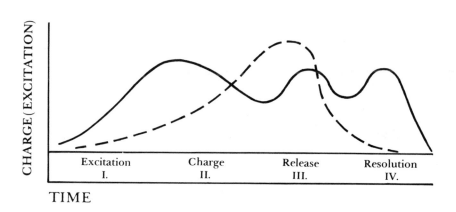

CHARGE (EXCITATION)

| Excitation | Charge | Release | Resolution |
| I. | II. | III. | IV. |

TIME

This person develops a high charge and can sustain excitement, maintain contact, and reach orgasm easily with minimal tension. This can be seen on a lifestyle level— this person has ups and downs, but moves from one event to the next, enjoying his or her life. This charge-discharge curve is similar to a multi-orgastic pattern.

The Breathing Process

A charge can be built up by altering a person's normal breathing pattern. To promote this excitement, he fires up the sympathetic nervous system by breathing into his upper chest (as opposed to diaphragmatic or belly breathing). Increasing the level of excitement increases the level of energy. Breathing is the most basic function of the body and is directly related to emotion. Any emotional response one has will immediately change one's breathing pattern. Conversely, by consciously changing one's breathing, it is possible to alter emotions and feelings.

A person should respond to an increase in excitement or charge by increasing his rate of breathing. Instead, many people are uncomfortable with the charge and they attempt to control their excitement so they can stay "calm, cool, and collected." They do this by curtailing their breathing. The reason that they do this is that breathing deeply and fully amplifies their awareness of feelings. Many of the feelings that emerge with the deep breathing are uncomfortable ones, so most people avoid awareness by restricting their breathing. Unfortunately, while restricting the breathing to repress uncomfortable feelings, they restrict feelings of pleasure as well. This is not just a reaction we see in therapy, but a common pattern of the average man- on- the- street. Most people breathe with only a portion of their lung capacity during the normal day and then hold their breath when they get tense or frightened. In order to continue this discussion of the breathing process, we must now talk about the effects of breathing on the autonomic nervous system.

Autonomic Nervous System

Reich's initial system of therapy, which grew out of character analysis, was called "vegeto- therapy," after the vegetative responses of the autonomic nervous system. The mobilization of feeling through breathing and movement of the musculature activates the vegetative centers (the ganglia of the autonomic nervous system) and thus liberates vegetative energy. The body has two nervous systems: the central nervous system, or the voluntary nervous system, and the autonomic nervous system, which is considered involuntary. The central nervous system controls muscular movement and voluntary responses; the autonomic nervous system controls the functions of organs, emotions (through the endocrine system), respiration, and is also concerned with sexual response (through the endocrine and circulatory systems). Reichian therapy is primarily concerned with the autonomic nervous system, Reich's theory being that the character resistances (armoring) are "automatic," and therefore locked into the autonomic nervous system.

The autonomic nervous system has two components: the sympathetic and the parasympathetic. The sympathetic nervous system (sometimes called the "fight or flight" system) serves to protect the person by mobilizing his resources: increasing adrenalin, heart rate, and respiration rate, and by readying muscles for action. This can be seen as a state of contraction. (See Chart 6). In this state, the person has increased energy to meet the stress.

The parasympathetic side is the subtler, relaxed side that mediates pleasure and free-flowing feelings. It can be seen as a state of expansion. Ideally, there is a balance between the two systems, and this can be achieved by changing a person's breathing pattern. If, for example, a person is tense and fearful, moving the breathing to the diaphragm and/or belly and slowing it will activate the parasympathetic system, and calm the person.

If a person has a toneless, apathetic personality and body, a goal would be to energize the sympathetic side by having him breathe from the upper chest, because this builds a charge that activates the sympathetic side. Breathing bridges the voluntary and involuntary nervous system; it is both a voluntary and involuntary activity. By voluntarily manipulating or controlling his breathing, a person can affect his involuntary responses.

The goal is balance. If a person is under psychological stress, the sympathetic nervous system of the body reacts as if he were in actual physical danger. This continued reaction can cause symptoms of stress and "diseases of adaptation," as Hans Selye calls it in *The Stress of Life*[3]. A person can be taught techniques to release the tension by learning to activate the parasympathetic nervous system, bringing it into balance with the sympathetic side.

Interruptions

Many people have difficulty building a charge. Muscular interruptions to the charge tend to occur during Phase I (excitation). (See Figure 9). They may take the form of thinking, dizziness and/or nausea (usually a sign of anxiety), splitting off, "spacing-out," fidgeting, scratching, squirming, yawning, falling asleep, muscle spasm, cramping, ear ringing, urge to urinate, talking, laughing, and a number of other responses that dissipate the intensity of the charge. Since the increased charge of energy in the body induces feelings of excitation and pleasure, we want to help the client tolerate these intensifed feelings of pleasure and increased amounts of energy without interruption. Rather than seeing interruptions as difficulties, we see them as expressions of resistance, and as indicators of where or at what point the therapy should be done. They are signs of blocks the client has. Because we are alert to his unconscious attempts to avoid painful impasses, we ask him to stay with the block, to experience the discomfort of the holding rather than changing or releasing it immediately.

For example, during Sara's session at the beginning of the chapter, she reached a point in her feelings where she wanted to cry,

Figure 14
The Nervous System

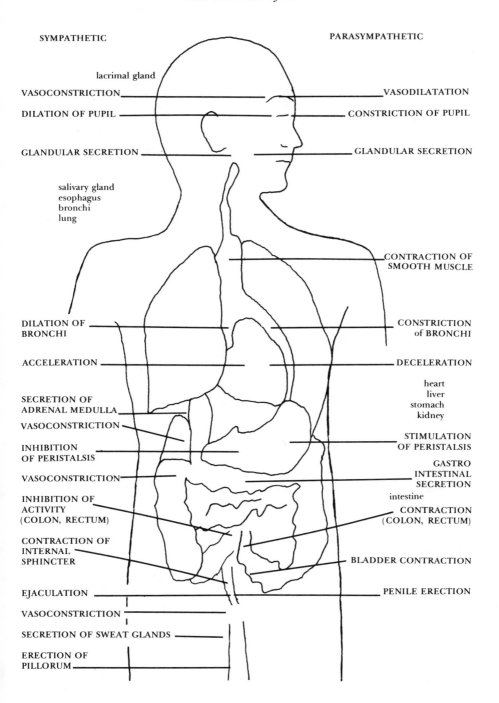

Figure 15: Functioning of the Autonomic Nervous System		
Sympathetic Effect	Organ	Parasympathetic Effect
Inhibition of the m. sphincter pupillae; *dilated pupils*	Musculature of the iris	Stimulation of the m. sphincter pupillae: *narrowing of the pupils.*
Inhibition of the lachrymal glands: "dry eyes." Depression	Lachrymal glands	Stimulation of the lachrymal glands: "glowing eyes." Joy
Inhibition of the salivary glands: "parched mouth"	Salivary glands	Stimulation and increased secretion of the salivary glands: "making mouth water"
Stimulation of the sweat glands in face and body: "skin is moist and cold"	Sweat glands	Inhibition of the sweat glands in face and body: "skin is dry"
Contraction of the arteries: "Cold sweat, " pallor, anxiety	Arteries	Dilation of the arteries: "freshness and flushing of skin, increased turgor without perspiration"
Musculature of hair follicle is stimulated: hair bristles, "goose pimples," chills	Arrectores pilorum	Inhibition of arrectores pilorum: skin becomes smooth and warm
Inhibition of the contractive musculater: bronchi are relaxed	Bronchial musculature	Stimulates the contraction of the bronchial musculature: bronchi are narrowed
Stimulates cardiac action: palpitation, rapid heart beat	Heart	Slows cardiac action: quiet heart, slower pulse
Inhibits peristalsis: reduces secretion of digestive glands	Digestive tract; liver, pancreas, kidneys, all digestive glands	Stimulates peristalsis: increases secretion of digestive glands
Increases adrenal secretion: anxiety reaction	Supradrenal gland	Reduces adrenal secretion: pleasure reaction
Inhibits musculature of the bladder, stimulates urinary sphincter: inhibits micturition	Urinary bladder	Stimulates musculature of the bladder, inhibits the sphincter: stimulates micturition
Tightening of the smooth musculature, reduces secretion of all glands, decrease of blood supply, dry vagina: reduction of sexual feeling	Female sex organs	Relaxation of the smooth musculature, stimulates all gland functions, increases blood flow, moist vagina: increase of sexual feeling
Tightening of the smooth musculature of the scrotum, reduction of gland functions, decrease of blood supply, flaccid penis: "diminished sexual desire."	Male sex organs	Relaxation of the smooth musculature of the scrotum, increases all secretions, increases blood flow, erection: "intensified sexual desire"

but she'd built up her armor against crying, so she resisted the feeling. The interruption came in the form of violent trembling and shaking. At this point her therapist could have either taken the course that was described — let her cry and talk about the feelings afterward — or the therapist would have had her confront the block. She could have done the latter by asking, "Can you feel anything? What's happening? What do you feel in your chest? Your throat? How are you feeling about the shaking?" she would have helped her see where the tension was — the tightness in her chest, the taut diaphragm, the clenched jaw, and the tightly constricted muscles around the eyes — then she would have asked Sara to concentrate on how she was blocking her feelings. The therapist might then have empathized, saying, "It must be terribly painful for you to be so close to your feelings and not be able to let them go."

The value in the second approach is that many people aren't aware that they are blocking. If the therapist lets them release their tears or their anger, the emotion dissipates, and the lesson is lost. This is like the cathartic release therapies: it brings temporary elation and relaxation but it is not the learning and re-learning process that we strive for.

As any school child knows, lessons learned under conditions of emotional excitement are the lessons remembered the longest. Who ever forgets his first love, his most embarrassing moment, or the things he learned from an inspired teacher? This is why the therapist gets so much mileage out of the interruptions to the breathing process. When a client is right up against strong emotions that are too painful for him to feel, he is extremely receptive. He is also vulnerable. The therapist must tread gently and not go any faster or deeper than the client can support. He must think of himself as a *guide*, assisting the client but not directing him. He *allows* the client to proceed but doesn't push, because even though his protective blocks are obsolete, they are part to his character structure and identity and mustn't be removed before he is ready. In fact, the therapist prefers to give him the responsibility for giving them up, rather as you let a child dive into the water when he is ready instead of pushing him before he gets over his fear.

Some interruptions are physiological in nature. They occur occasionally among clients in the early stages of body work. The rapid stimulation from the deep breathing changes the blood chemistry, leading to a decrease in calcium levels. This causes nerve symptoms such as numbness and tingling in the fingers and around the mouth and, sometimes, muscle spasm or cramping (tetanae). It may cause reduction in blood flow to the brain, which may result in light-headedness (dizziness) and in extreme cases, brief spells of unconsciousness, fainting, or syncope.

Once the body becomes used to high levels of oxygenation and the corresponding sense of aliveness throughout, these reactions seldom occur.

These symptoms are temporary and not dangerous, so they can be ignored if the client isn't distracted. However, if he is, the therapist should define what is happening and put it into perspective so the client can cope with the sensations of hyperventilation. Also, slowing or stopping the exaggerated breathing will correct the imbalance that is causing it almost immediately.

Muscular interruptions, or tetanae, may cause discomfort and some degree of loss of control. Pain or numbness are minor examples of this condition and feelings of paralysis or of the hands rising off the mat are more extreme. Spasm, or tetanae of the hand (Figure 3) and tightening of the sphincter muscles (eyes, mouth, vagina, anus) may occur, causing moderate fright to a client. This can be a valuable experience to people who have never allowed themselves to lose control.

For example, Ruth was a gifted cellist, a beautiful young woman with long blond hair and a perennially soulful expression. During her first breathing session, her hands went into spasm and she was terrified. "My God," she cried, "I'll never play again — I can't move my hands!" Her fear was real and intense and she came to realize as she talked about it that it was a chronic fear, not a sudden fear evoked by the spasm. "I dream about things happening to my hands." she said. "I always have, since I first knew I was good. The night before my first solo I woke up screaming because I dreamed that I was in Turkey and stole some food and had my right hand cut off as punishment. It came from a story I'd just read and I knew it was a far worse punishment than being put to death." Ruth hadn't known consciously how much tension she carried in her hands and how much fear was behind that tension, but her new awareness allowed her to give it up. The spasm that so frightened her not only didn't prevent her playing but ultimately allowed her to play even better.

Tetanae of the hand can be relieved in several ways: by simultaneous use of the energetic pressure points in the web of the hand and in the elbows (See Figure 19), by having the client slap his hands on the mat or table, or by having him massage them or rub them together.

Another interruption to the breathing process is *muscle vibration.*

Figure 16
Spasm or Tetanae of the Hand

This happens when a muscle begins to let go of its fixed pattern of tension, and it is similar to muscle fatigue, such as Sara's experience. The vibration may begin as gross jerking of the muscle, which eventually smoothes out into a pleasurable sensation. It is as though the fixed muscular pattern is shaken or melted, and as this happens, a sense of muscle aliveness begins. The muscles that are held most tightly will start to vibrate first, and we encourage this vibration to let the muscle relax.

Once the physical interruptions have been focused on and released and the charge proceeds, involuntary movements and pleasurable sensations will occur in the person's body. His energy field will be expanded and he will seem to glow. His whole body may vibrate. These sensations are from the energy flowing through the body. Reich called it *streaming*. Although the involuntary movements are called the "orgasm reflex," it isn't a true orgasm but something that can occur when the breathing is completely free and a person surrenders to the energy or the charge in his body.

The ability to be flexible enough to expand muscularly and to sustain one's charge is called *containment*. To go back to the balloon analogy, imagine a balloon with a tiny hole in it. It can be blown up, but it won't stay that way because the pressure is released in a thin stream from the pinhole. Some people release the charge the same way, letting it dissipate before it's even fully built up. Containment is an important ability to develop in this early stage of the work because maintaining a sense of well-being is necessary to facilitate and sustain the therapeutic relationship.

Emotional interruptions may occur in Phase II when a client is flooded with the emotions triggered by the release of old, fixed patterns. It is important to stay with the emotion until it subsides, allowing it full expression without cutting it off prematurely.

The physical and emotional interruptions are different expressions of the same inability to tolerate the excitement and pleasure of the charge. We discuss them separately to aid in recognition, but they may occur simultaneously and for the same purpose.

As the client begins to develop the capacity to tolerate higher levels of excitation and oxygenation through deeper breathing, the tingling of the charge tends to diminish, leaving only a charge of energy. This is a feeling of excitement and pleasure, a sense of vitality not unlike the feeling that follows an orgasm. The pleasure is in a profound sense of Self and well-being, and this can support a more intensified exploration of emotions. When a client has this sense of well-being deep within his body, he can begin to grow, to move forward both in therapy and in his life. Without this, he won't be able to sustain the changes he makes.

Chapter 5
Looking at the Body

Energy flows in the body from head to feet and feet to head. When that energy flow is blocked by fixed muscular patterns, it is called armoring. Muscular armoring runs laterally across the body and divides the body into segments. Each of the segments represents areas of the body where blockages of energy can occur.

The Segments

Reich organized the body into seven lateral segments as follows:

1. Ocular (eyes, brows, and forehead)
2. Oral (mouth and chin)
3. Cervical (neck, throat, and upper shoulders)
4. Thoracic (chest and back)
5. Diaphragmatic (lower chest and diaphragm)
6. Abdominal
7. Pelvic

In addition to Reich's seven segments, we divide the ocular, oral, and part of the cervical segments into four bands (see Figure 8).

It is interesting to note that in Hindu, and other mystical traditions, the body is seen as seven energy centers, which correspond to these segments. We will discuss the possible implications of these similarities in the Transpersonal Chapter.

All these segments are connected with varying degrees of interdependence. In a chronic state, armoring usually involves more than one adjacent segment. Therefore, even though we work with the segments separately, we keep in mind the whole body concept. As the armor in each segment is softened we work with associated and adjacent segments to maintain the openness and to prevent the armor from reforming.

Figure 17
Segments

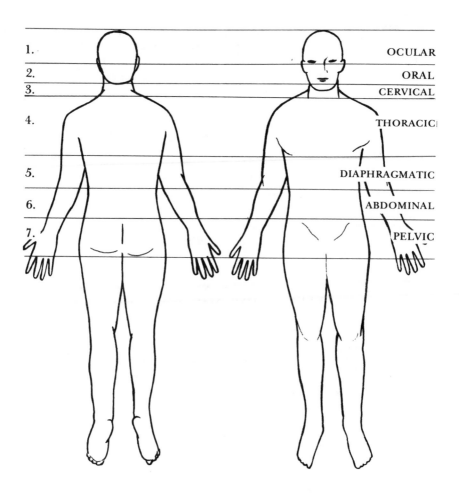

1.	OCULAR
2.	ORAL
3.	CERVICAL
4.	THORACIC
5.	DIAPHRAGMATIC
6.	ABDOMINAL
7.	PELVIC

Figure 18
Bands

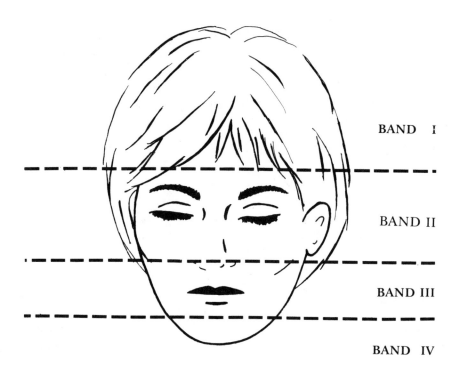

BAND I

BAND II

BAND III

BAND IV

In Reichian therapy, the general rule is to follow the segments sequentially from top to bottom. We follow a different sequence because the Reichian system seems too rigid, too contrary to the natural emergence of the client's repressed material. Instead, because contact is such an important issue in IBP, we begin each session by focusing on the ocular segment. Then we focus on the chest to facilitate breathing and to promote the sense of Self and well-being associated with this area (the heart). Opening these two areas is all that is needed for the client to be a full participant in the therapeutic process and to foster the therapeutic alliance.

We are very cautious in approaching the pelvic segment since such powerful emotions are held there that any premature opening may intensify resistance to the therapy. (In chapter 8 we will discuss particular ways of working with sexuality.) What we are talking about in essence, is the Gestalt theory of Organismic Self-Regulation. This means that the repressed material will emerge in a natural way and that the unfinished Gestalten, or situations, which are closest to the surface will be expressed first. By following and trusting the natural rhythm of the organism, we guard against moving too deeply and too quickly into the defended painful experiences, thereby respecting the defensive boundary of the client.

As we discuss the segments, it is important to remember that the person is an organismic whole. For purposes of explanation we present the segments separately, but it is the relationship of the segments to each other and to the whole body that gives us the clues to each person's unique character.

Release Techniques

There are a number of ways of working with the armor in each segment: verbal/cognitive, muscular, energetic, and stress movements, and subtle energy level (Kundalini). All of these approaches may be used at one time or another.

Verbal/Cognitive

Any therapy that directly involves the body leaves the client extremely vulnerable. Approaching the client on a verbal level is the least invasive method and leaves his defenses most intact. Therapy begins at this verbal level to establish contact and rapport. The therapist's empathic responses and acknowledgment of the client's pain can help him release his feelings. Only with this contact is it possible to address the body.

Muscular

Muscular release techniques are the most invasive and should be used only with certain character structures and when chronic armor resists other methods. When we discuss the muscular approach, we mean direct manipulation of the muscles through deep massage. There are five different ways of releasing tension in a muscle: stretch, press, massage, vibrate (shake), and stress (fatigue).

Energetic

Another way of releasing the body is the energetic approach, which is similar to the Oriental practice of acupressure. According to this system, energy moves along pathways called meridians and can be influenced by finger pressure applied to specific points along these pathways. Our approach differs from formal acupressure in that we do not follow the meridian system of stimulating the specific points related to various organs. Our method is similar to the Tantric system: we are concerned with moving energy *through* the body. The energetic pressure points that we use are usually relative to each specific segment in which we want to release blocked energy. Once a person has developed a charge through breathing, we can then move energy through blocked muscles by stimulating relevant pressure points (Figure 19), thereby allowing the charge to distribute evenly through the body. We use this method more often than the muscular or stress/ movement approaches.

Stress/ Movement

The stress/ movement approach refers to positions and movements used to induce muscle fatigue in specific segments in order to release blockages and the underlying emotions. These positions and movements (see IBP Release Techniques, Chart A, Appendix) push the muscles at a maximum stress so they will tire enough to release their chronic holding patterns. We use this approach with chronic, long- term holding that doesn't respond to gentler methods.

The major problem we see with this method is that it releases large amounts of emotional energy too fast, so that the repressed material associated with the holding cannot be dealt with in a subtle way. This approach can be overwhelming to the client, as opposed to the slower, more subtle approaches.

The Subtle Energy Level

The subtle energy level is defined by the building of Kundalini energy which is often experienced as heat in the body, usually along the back. The energy field around the body expands dramatically as well. This type of energy release is usually spontaneous, and if it occurs, it will be after most body blockages have been dissolved. We discuss it at more length in Chapter 9.

The Face

The face is a particularly important segment because it shows the most direct affect. Tomkins[1] views the face as a primary organ of manipulation and explorations. The face (and to a lesser extent the hand) is engaged in a very heavy two- way traffic communication.

Whatever it sends via tongue and facial muscles it also receives as feedback. For example, changes in blood flow to the face which produce changes in the temperature of the face are also received as feedback, most notably in the blush.

Figure 19
Pressure Points

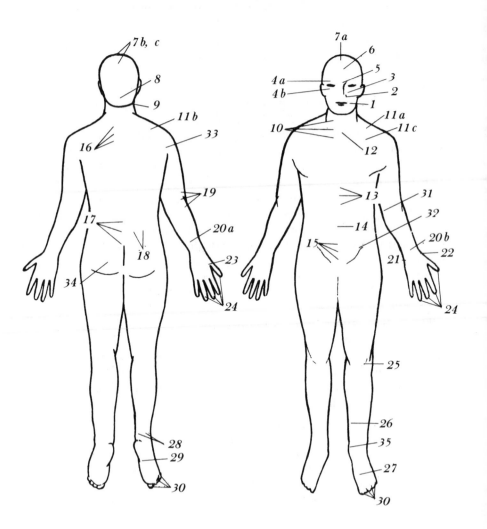

A person's face leads directly to his core; too much manipulation of the face is invasive. We would like to share a piece by Ranier Maria Rilke to help the reader get a feeling for the importance of the face:

Have I said it before? I am learning to see. Yes, I am beginning. It still goes badly. But I intend to make the most of my time.

To think, for instance, that I have never been aware before how many faces there are. There are quantities of human beings, but there are many more faces, for each person has several. There are people who wear the same face for years; naturally it wears out, it gets dirty, it splits at the folds, it stretches like gloves one has worn on a journey. These are thrifty, simple people; they do not change their face; they never even have it cleaned. It is good enough, they say, and who can prove to them the contrary? The question, of course, arises, since they have several faces, what do they do with the others? They store them up. Their children will wear them. But sometimes, too, it happens that their dogs go out with them on. And why not? A face is a face.

Other people put their faces on, one after the other, with uncanny rapidity, and wear them out. At first it seems to them they are provided for always; but they scarcely reach forth— and they have come to the last. This naturally has something tragic. They are not accustomed to taking care of faces, their last is worn through in a week, has holes, and in many places is thin as paper; and then little by little the under layer, the no-face, comes through, and they go about with that.

But the woman, the woman; she had completely collapsed into herself, forward into her hands. It was at the corner of Rue Notre-Dame-des-Champes. I began to walk softly as soon as I saw her. When poor people are reflecting they should not be disturbed. Perhaps their idea will yet occur to them.

The street was too empty; its emptiness was bored; it caught my step from under my feet and clattered about with it hither and yon, as with a wooden clog. The woman startled and pulled away too quickly out of herself, too violently, so that her face remained in her two hands. I could see it lying in them, its hollow form. It cost me indescribable effort to stay with those hands and not to look at what had torn itself out of them. I shuddered to see a face from the inside, but still I was much more afraid of the naked flayed head without a face.

— The Notebooks of Malta Laurids Brigge

We find it useful in IBP to divide the face and head into four bands, which fit into the Reichian ocular, oral, and cervical segments. All affect shows in a person's face, but some emotions show more in one band than in others.

Hand-face gestures are extremely important because they often show affective expression not understood unless seen in combination, such as hand over eyes, hand over mouth, hand to head, etc.

Working with the face is delicate because more efferent nerve fibers lead from the face to the brain than from any other part of the body, and they can easily be overstimulated. Also, because facial muscles attach directly to the skin with no protective fascia, massaging the face must be done with great care lest muscle fibers be injured. The face is composed of a multitude of very fine muscle fibers making great subleties of movement possible in displaying affect.

Band I: Top of Head and Forehead.

(See figure 18.) Included in this uppermost section are the entire scalp, temples, and occipital area. A fascial sheath connects the forehead muscles (frontalis) with the muscle at the back of the head (occipitalis). Thus, the frontalis and occipitalis are one muscle, running across the front and around the top to the back of the head. The therapist must massage the occipital area in order to release the frontalis (forehead). It is very useful for the therapist to observe the forehead since it reveals tension at the back of the head and the base of the skull. Mental states associated with the contraction of the forehead include: wondering, worrying, perplexity, despair, any intense form of thinking, and feelings of suffocation.

Another muscle connected to this area is the temporal muscle or temporalis. This muscle fans up alongside the head connecting the temple and the jaw, and is one of the five muscles that closes the jaw. It is possible to keep this muscle contracted even when the jaw is relaxed. Not surprisingly, anger is often associated with the release of the temporalis. To relieve temporal headaches, massage the temporalis horizontally above the temporal ridge.

The release of Band 1 allows the client to move energy into Band 2 (the eyes) for contact and expression. At this point in the therapy, our main interest is in helping the client to make contact with us, for it is of no use to do therapy with a person who isn't present. While the release of energy in the top of the head provides relief of headaches in this area, the treatment of psychosomatic disorders is not our focus. Releasing Band 1 often releases pent up emotions held in this area, which can result in a client "blowing his top." This is of value only if the client can make contact with the therapist as the venting occurs.

Other non-invasive ways of releasing the head include deep relaxation and sensory awareness. These techniques work especially well for migraine, since they relax constriction. Sensory awareness work allows the person to create a sense of space inside his head. Most people come in feeling as though their heads were stuffed with thoughts and emotions. Just creating some space in that area seems to provide relief, and it is a technique that people can learn to do for themselves whenever they feel pressure building up in their heads.

Band II: Eyes; Ocular Segment
   The eyes are probably the most exciting place to work because this is where the sense of aliveness, soul, and being shine through. Even before a client is able to cry, or to smile fully, we can make some contact with the person that we're seeking in his eyes. There are two levels of working with the eyes. First, contact: a softening of the intrinsic muscles of the eyes to allow the person to see you. Second, expression: allowing the aliveness to come through.
   There are two levels of ocular blocking. One is superficial, and the other is deeper. Blockage of the intrinsic muscles will cause a deadness of the eyes. In this case there is no expression or affect coming through — it is as if no one is there. A glazed look in the eye is more superficial, and when removed, the deeper level of blockage must be worked with as well. In the deeper block there is "no one home," and this is symptomatic of the split-off personality (see Chapter 6).
   We agree with Ellsworth Baker, when he says that armoring in this area "consists of a contraction and immobilization of the greater part of all the muscles around the eyes, eyelids, forehead, and tear glands, as well as the deep muscles at the base of the occiput — involving even the brain itself."[2]
   The eyes have both expressive and retentive functions. As the window to the soul, the eyes are always expressing, even when they appear blank. The eyes are a very private place, and much emotion is held in them. The predominant emotions manifested or suppressed in the eyes are love, joy, shame, anger, fear, and sadness. Anger is often shown by a wide-open glaring look, or a contracted look, while fear looks similar, but without the glare. With sadness we see misty, red, moist constricted eyes, and with shame we see moist downturned eyes.
   At the onset of breathing work, the first area of blockage will be the sphincter muscles of the eyes. Since the eyes are so important, this is one of the first places we work in order to relieve the contraction, and to make contact. We ask the person to look at us, and make sure that he can see us (i.e., to make contact). We ask him to use his eyes: to look around the room and then look back at us.
   To work with the eyes we massage the top and back of the head because holding in the eyes often results from stiffness and rigidity in the neck and head, since the ocular band goes all the way around the

head. We also massage the temporal area around the eyes, allowing
the Self to be expressed.

According to Reichian theory, if certain emotions have been
chronically repressed, protective patterns patterned in the eyes are
created and visual defects such as nearsightedness (myopia) and
farsightedness (hyperopia) may develop. We believe that myopia is
similar to splitting off: keeping others out, withdrawal from contact.
Conversely, hyperopia is pushing others away with the eyes. Since
much tension is necessary to do this and this tension is released
when we begin to work with the eyes, there is often significant
improvement in vision with IBP work.

When someone has a fixed stare, we attempt to break this pattern
by mobilizing the eyes. We ask the client to limber up the eyes by
rolling them up to the top of the head on inhalation, or looking
around to the corners of the room without moving his head.

We want to determine which is the client's dominant eye. By
looking into the dominant eye, we can contact the individual's
intellectual side; by looking into the passive eye, we can more readily
contact his emotions. To establish which is the client's dominant eye,
we ask him to look through a rolled paper. He will spontaneously
look through the dominant eye and close the other eye.

The most obvious place to see that a client is split off (out of
contact) is in his eyes. We watch for a change in pupil size to indicate
intellectual or emotional activity, which signifies interruptions of the
charge, and we ask the client what he is experiencing. If the client
has a blank or glassy stare, this indicates splitting off, and the first
task is to get the client present. We use Gestalt awareness techniques
to ground the client, asking him to look around the room and name
the colors of objects, and so on. When a client seems to be
withdrawing from contact by not looking at the therapist, we ask him
to make this behavior explicit by stating his refusal to make contact
or by closing his eyes and actually withdrawing from contact.

No one can stay in continual contact. Actually, true contact is a
shuttling back and forth between contact and withdrawal. The withdrawal is to give a person a chance to make "inner" contact. He may
need to go inside to check his reactions or find an answer or just to
feel. Then he has something to take back to the outer contact. When
a person becomes glassy-eyed and stares at the person with whom
he's in contact, he is split off behind his eyes. Other people cannot
get present at all and are withdrawn. So, when asking people to make
contact with us, we allow them to withdraw explicitly, to avoid their
splitting off behind their eyes when they can't remain present. When

a person closes his eyes, he is instructed to go inside himself so that the withdrawal is not a splitting off but a conscious moving from outer to inner contact, a definite going towards something rather than a going away from something. Once people are able to make contact, we begin to work with boundaries and other emotional issues: issues of contact and confluence.

The best way of releasing the eyes is through crying, and depending on the client, we almost always encourage this. People who cry very easily may have to learn greater control (containment). Cupping the hands over the eyes is a good way for the person to contact the feelings inside and allow him to choose whether to express them or not. Again, working on the muscles at the back of the neck then will also reduce ocular constriction.

In general, glasses should be removed during body work. The only exception would be if the correction were so strong that the client would not be able to see clearly at close range without them. If he has soft contact lenses, he can leave them in. If he has hard contacts, the situation is the same as with regular glasses. The problem with hard lenses is that if the client becomes tearful, the fluid buildup makes them slide around the eyeball, causing irritation.

There are great subtleties of expression possible in the eyes. Releasing an ocular block will result both in greater freedom of movement of the eyes, and most important, a greater ability to contact and express the emotions within.

Band III: Jaw and Mouth; Oral Segment

Band 3, the mouth, is an extremely important aspect of our whole being. This is the part of the body that has the most and the earliest contact with the world. A baby gets his first nourishment and nurturing from the mother with his mouth. Later he puts everything he can into his mouth to test. The mouth has many functions: expression, aggression, nourishment, respiration, sexuality. The mouth is a very vulnerable area, so it is important to be aware that much emotion can be released when a block here is opened. Some of the expressive functions connected with the mouth are talking, crying, laughing, and smiling. It's also used for biting, spitting, gagging, swallowing, and sucking. Some of the related attitudes are aggression, helplessness, dependency, holding on, and sexual feelings.

It is thus understandable that so many problems are associated with the mouth. In the beginning it is probably advisable to work by stimulating expression through exaggerated movement of the mouth, rather than massage of the mouth itself, since too much affect can be released when the therapist works directly on a muscular level.

Since the mouth is such an important area, it is necessary to observe whether there is a split between the person's eyes (Band 2) and his mouth (Band 3): is the person smiling, but expressing sadness in the eyes? When beginning to work with expressions of the mouth, we may notice that the eyes start to harden again. This is due to the association between the two bands and is true of any and all adjacent segments. So, it will always be necessary to go back to the eyes, re-release the ocular block, and make contact again as we work with each segment. In this way we will keep the emotion flowing through the eyes. Since the eyes are the major organ of affect, they will close up most often, so it is important to remember to return to them.

The mouth is also involved with the pelvis and is considered a sexual organ, so the mouth can be used to release the pelvis by sucking and so on. Sucking is an earlier developmental pattern than biting, and is associated with earlier repressed memories than is biting.

The mouth and jaw can also contain repressed anger and rage, due to withheld aggression. According to Perls' theory of dental aggression,[3] the development of teeth causes the interruption of the pleasurable activity of sucking at the mother's breast. The infant must withhold his aggression (biting) in order to receive nourishment. This causes enormous frustration and rage. If a person represses his aggression and is stuck at the earlier stage of sucking, he will tend to "swallow whole" ideas and attitudes without really "chewing" (assimilating) them and making them his own. This aggression is often retroflected (turned back on the individual), as in fingernail-biting. Many people exhibit, as adults, infantile oral patterns such as lip biting and sucking, tongue thrusting, as well as the more obvious activities associated with the mouth, such as overeating, smoking, and alcoholism. In IBP, we see evidence of Perls's theory very clearly as we work with Band 3.

Fixed patterns of the jaw are often associated with the characteristics of holding on and of repressed anger and may have to do with maintaining control. When a person is clenching the jaw, the therapist may suspect the person is repressing expression of this anger.

Circling the mouth is the orbicularis oris. This muscle is attached to a number of smaller muscles, which can be massaged to release tension in the mouth. These muscles are responsible for movement of the mouth and, in fact, create expression of the mouth. The orbicularis oris is a sphincter, and like other sphincters, it will tend to contract early in the breathing process. Having a client move his mouth (by pursing his lips, extending his lips and tongue, or making any sort of grimace using the mouth) or suck on something are less invasive release techniques for the mouth and are preferable to massage. Certain exercises can be used to stress the holding patterns of the mouth and jaw and cause a release. One such exercise is to ask the client to bite down with the molars on a towel held by the therapist (much like a puppy playing with a towel) and pull against the therapist. When the therapist tells the client to let go suddenly, the client falls back onto a pillow and can experience a sense of release that he may never have experienced before. (Be wary of damaging bridgework or dentures when this exercise is tried.)

Much emotion may be released when the mouth and jaw are freed. It is important to focus this emotion by making sure the client keeps his eyes open and stays in contact with the therapist. Since anger, screaming, and so on may be expressed with the release of this area, it is important to emphasize again that venting the emotion alone is not our goal. We want to remember to focus on the injury that underlies the anger.

To get clients in touch with emotions associated with biting and sucking, we have them use the heel of their hand to either bite or suck on. They can bite fairly hard on this area of the hand without causing pain. The web of the hand can also be used for sucking, and of course the thumb or fingers are always available! Sucking may result either in very pleasurable feelings or in anxiety.

When the mouth is held in a pattern of disgust, we may ask the client to release this by poking his fingers down his throat to stimulate the gag reflex. Gagging will also release the diaphragm.

Band IV: Mouth and Throat

This band contains the supra-hyoid muscles of the floor of the mouth and connects the mouth to the throat. Blockage in this band is formed to resist crying as well as other forms of expression. The floor of the mouth often holds sadness from times when tears have been held back and swallowed. Releasing this area can result in crying and also in expressions of disgust, since the muscles that pull the corners of the mouth down reside in this segment. These muscles can be massaged externally by using several fingers and pressing up into the floor of the mouth under the jaw. Pressure

points at the back of the head and neck also release this segment
(#9).

The mentalis is a small muscle on the bottom of the chin. This
muscle often controls crying and can be seen to quiver, especially in
children when they resist crying.

Cervical Segment (Throat and Neck)

In the throat and neck there are many vital and sensitive structures:
the jugular vein, the thyroid and parathyroid glands, the carotid
arteries, and the carotid sinus (which regulates blood pressure). It is
better to use acupressure and movement with this area than to
massage it directly. Muscular release can be done at the back of the
neck.

The functions of the throat include: swallowing, speaking, crying,
screaming, and so on. There are a number of ways to release the
throat: gagging, hanging the head backward over the edge of a bed
or pillow, or by protuding the tongue on inhalation. An important
diagnostic factor in locating a throat block is to listen carefully to the
quality of the breath, especially the exhalation. Notice where the
breath is catching (making a rasping sound), and this will show
where the throat block is located. Screaming, yelling, coughing, and
crying will also release the throat and are valuable if done for release
and not just for the sake of venting.

There are a number of deep muscles in the throat and neck
segment, but we center our attention on two of them: the trapezius,
a very large muscle that runs from the back of the neck across the
shoulders to the center of the spine; and the sterno-cleido-mastoid,
extending from the mastoid bone (behind the ear) to the sternum
and the clavicle. Stretching the trapezius is really the best way to
release the neck. Rolling the head from side to side will often also
loosen the neck.

The intrinsic muscles of the throat are important because a
reciprocal relationship exists between a throat block and a pelvic
block. Removal of either of these blocks may intensify blockage in
the other area. That is, if the neck loosens, the pelvis tightens, and
vice versa. This relationship between the throat and the pelvis will be
discussed more fully in the pelvic segment (see p. 134). It is not
merely a theoretical relationship, but an anatomical, functional, and
energetic one as well, and this relationship can be found as a concept
in all body systems.

Thoracic Segment (The Chest)

Besides its function of breathing, the thoracic area is important as the home of the heart, doorway to the sense of Self, well-being and compassion. Opening the eyes is the first task of therapy, but opening the heart is of equal importance. When this is done, a connection is made between therapist and client that is often the start of the trusting relationship. Never consider opening other segments (especially the pelvis) before the heart center is opened. This creates a softening and releasing that allows the work to proceed. When we move to the pelvis, there may be a separation between the feelings of the two segments (love vs. sex, for example) so we will have to open the thoracic segment again.

Once the person has opened his chest and felt the concomitant sense of well-being, it is always possible to return to that area and to re-establish the connection between client and therapist in order to continue further opening of the rest of the body. Building the sense of Self in the body is important because it becomes the support for doing the psychological work (see chapter 5). Splitting off will often occur with the opening of the chest as well as with the eyes. Here is where we will see a connection between the eyes and the chest. This is a withdrawal of the Self from the world, in a protective mode. Opening the chest will reduce splitting off and will further the relationship between the client and therapist.

The thoracic segment extends from the diaphragm to the clavicle and consists of the rib cage, lungs, heart, arms, and hands. Remember that the arms and hands are extensions of the chest and are used for reaching out and for protection.

This segment is, of course, concerned with breathing, which we have discussed in the first half of this chapter. Psychologically, because the chest contains the heart it is the seat of interpersonal, passionate, soft, yielding, trusting, joyful, compassionate, affectionate, and loving emotions. An injured or "broken" heart may also harbor sadness, longing, pity, pain, and sorrow. The chest, hands, and arms express these emotions. The individual who holds tension in the chest shows a protective attitude that guards against injury but also keeps out warmth and nourishment. This protective attitude can be seen in a concave chest with shoulders rounded forward or raised in fear. This tension develops into fixed muscular patterns that limit expression, cause pain, and affect breathing, thereby affecting health. These fixed muscular patterns also reduce the flow of energy and feeling to the area resulting in underdeveloped pectoral muscles and breasts. The collapsed chest shows reduced breathing activity, with minimal inhalation, making it difficult for the person to build and sustain a charge. People with this fixed pattern may have feelings of insecurity, sadness, depression, fear, inferiority, and passivity, as well as low energy levels due to insufficient breathing. Releasing the chest allows the person to breathe properly and to begin to feel.

The opposite thoracic pattern — a barrel chest — is large and over-developed from being stuck in expansion. This can be seen in someone who is "holding himself up" and putting up a "front" in order to repress feelings of fear. He presents an attitude of aggression, power, strength, and toughness, but it's all just a cover for the injured child beneath. This fixed pattern is often accompanied by a narrow pelvis, indicating an excess of energy held in the upper portion of the body with a lack of energy in the lower portion. This results from a habitual over-retention of air when breathing and creates a tight, rigid diaphragm and abdomen, cutting off feelings from these areas and below.

Both of these positions result in rigidity of the chest caused by the suppression of anxiety and fear. Bronchitis, asthma, and other related respiratory dysfunctions are often psychosomatic manifestations of this rigidity. Optimal functioning of the chest must include the full range of mobility, with unrestricted inhalation and exhalation.

Even though the chest is seen as one segment, we sometimes divide it into upper and lower segments because often we see that only one portion moves freely, while the other remains rigid. Frequently there is little movement in the upper chest. We want to open this portion of the chest, because breathing here will stimulate the sympathetic nervous system and help to build a charge. At the beginning of the work, we indicate certain reference points on which the client may focus while breathing. These points are between the clavicle and the first rib. These are pressure points #11 C (see Figure 19, page 120) and can be tender to pressure. The therapist should ask the client to bring the breath up to these points so he can feel his chest expanding under the therapist's fingers. We may ask the client to pant or to use other breathing techniques to deepen either the inhalation or the exhalation, depending on which is appropriate for the client.

Remember to think of the chest as a band that goes all the way around the body and includes the back. Since the back is less sensitive than the chest, deep massage and other muscular release techniques are appropriate for releasing it.

A way of determining which back muscles are blocked is to run your hands over the back and note areas of coolness, or small bumps or knots on the back. These knots may be released by firm pressure with fingers or thumb. Pressing on the rhomboids will also open the chest. The therapist should massage the paraspinal muscles (along the spine). When massaging the back, firm pressure should be applied; these are solid muscles and they respond to a vigorous approach. Holding, squeezing, and massaging "dead" areas brings awareness and energizes these areas.

It is important that the therapist remind the person to breathe deeply at all times when using release techniques. This will greatly assist in the release of the muscles and the held emotion.

For a person with a very tight back, there is a technique called the "back roll" or finger roll/pinch process. The therapist gently pinches some tissue between the fingers and thumb and rolls the tissue up the person's back to the shoulders. The skin is connected to the parasympathetic system, which is why stimulating the skin of the back, the largest area of skin on the body, relaxes and releases a person. Nipple erection and goose bumps indicate a sympathetic release leading to a parasympathetic condition. It is important to remember that the client may encounter his repressed anger when his back is released (as with the jaw), and it is essential that the therapist have him maintain eye contact during the discharge of the anger. Possibly the expression "getting his back up" comes from this common tendency to harbor anger in the back. Shoulders may be held up, arched, and rigid in an attitude of fear, with the body frozen in this attitude. Bowed, rounded shoulders indicate overburden, and the inability to reach out indicates repressed longing.

The next techniques are the most invasive. These are the stress positions and movement patterns (hitting and so on). Stress positions work to exaggerate an open position of the chest. Rolling back over a barrel, accompanied by breathing, (see *Total Orgasm*, by Jack Rosenberg, and the IBP Release Technique, Chart A) is one of the best ways to open the chest. Each roll back or arch should always be followed by leaning forward. This facilitates the breathing process by expanding the chest and diaphragm. Twisting a towel with the arms exaggerates the closed chest and retroflected anger and tiring these muscles facilitates release.

One way of releasing the shoulders and arms is by reaching out. This should be accompanied by deep breathing, and making a sound. When the urge to strike out has been inhibited, chronic tension in the shoulders, arms, and hands may be the result and can be released by striking and hitting (a pillow). Growling, yelling, and so on will facilitate the release.

We would like to caution again that venting or catharsis is not the goal of IBP. It simply allows us to uncover the underlying emotions and injuries so we can work with them. These blocks originated to defend and protect the organism against the pain of these early injuries. Our purpose is not to remove blocks, but to help the client to understand their function in protecting him from psychic and physical trauma suffered during formative times.

Diaphragmatic Segment

The diaphragm is directly related to breathing, so it is a very important segment and extremely resistant to change. The diaphragm itself is a broad, flat, sheetlike muscle that attaches directly under the rib cage and extends through the body to the spinal column. It rests below the lungs and just above the abdominal organs.

The diaphragm functionally separates the two halves of the body. Deep diaphragmatic blocks are very common and certain activities may lead to diaphragmatic rigidity. Many practitioners of certain types of yoga, for instance, have learned a breathing technique as part of their training that effectively immobilizes the diaphragm by locking it in one position. Wind instrument players and singers also often have diaphragmatic blocks.

Because the diaphragm controls breathing, any tightness and rigidity restricts feeling as well. Because of its position as a "lid" over the abdominal cavity, the diaphragm can hold down "gut" feelings in the belly and sexual feelings in the pelvis. When it moves freely, the energy from the lower half of the body is allowed to flow to the upper portion of the body (chest, arms, throat, eyes) for expression.

The diaphragm plays a central role in the breathing process. It is the place where the autonomic and central nervous systems come together, meaning that breathing can be either unconsciously or consciously controlled. It is extremely important to the whole organism that the diaphragm be healthy and move freely. The interrelatedness of the belly, diaphragm, and lungs becomes very apparent when we understand the functioning of the diaphragm. The healthy functioning of the thoracic and abdominal segments depends upon unrestricted movement of the diaphragm. Many people experience anxiety as they begin to breathe in therapy and may attempt to lessen the anxiety by tightening the diaphragm. Releasing the diaphragm may bring these feelings of anxiety into awareness.

Release techniques in this segment include massaging the diaphragm under the rib cage during exhalation when the diaphragm is most accessible. Breathing will then increase and deepen. Deep massage of this area can be painful, so the therapist should stay superficial at first and feel for the degree of tension. The therapist may place a pillow under the client's back directly beneath the diaphragm area, and this will allow the diaphragm to stretch gently. Or the client can roll backward over a padded barrel to stretch the diaphragm.

Since the gag reflex affects the diaphragm, inducing gagging will help release the diaphragm and allow feelings that are stuck in the belly and throat to be released into expression.

Abdominal Segment

This segment begins at the diaphragm and ends at the top of the pelvis. Although this is the most unprotected and vulnerable area of the body, many vital organs are contained here. So it is understandable that many people contract their abdomen during times of stress. The abdomen constitutes the core of the body in most Asian systems (see chapter 9. "Chakra System"). Many emotions originate here, and people often tighten the abdomen in an effort to control them.

The primary muscle in the abdominal segment is the rectus abdominus, which attaches to the sternum and the pubic bone, and shields the abdominal organs. Massage of this muscle should be done in a kneading manner rather than with deep pressure because of the vital organs beneath it. Caution should be used if the client has a history of back problems or injury. Weakness and lack of tone of the abdominal muscless will stress the lower back and cause pain in the muscles in the lower back.

The most important thing that occurs in releasing the abdomen is a flooding of withheld emotions, usually expressed by sobbing and deep infant-like crying. When this happens, the abdomen will move convulsively.

Release of the diaphragmatic and abdominal segments can be assisted by teaching the client how to breathe into these areas. Abdominal breathing stimulates the parasympathetic response so it has a calming effect. Remember, breathing is an activity that involves the entire torso, and, ideally, proceeds in a wave involving the chest, diaphragm, and abdomen.

Pelvic Segment

Work with the pelvic segment is probably the most important and the most difficult of all. Opening the pelvis can be very invasive, and for that reason we have devoted an entire chapter to our approach to sexuality (see chapter 8).

As we stated earlier, the pelvis should not be opened early in therapy. Even clients who have experienced some degree of physical and emotional opening in the therapy may begin to close up and block again at the onset of pelvic release work. For example, the eyes may begin to block again (splitting off). Since pelvic blocks are reciprocally related to neck, throat, mouth, and shoulder blocks, freeing one area may be associated with increased blockage in the other. Therefore, we pay close attention to the upper body while opening the pelvis.

The important part to remember is that the holding in the pelvis is there for a reason, and we don't want to work in the pelvis without paying attention to the *reason* that a person has blocked off that area. We want to remember to *respect his defenses*. This is particularly true for working with someone whose defense mechanism is one of splitting off from sexual feelings. Often people believe that they're splitting off, but what they're actually doing is cutting off their feelings in their pelvis and in their body.

Remember that as we start working directly with the body, we begin with the *least invasive* technique first. So, in opening the pelvis, we start at the verbal level, and we address the mouth, throat, and neck area before we begin actual work in the pelvis itself.

First we have the client breathe and build up a charge. When he gets charged, we often notice tightening of the throat, or in the mouth, which will be the first sign of blockage. This is parallel to a tightening in the pelvis, but the place to work is *not* in the pelvis, but in the neck or mouth. And so, as someone breathes, movement of the neck is encouraged so that the neck becomes mobile.

Pelvic blocking may be indicated by a general unawareness of the pelvic region, or a sense of deadness. During the charging process we may hear such comments as, "I don't feel a thing *down there*," or "I feel everything down to my waist and then nothing until my knees." The first step in opening the pelvis, therefore, is the bring awareness to the area. As the work begins, the person may often report no sensation in the anus, vagina, labia, clitoris, penis, scrotum, etc. To determine the amount of blockage, it is necessary to ask *very specific* questions regarding the distribution of the charge. Increased pelvic openness is related to the depth to which the person experiences the charge, beginning with the external genitalia, and proceeding inwards. If the charge is superficial, the person will experience what has been called a genital orgasm. If the charge has moved more deeply into the pelvis and into the whole body, including the mouth and neck, the orgasm will be felt in all the areas of charge. It is probably the extent of the charge that made Freud see two distinct kinds of orgasm in women: the clitoral and the vaginal. By deepening the charge and spreading it evenly thoughout the body, it is possible to bring awareness to the *total body*, not just the genitals and the pelvic area.

Before beginning pelvic release work, we notice the person's reaction to the knees- up, hip- width- apart position that we ask him to assume. The act of raising the knees, in itself, may bring up negative sexual connotations. We watch the legs for jerkiness and other signs of holding. Sara, for instance, unconsciously held her knees tightly together until made aware of this fact. For some people it may be a very powerful experience just to lie on their backs with their knees up. Some women may be resistant for reasons of modesty or traumatic sexual experiences.

If an emotional experience results from this position we will work with it verbally. We will discuss what kinds of experiences this position reminds the person of, such as childbirth, gynecological examinations, intercourse, and other related experience of vulnerability. Traumas connected with experiences may have been repressed and held in the pelvis and legs, and it is important to bring them into awareness. Achieving some resolution of them at the beginning of pelvic release work helps bring awareness to a person's attitude toward his sexuality.

Sometimes we ask a person to bounce his pelvis gently on the mat to bring awareness to the area. This will often awaken the pelvis and bring sensation to the anus. *It is important to remember that the pelvic block goes all the way around the body and includes holding in the buttocks and anus.*

A frequent cause of pelvic blocks for both men and women is *premature toilet training.* The child's only way of controlling his anal sphincter is to tighten the entire pelvis. The child thus learns how to stop bowel movements by developing a chronically tight pelvis, which is then cut off from awareness. According to Dr. Ellsworth

Baker, a student and colleague of Reich:

> Life is further blocked by early toilet training. . . . Sphincter
> control is not attained until eight months of age so that earlier
> toilet training (some mothers start at four months) requires
> contraction of the body musculature, especially the muscles of
> the thighs, buttocks, pelvic floor, as well as retraction of the
> pelvis and further respiratory inhibition. This is familiar ex-
> ample of the armoring process. It effectively diminishes natural
> emotional expression, and especially the pleasureable sensa-
> tions from the pelvis.[4]

A different kind of early trauma in the pelvic segment was
described by a client:

> My buttocks are chronically pinched and the muscles con-
> tracted in the rotator area. The therapist manipulated the area,
> including my legs, so as to relieve the muscular contraction. He
> commented that the very tightly held pinched areas greatly
> relaxed and appeared to look markedly different. I first became
> aware of the difference as I was lying on my stomach. I noticed
> that my heels, which rolled inward toward each other when I
> first lay down now rotated to an outward position. For approx-
> imately an hour after the session, I continued to experience
> a heightened sensation of movement and vibration in my but-
> tocks. I was aware of the energy moving through that area,
> giving a warm tingling effect. During this time I was in touch
> with a deep sense of fear. While allowing myself to have these
> feelings I suddenly remembered an incident that occurred when
> I was approximately ten years old. My brother had chicken pox
> and it was decided by the doctor and my mother that I should
> contract the disease and be given a gamma globulin injection to
> reduce its severity and the potentiality of scarring. When my
> mother conveyed this decision to me, she did so in a manner
> that communicated her anxiety and discomfort about it. I
> remember feeling a terror about this, screaming my objections,
> yet remaining powerless to alter my fate. By the time I finally
> got these dreaded shots, my body was contracted and frozen in
> terror. It wasn't surprising, therefore, to feel the terror and
> sadness when these muscles finally relaxed."

Orgastic Reflex

Since the pelvis is such a delicate area, we want to recreate, as nearly as possible, what it was like before it became inhibited. The orgasm is simply a reflex, just as sneezing is a reflex. So we teach the body to move in a normal, healthy pattern that simulates the orgastic reflex pattern. In this way, the body will let go of fixed muscular patterns that inhibit the orgastic release.

We now begin to have someone breathe until he has a complete charge. After he has complete charge, we begin *to pattern in the orgastic reflex.* The orgastic reflex is one in which the *pelvis moves forward and the breath goes out.* This healthy orgastic reflex will be neuro- muscularly patterned as a result of doing this movement and breathing pattern. The person' s energy will begin to flow at much greater levels, and he may even have an orgastic release of the whole body in the therapy session, but not necessarily an ejaculation. If the person is not able to let go into an orgastic release in this exercise, it is important to remember that *the holding may be in the neck, throat, or mouth,* and that letting go is less threatening in the oral segment than in the pelvis. Moving the pelvis forward will also allow the neck to move, and if this doesn' t happen, we help the person *move his neck on the exhalation* to make him aware of this connection as he *moves his pelvis.* The therapist may also ask the person *to suck as he does the pelvic rocking.*

Release of the throat through sucking will allow the pelvis to open. This is why orgasm is often more intense during intercourse if deep kissing is also involved. Oral inhibition or blocks may not be sexual blocks, even though they may be expressed sexually. Very often they are feelings of longing that result from early lack of nurturing and actually express the "needy child." This is because sucking is associated with early satisfaction and hunger as well as with sexual feelings. Overemphasis on the oral aspects of sex can often be traced directly to the Primary Scenario. By working with the holding patterns in the mouth and the Primary Scenario, IBP can help a client resolve deep longings that are sexualized by sucking.

Often people try to push for the orgastic release. Both men and women contract the rectus abdominus in order to move the pelvis forward. This pattern of tensing in order to achieve an orgastic release is often encouraged by therapists who view sexuality from a genital or orgastic point of view. Tensing will cause a release, but you can only release the amount of charge you have built up. What happens is that tensing or contracting begins well before enough excitement has been built up. *When we pattern the orgastic reflex, we teach the person to use the psoas (the internal muscle which surrounds the pelvis) to move the pelvis forward, and to keep the rectus abdominus loose.* The movement then becomes one of *opening rather than closing, and thereby heightens the charge.* In order to move the psoas, the person must use his feet for leverage, and this allows awareness of the connection between the feet and the pelvis. It is extremely important *that feet be grounded in the body session and during intercourse* for heightened ability to build and release a charge.

An example of similar grounding is swinging on a tire from a tree and pumping to get the tire going. If you can get just one toe on the ground and give yourself a push, you really fly. But, if you try to move it with your stomach muscles alone by pumping, you won't get very far! We bring the energy (charge) into the feet from the pelvis by using the movement/ release technique of *lifting the pelvis off the mat and pushing into the ground with the heels and rocking the pelvis* (without tensing the abdominal muscles or gluteus maximus). All the muscles of the legs and pelvis will begin to tire in this position, thus causing them to vibrate. This will allow the charge to move from the pelvis into the legs. *This can be more effective with the feet up on a wall as well as on the floor.*

One of the best ways to bring energy into any area of the body is by using the pressure points we have mentioned. *The pelvis, in particular, is sensitive to its pressure points,* so we want to remember to use them all, *both front and back,* on the pelvis, as well as the *points on the feet and legs. This will bring energy to the pelvis.* Since the points we use are similar to those in the Tantric system, they can also be used during love-making to heighten pleasure.

The pelvis should never be opened forcefully! This could be tantamount to rape. The techniques we have mentioned so far are subtle and work to bring awareness to the pelvis. *Opening of the pelvis frequently results in the release of considerable repressed emotional material, especially hurt, anger, and rage.* If the repressed anger has been retroflected (turned back on the self), this then becomes spite, and the person cannot relax into pleasurable feelings. While he may express some anger toward his partner, it is spiteful in the sense that the person prevents himself from experiencing his own pleasure ("cutting off one's nose to spite one's face"). Simply expressing the anger is not enough; it has to be focused. Often the person is really angry at a parent rather than the sexual partner. So, part of the anger that is held in the pelvis has to do with blaming the parent (see chapter 8). When that association is made, often there is a release and the spiteful behavior is given up. We also know that people become identified with their anger; they know who they are when they are angry. The work in establishing a sense of Self will help a person shift into allowing himself pleasure when the anger is released.

Although we do work with anger we see it as a bandage to cover up hurt. The most effective way to deal with anger is to get to the injury and hurt beneath it.

Chapter 6
Growing Up:
The Development of the Self

In the past two chapters we showed how we use physical interruptions in the breathing work to help a client see how he held emotions in his body. As the work continues, the physical interruptions don't occur as much, and we can begin to tackle the psychological interruptions, using them as we did the physical ones, to move the person toward a deeper and stronger experience of the Self.

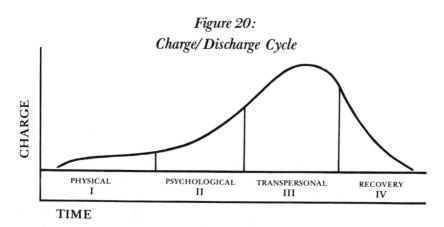

Figure 20:
Charge/Discharge Cycle

We use Figure 20 to emphasize the parallel courses of therapy and the charge/orgastic cycle. The psychological stage of therapy corresponds to the second portion of the curve, or the excitation phase of the charge/orgastic cycle described in chapter 4.

Here the interruptions are similar to but different from the physical ones. The physical ones— the fits of giggling, hyperventilation, cramps in the hands, splitting off, and so on— stall the body work. They happen when the client and the therapist get close to the emotions underlying the holding patterns in the client's body.

In a similar way, psychological interruptions occur when the client wants, at some level, to protect or hide his feelings. These interruptions also follow predictable patterns in a particular person. They differ in that the psychological interruptions pervade the person's entire life pattern. They are rigidified into defensive character styles that protect his underlying Self from painful emotions. They protect it day by day, year after year. While they are reflected and maintained in the body, they are most visible or observable in the way a person forms and conducts close relationships.

We call them interruptions because they interrupt a person in his conscious or unconscious attempts to experience his true Self and his sense of aliveness. They are barricades thrown up to thwart real and imaginary invaders from within and from without. This over-zealous protection keeps a person from being in touch with his Self and keeps the Self from being constituted.

The Self, as you know by now, is a nonverbal sense of well-being in the body coupled with the verbal overlays of his cognitive process. It is that healthy narcissism a child develops, that permanent core of being inside him, into which he can retreat for comfort and self-support.

The Self is different from the functioning ego, which can develop intact, despite injuries to the Self. The ego is the personality with which one functions in the outside world. It masks developmental injuries and allows one to be successful in dealing with the outside world. Someone may, for instance, meet or surpass outer standards of achievement, and his injuries will show up only in his inner world— and in his intimate relationships. If his Self isn't intact, he can't feel a great satisfaction in his achievements, nor can he sustain an internal sense of well-being.

The sense of Self provides a continuity of internal identity. When it is intact, a person knows who he truly is, independent of the rest of the world. Integrative Body Psychotherapy is aimed at disturbances in this continuity.

A great deal has been written recently about object relations theory and Kohut's psychology of the self (see bibliography). IBP developed independent but parallel to both and is similar to both in that the primary goal is to help an individual develop and sustain a whole, integrated self. IBP differs from the others in the definition of the Self. Object relations and the psychology of the self describe the Self as a structure of the mind. IBP defines the Self as a nonverbal experience of well-being in the body as well as a cognitive process.

Another way IBP differs is that IBP is basically a transpersonal model. That is, our work assumes that there is something beyond the individual and his body/mind. We believe that a person is born with an essence or a soul, and that is what IBP works with. We believe that this essence becomes overlaid with experiences, either nurturing or destructive to the expression of this essence, but the experiences themselves are not the Self. They are what we call the character structure, which often obscures the Self, preventing its expression. Our work is to uncover the Self, make contact with it, and free it from the overlaid experiences that limit its expression.

The psychological part of the therapy in IBP deals with these limiting experiences as interruptions in the individual's contact with his Self, interruptions that occurred in early childhood.

Since language is undeveloped in the child at this time, therapy can find evidence of these early life experiences only in the body and through images. Through the breathing and body work, in a compassionate relationship with the therapist, these early life experiences are not merely remembered, but *relived* in the body and in imagery. The client's gestures, body movements, voice, and demeanor change to childlike ones. When we ask him how old he feels, he verifies this regression, saying "I'm very young" or "I'm a baby." His imagery, too, shows the regressed perceptions. For instance, he might say: "People are very big," "Giant hands are holding me," "I have to look up very far," "My feet can't touch the ground," or "There are huge bars around me."

Reliving an early episode made a big difference in understanding and growth for Ella. She was, at 45, a self-described "slob and klutz." An aerobics class ended with her third pulled muscle. According to the exasperated teacher, Ella pulled muscles because she never did the exercises correctly. It was clear to anybody watching Ella that she didn't use her body well. She admitted this, saying, "I often ignored the signals that I was doing those damned exercises wrong. I would decide in my head that I would keep going no matter how much it hurt."

Her therapist noticed in the body work that Ella was tightly contracted on her left side. She listed slightly when she walked, and her handwriting— she was left-handed— was tight and crabbed. When she regressed, she relived a frustrating moment with her mother when Ella was about three.

They were sitting on the front porch and her mother was holding a bowl of orange sections. Ella reached for one with her left hand and her mother pushed her hand away. She reached again, and her mother moved the bowl out of reach. The third time she reached, her mother pushed her left hand aside and told her to use her right hand, but her right hand was dirty so she couldn' t have any oranges. The hand she *could* use, and *wanted* to use, was unacceptable. The lesson was indelible.

From then on, Ella' s mother tried to train her out of being left-handed. These later attempts Ella had rebelled against and remembered, but the earliest one was forgotten by everything but her body. Reliving that early lesson was the beginning of her trusting and enjoying her physical self. Although she never learned to love aerobics, she began to walk straight, and eventually, to jog with enthusiasm.

The value of the reliving experience is two-fold. It makes it possible to understand the early life events in terms of the Primary Scenario. It also makes it possible to begin healing the wounds that occurred at that time and to find closure for the unfinished early events. Often these early experiences have been missed in previous therapy due to their inaccessibility and pre-verbal nature.

Stages of Development of the Self

We identify four stages in the development of the Self. The first is the attachment stage, followed by three separation stages: mirroring, healthy introversion, and rapprochement. A fifth stage would be the constituted Self of adulthood.

For each stage, there is a task or a process. The task of the attachment phase is bonding of the mother and the child. For the mirroring stage, the task is reflecting the child so he can experience who he is as he separates from the unity with his mother. In the healthy introversion stage, the task is the child' s: through proper bonding and reflection, coupled with the consistent availability of his mother, he reinforces his sense of Self. The resulting "healthy narcissism" means that he had a fairly stable, accurate, and comfortable sense of his own identity— cognitively as well as in the body. He also has an internalized assurance of his mother' s consistent presence. In the rapprochement stage the task is reality testing, in which the child tests his inner belief and his competence and power against the outside world.

In Figure 21 we show the developmental stages with the necessary tasks for each. When the developmental task is interrupted or done inadequately, injuries occur, and certain defensive character styles are developed. Corresponding to the developmental stages are the stages a person might go through in his relationship with his therapist. The stages and activities of therapeutic intervention (shown in dotted lines) suggest how a therapist helps a client develop a sense of Self by going back to the point at which damage was done.

Attachment Stage (Birth to 4 or 5 Months) Task: Bonding

The first stage, total unity with the mother, is a nonverbal, physical experience and actually begins well before the child is born. The mother's experiences during pregnancy and her attitude about her child affect him even in utero. This is why we ask about the mother's pregnancy when we gather the Primary Scenario, and why we ask if his parents wanted him.

In the beginning, inside his mother, the child's awareness of himself is simultaneous with his awareness of his mother. She is his total environment and his food supply. Through unity with her, he is united as well with the flow of life. After he is born, this bonding is continued and reinforced by the contact between their eyes during nursing and by intimate holding, touching, and caressing. In some cultures, babies are held close to the mother's bodies at all times, and the mothers become instinctively aware of their needs. A client of ours who had visited Uganda described this close bonding:

"A mother keeps her baby wrapped in a sling, right close to her breast, all the time. Every once in a while, no matter what she's doing, she'll slip the baby out of the sling and hold him over the bushes, whereupon he urinates or defecates. There's never an accident. I finally asked one of the mothers how she knew when her baby had to relieve himself. She looked at me as if I were really dense, then answered, 'Well, how do *you* know when *you* have to go?' "

In our culture, recent advances in childbirth practices are replacing the hospital practice of separating mother and child at birth. More and more the child and mother are allowed to remain together so that bonding will be fostered rather than destroyed. As fathers begin to participate in the birthing process, we see a bonded relationship developing with the father also.

Figure 21
Stages in Ideal Development of Self

An injury during development leads to fragmentation, and the pain of fragmentation leads to the adoption of a defensive character style, either Split Off (As-If or Trance), Constellated (Never Enougher), or Cut Off (Super Trouper).

Therapeutic intervention takes advantage of the similarities between development and transference stages to substitute proper bonding and mirroring to help a client belatedly develop a healthy introversion.

DEFENSIVE CHARACTER STYLES

SPLIT OFF

Trance

As If

CONSTELLATED

Never — Enougher

CUT OFF

Super Trouper

FRAGMENTATION

Therapeutic Intervention

Healthy Narcissism

Injuries from improper reflection

Proper supportive reflection

Borderline Personality
Schizophrenia

Injuries from insufficient bonding

STAGES IN IDEAL DEVELOPMENT OF SELF

S
Constituted Self
Individuating

Merging fantasy with reality

Reality Testing

Reinforcing self

Mirroring

C

M

Unity with Mother/Life

Bonding

ADULTHOOD

RAPPROCHEMENT — 3 yrs.

HEALTHY INTROVERSION

REFLECTION — 6 mos.

MAGIC

LEANING

CORRESPONDENCE SELF-RELIANT

STAGES OF TRANSFERENCE

CORRESPONDING

ATTACHMENT In utero — 6 mos

© 1985 Jack L. Rosenberg, Marjorie L. Rand, Diane Asay

After four or five months of intense bonding with the mother, the baby develops the need, the strength, and the perceptions to acknowledge his separateness. From being one with his mother, he become an individual on his own. He becomes aware of himself as separate from the universal consciousness, symbolized by his mother, even while he remains a part of it.

The frustration and traumas of life that occur in the development of the child's sense of Self may cause him to flee back to the safety of unity with his mother. Yet the process of development pulls him continually into life, away from the unity, the womb, the mother, and toward a greater and greater individual sense of identity. It is in the fragile Selfhood of the first few years of life that the problems we observe in ourselves and in our clients start.

Bonding Injuries

If the early bonding relationship breaks down completely, the type of disturbance to the Self can be so severe that treatment is difficult or futile. Jodi T. Samuels, in an unpublished doctoral dissertation, describes this disturbance:

> "Harry Harlow illustrated this point(1967) in his well-known experiments with monkeys. In one experiment, monkeys were separated from their mothers at birth. Each monkey was then placed in a cage with a "surrogate" artificial mother(wire frame covered with terry cloth, two eyes, a nose and a mouth). The monkeys clung to these "mothers" as though they were real. These monkeys appeared to develop normally until maturity at which time they failed to establish normal sexual relations, and those that did bear young were completely helpless and dangerous mothers."

If a human baby is virtually abandoned when he is born— that is, fed enough so he doesn't starve but otherwise left alone— he will most likely end up in an institution and/or suffer psychosis.

Most bonding injuries aren't that severe, however. Even parents who are badly injured themselves have what it takes to bond satisfactorily with their infants.

Injuries sometimes occur when a mother and baby are separated immediately after delivery. If a baby is left in the hospital because he is ill or must be kept in an incubator, he usually has many different caretakers. This inconsistency in contact denies him the opportunity to form a bond with one special person. Similarly, a child put up for adoption at birth loses valuable bonding time. The sooner adoption takes place, the better, for bonding and bonding injuries occur the first few minutes of life through the first four or five months.

Some bonding injuries come about because of the mother's damaged Self. If she didn't get what she needed when she was very young, she is likely to pass along the same unmet needs to her children. If she is consistently "a million miles away" when she is nursing her baby or changing him, he won't get the close contact he needs. It should be pointed out that it is the mother's *energetic* presence that is necessary. She can make physical eye contact, but it won't be real contact if her energy isn't there. A blind mother who was "all there" would make a better contact than a sighted mother who didn't actually see her child. Most mothers develop an instinctive awareness of their babies' rhythms. Like the Ugandan women, they may appear to be wholly involved in tasks or sleep or conversation, yet will respond instantaneously to the slightest murmur or change in their babies' breathing.

All children, in turn, have a keen sensitivity to the degree of their mothers' availability. Every mother knows that a child playing contentedly four houses away heads for home the exact moment she telephones a friend, thereby rendering herself unavailable. This sensitivity is most profound in the early days when the mother is the prime figure in a baby's life. Thus a mother who isn't "there" for whatever reason can make an enormous impact on her child's need for bonding.

People who didn't get enough close contact as babies grow up with a desperate need for closeness. They tend to merge completely with other people, losing their separate identities, and cannot tolerate separating again, for they didn't get the thorough bonding that makes separation possible.

Sometimes, when the nurturing is barely adequate, or if the mother is unable to let her baby become separate from her, the bonding stage is over-extended. One such example is Rhoda, a talented movie script writer. She had a strong functioning ego, but her inner identity was not well-formed. She had a desperate need to be close to someone all the time. "When I was a little girl, my mother held my hand every day while I picked up my toys. We were very close. I couldn't stand not being right next to her all the time."

That closeness was shattered when Rhoda's parents stopped supporting her financially. She was thirty-four and the blow brought her into therapy. In reality she supported herself with no trouble, but she felt an acute need to be taken care of. Being forced to be independent, even so belatedly, was devastating. The therapist could see her pain, but also saw that she found it hard to maintain contact with him and to stay present with her feelings.

This tendency to split off is a defensive style that can be indicative of some injury in the bonding stage. Since the infant has no resources to deal with painful feelings, he simply splits off from them. It's possible that Rhoda's mother was not able to allow her to separate, so the bonding stage become over-extended and Rhoda never developed an *internal* security.

Bonding injuries are the most difficult to treat, because the earlier the injury, the harder it is to shift the responsibility for healthy "Self" development to the individual. In our work, though, a client can relive these early traumas. This gives us the advantage of starting the work on the Self at the point at which its development was interrupted.

All of our clients in IBP had more or less adequate bonding, or they wouldn't be functioning in the world. The injuries they have are in other stages.

Reflection Stage (6 Months to 1½ Years)
Task: Mirroring

As a baby grows, his need for unity with his mother diminishes. His senses develop, calling him out beyond the perimeter of that unity. He can focus clearly on objects that were once a blur and learns that fingers and toes are subject to some sort of control from within. The day comes when he triumphantly draws an elusive foot into his mouth and his mother laughs with delight, having watched the struggle for weeks.

That's what mirroring is: the mother giving back to the child a picture of what he is, and making him feel good about it. It's more than that, though. It's also saying, "Once we were one, and that was good. Now you are *you*, and that is good, too." It allows the child's Self to continue expanding, and it gives him permission to *be* himself, to be different from his mother. He depends on his mother for this reflection and for the verification of the Self he is experiencing within. It's as if the mother who was once the same Self as the child is now the custodian of the child's Self. She *contains* his feelings of Self and of well-being for him, much as she might hold his jacket while he goes off to play. When he finds himself away from her and a little unsure, he comes back to her for a reminder of who he is. She gives him a quick glimpse of his Self, a smile, and he's off again, replenished.

Most mothers are pleased at their babies' attempts to control their bodies and explore their environments, so proper mirroring would seem to be inevitable. However, some mothers were so injured themselves at this stage that they are unable to mirror their children properly. They may have gotten enough of what they need to bond properly, but not enough to be able to mirror their own children adequately.

We said that it was an energetic quality of the mother that made for successful bonding, rather than her mere physical presence. Sometimes we describe proper reflection in energetic terms by likening the mother's quality to a "Blue Light." If she had adequate bonding and proper reflection, then she "got the Blue Light" and gives it to her children, and they pass it on to their children. It is compounded of many things: warmth, love, acceptance, humor, respect, and trust. Children who were raised in a Blue Light feel generally good about themselves and understand that children can be a joy to raise. This personal sense of adequacy coupled with honest pleasure in a child's existence makes for proper mirroring.

If a child doesn't get the proper reflection when he needs it, he loses touch with his fragile developing Self. The loss of this connection leads to fragmentation, or loss of identity accompaned by a total body/mind/emotional experience of annihilation.

Mirroring Injuries

There are infinite opportunities for proper mirroring to fail, but the injuries fall into three basic categories: under-mirroring, over-mirroring, and improper or distorted reflection.

In *under-mirroring*, the parent is too critical. Long before she would think to criticize in words, a mother reveals her attitudes in facial expressions and sub-verbal noises such as scowls and snorts of disgust. The mother who found her baby's curiosity adorable in the crib may find it irritating and destructive when he begins to crawl. The mother obsessed with cleanliness will not reflect the basic goodness of the child she fishes from the mudhole.

The critical parent tends to overlook what a child's activity means in terms of his learning and sees only how it affects her. A non-critical parent is more likely to see that a baby's new interests reflect new capabilities and a readiness for new toys or opportunities. A young mother ruefully told this story about herself:

> "My ten month old, David, emptied all the detergents onto my kitchen floor, so I flew into a rage and left him with my

neighbor while I cleaned up. When I returned two hours later, guess what I saw! David and Adam had emptied out Martha's cupboards, including a canister of flour, which they had spread out on the dark linoleum. They were sitting in the midst of the mess making designs in the flour. Where was Martha? She was taking pictures! Every once in a while she sprinkled a little more flour over the kids' designs so they could start over. She laughed when she saw my expression and said, 'I think they're ready for a sandbox, don't you?' Four days later she invited David over to play in their new sandbox and showed me the funny pictures she had taken, one of which she sent out in her Christmas cards that year." She sighed. "I think there is a moral there, because David always wants to play at their house, not at ours."

As the child grows older, the parents tend to criticize more in words. The scowls and groans that greeted spilled food and torn pages are augmented by words like "clumsy" and "naughty." An innocent two year old wanders up the street in her ragged underpants and is asked by her mother, "How can you shame me so?" A two and a half year old bites his friend and is called "vicious."

If the parent is continually critical, a negative introject will be created; that is, an inner voice or feeling stays with the child, always criticizing. It makes it impossible for the child to accomplish any task well enough or ever to feel that he *is* enough. The child swallows the critical parent whole and it remains undigested, constantly telling him that he is "bad" or "dumb" or "clumsy." This feeling, once created, remains long after the real parent is gone.

Sometimes the parent isn't exactly critical but is never quite satisfied, no matter what the child does. The parent always has yet another expectation, so the child never has a sense of closure. A brilliant, creative physicist described how this worked in her family:

"I was so excited when I made Phi Beta Kappa that I called home right away. 'Mama,' I said, 'I just found out! I made it!' My mother said, 'Fine, dear, your father will want to speak to you,' and she handed my father the phone, saying, 'Bridget just made Phi Beta Kappa.' My father came on the phone and said, 'Fine; now when are you getting your Ph. D.?'

"I was terribly let down," Bridget said, "but I wasn't surprised. It was just like when I finished the first piece in a piano book, they never said 'How wonderful'; they only wanted to know when I was going to start the next book. And when I learned how to ride my trike, my father started planning for my first bike. They never thought what I did was good for itself, just as preparation for the next step."

It is as if a mother, seeing her child take his first steps, fails to acknowledge his joy and triumph, and only asks, "Why don't you run?" The child is always pushed to the next performance level without the needed appreciation and closure for the current achievement. The closure comes with getting a sense of well-being for what he did. It finished the "unfinished business" and provides a foundation for the next achievement.

In *over-mirroring*, the parent is overly positive, reflecting the child in a grandiose manner. The child may develop a need to live up to the parent's grandiose expectations and, in failing to do so, will have a sense of dissatisfaction in himself, no matter what he actually does achieve. If a child's aptitudes are extremely over-evaluated, it will interfere with his ability to merge with reality. For instance, a child whose parents insist he can do anything, jumps off the roof, certain he can fly. After breaking both ankles, he still insists he can fly, blaming the accident on a "poor landing." Or there is the mother who insists that her son is so terrific he can even walk on water. The boy hears this once too often and decides to try it in their sluggish suburban creek. He sinks, of course. His mother dries him off and comforts him, saying, "It must have been bad water; you know how they pollute everything nowadays."

Even if the over-mirroring isn't always dangerous or foolish, it is just as injurious to the developing Self as under-mirroring is. In both cases, the injury is caused because the reflection isn't accurate. When the child with the inflated or grandiose self-image faces the reality outside his family, he meets a more accurate, less supportive reflection than he gets at home. He is cut down to size. Now if he goes home crying "they said I couldn't walk on water and they were right," and his mother insists the water was polluted, he's in trouble. On the one hand, he has the word of his mother who has been his ultimate authority. On the other hand, he got wet and a lot of people laughed at him. This puts him in a bind. If it happens consistently, he will retain *only* his mother's opinion but at the price of blocking reality in order to sustain his support.

If, however, he runs home wet and tearful and his mother hugs him, saying, "Oh, honey, when I say you can walk on water, that just means that I think you're wonderful. But we'll have to get you a boat if you want to stay dry," then he will be all right. He can keep the grandiose reflection that he is wonderful, but he also gets a usefully accurate reflection that jibes with external reality.

In the first case, the child will always have the problem of trying to make things come out the way he thinks his mother expects. Since he will never be able to walk on water, he will always have a sense of failure. When *he* has children, he may possibly project onto them his own unintegrated grandiosity and do them the same injury of over-mirroring.

Such patterns tend to be passed on through the generations. The childhood Self is taken from the sense of Self of the mother with whom the child is bonded.

Distorted Mirroring is like the reflection from the kind of bent mirror found in a carnival's House of Mirrors. Sometimes the child appears much larger than he is, and sometimes much smaller. He may appear utterly grotesque sometimes, and perfectly normal at other times. Because of its inconsistency, the child never gets a picture of himself that he can consistently rely on, as is necessary in the next stage for healthy narcissism.

Since the mother is the primary mirroring object, the injury occurs because of the distortion in the mirror — that is, the mother's own distorted perceptions of herself due to her own injuries. If she over-reflects her child, it may be in response to the under-mirroring she received as a child. If she sees herself as distorted and strange, she may reflect her own image onto her child. The mother, as the mirror, may reflect either an exact replica of herself or whatever was missing in her own development, both of which are inaccurate reflections of the child.

The father can participate in the distorted mirroring by going along with the mother's distortion or he can counter it. For example, a fearful mother tells her strong, agile three year old that he mustn't climb on the jungle gym because he will break his neck. The father can allow the distortion of the child's abilities and the probable consequences by taking the mother's side and telling the kid to mind. Or, if he has the wit and clarity, he will balance the mother's distortion and say, "Don't worry, it's your mother who's afraid of heights, not you. Besides, I'll catch you if you fall."

Other mirrors that cause distorted reflection of the child's self-image are those representing the father and society. An example is the Olson family, a rough and tumble family whose life centered on the Oregon logging industry. The father was the chief foreman of the logging camp, and the mother was a waitress there. They had four boys, three of whom were dyed-in-the-wool loggers. The youngest Olson was a logger, but he wrote poetry in his spare time. He hated the logging camp, chain saws, and Pendleton shirts, but at the same time, he thought of his writing as a deviation, not a talent. His whole life had been an example of poor mirroring. When he was little and wanted to read indoors, he was told to "get out there and play baseball like the other boys do." When he was older and read a poem he had written, his mother asked, "Now what are you going to do with dreamy foolishness like that in a logging camp?"

His family not only never honored the expression of his true Self, but they made it a negative quality. The only thing they honored was the logging life, and because he didn't fit that, he grew up feeling inadequate and abnormal.

The same thing happens sometimes to people who are born the wrong sex — that is, not the sex the parents wanted. No matter what the child does, it can't be right. A girl, for instance, born when her parents wanted a boy, can never throw a ball right, even if she throws better than any boy on the team. Her girlish accomplishments are considered unimportant and her boyish ones inadequate. No matter what she does, she can't grow up feeling adequate because she is never mirrored for what she is and allowed to feel good about it.

In discussing mirroring in *Prisoners of Childhood: The Drama of the Gifted Child*, Alice Miller states:

> "Every child has a need to be noticed, understood, taken seriously, and respected by his mother. In the first weeks and months of life he needs to have the mother at his disposal, must be able to use her to be mirrored by her. This is illustrated by an image of Winnicott's: the mother gazes at the baby in her arms, and baby gazes at his mother's face and finds himself therein. . . provided that the other really is looking at the unique, small, helpless being and not projecting her own introjects onto the child, nor her expectations, fears, and plans for the child. In that case the child would not find himself in his mother's face but rather the mother's own predicaments. This child would remain without a mirror, and for the rest of his life would be seeking this mirror in vain."

In summary, mirroring should be accurate, neither over- nor under-done. It should also be consistent. The consistency is essential to the goal of the next developmental stage: a healthy narcissism.

This is similar to the notion of "object constancy" from Object Relations theory. It means that a child has a continuous relationship with one person, which allows him to grow in a healthy way, knowing who he is. This certainty of identity must be reinforced day by day through proper mirroring.

Mirroring goes on forever. We all continue to need it, even as adults. The young child, however, is in a survival situation. A parent who doesn't see him accurately can neglect his needs and endanger his health. One who cannot or will not not see her child as anything but perfect might overlook the signs of serious disorders. One accustomed to constant annoyance by the child will dismiss those signs. Either way, the child's needs aren't met. The physical trauma is closely intertwined with emotional trauma. Improper reflection, when experienced repeatedly, will move the child into fragmentation and he will see himself— his developing Self— as though he were reflected by the scattered pieces of a broken mirror. This lack of a cohesive identity is extremely painful and motivates the child to create a variety of defensive behaviors. A discussion of these ways of avoiding the pain of fragmentation comprises the bulk of this chapter.

Solipsism: A Special Kind of Injury

Solipsism can be seen as an over- extension of the bonding phase that interferes with the mirroring or reflective stage of the development relationship. If the mother has a damaged sense of Self, the bonded relationship with her child may provide the last hope for the wholeness she lacks on her own.

Solipsism is a philosophical term for the belief that the world exists only in the mind of the individual or that it consists solely of the individual himself and his own experiences. It's the old tree- falling- in- the- forest argument: if a tree falls and there's no one there to hear it, was there actually any sound? We use the term here to describe the cases in which a mother treats her child as though he doesn't exist except in relationship to her. The child then feels as though he doesn't exist as a separate being— that he exists only as part of his mother. The feeling is so profound that he loses his sense of identity. The diagram below shows that this is not purely illusion on his part. Neither the mother nor child has a separate identity.

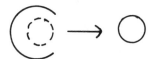

Child inside
of mother

Child born; now
separate from mother

Child engulfed; emotionally
part of mother again

In a solipsistic relationship, the child isn't an entity of his own but an extension of the mother, much like an additional limb. It is through the child that the mother lives and hopes to fulfill her unmet needs. When this happens, the mother can't afford to let her child separate, and he becomes a self-object (a term from Kohut's Self Psychology). As a self-object, he is used to fulfill the mother's desires, to temper her longings, to relieve the pain of her life.

It is rather like the relationship between a blind man and his cane. When he holds it tightly to explore the terrain ahead, the cane is almost a part of him. Because he receives information through it directly, he might forget that it is a separate object and think of it as part of himself. When he's not using the cane, he loosens his grip on it. Then he can feel it with his hand and fingers. He becomes aware, again, of its texture and shape. He no longer thinks of it as part of himself, but as something different and separate.

But the mother in this type of relationship can't bear to think of the child as something separate. To fulfill her needs, the child must be under control. In this tight relationship, the child feels used, not intensely loved. He knows that he is nothing more than his mother's window on the world or her bridge to that world. His value lies in his being an effective tool.

When the bonding stage gives way to the mirroring stage, the mother can't give him proper reflection because that would acknowledge his separateness from her and give him permission to enjoy it. So she frowns at every normal gesture of independence and smiles at every abnormal display of cohesiveness or clinging. She disciplines him saying, "No, no, *we* don't *do* that." She praises him saying, "My, didn't *we* do well in school today! She emphasizes at all times that *he* does what *she* does, and that she "owns" whatever he does. His victories are hers and his failures, God forbid, are hers, too.

It is very hard on the mother when her self-object doesn't or can't cooperate. Galina was such a child. Her mother had wanted to be a ballerina, but the turmoil of war had disrupted her training. Her family had fled to the United States where Galina's mother married a wealthy man older than herself. "Mama was very bitter," Galina said, "and she was determined to make everything right this time. She was so relieved that I was a girl. . . . She named me after a famous ballerina and bought me a tiny pair of toe shoes when I was two weeks old. By the time I was a year old, I was walking in them. I was the youngest child in the ballet school, but I was never afraid because Mama was always there with me. She would have been on the stage when I performed in recitals, too, if they had let her, but she sat in the first row and clapped like crazy. She was so proud of me, and it made me feel good to dance beautifully because she took such pleasure in it."

All went well through Galina's childhood because she did as her mother wanted her to. She danced eagerly and studied hard and her reward was always there in her mother's eyes. When she was thirteen the ballet teacher took them aside for counseling. "Madame Barlova had tears in her eyes." Galina said, "she knew it meant so much to Mama, but she said, 'Galina is five-feet-nine now and growing. She will never be a prima ballerina.' It was like a death blow to Mama. She didn't speak to me for three weeks. I became a choreographer, a very good one, but it wasn't the same thing. She was polite about it, that's all. So now I'm going to finish my degree and be what *I* need to be."

It's hard for people to recover from solipsistic injuries, because they occur so early and the victims don't always question the joint-identity they are subjected to. A typical response to the questions "Why did your parents want you?" was "To make my mother's life complete, of course. To get her all the things she never got for herself— why else would anyone want to have a child? Isn't that what children are for?" That response came from the thirty-four-year-old woman who was so crushed when her parents stopped supporting her financially. She had never seen a purpose to her existence beyond satisfying her mother's needs.

There is no real way out of this sort of situation— no truly effective way of coping that doesn't involve some damage to the child's Self. Nevertheless, children react in a number of ways that allow them some salvation of their Selves.

Rebellion and Spitefulness

One way is to rebel, to fight the mother, An older child does this in obvious ways— refusing to study, having an unusual hair style, defying curfews, or leaving home. A younger child is too young to act out his rebellion so obviously and may turn his anger onto himself. This retroflected anger results in self-destructive behavior, such as the little boy who rode his bicycle down a flight of stairs, driving his mother crazy with concern. The more she cried out, the more he did it, and the more she pleaded, "Stop! You're all I have to live for!"

Such an extreme display of spitefulness may force a mother to loosen her grip in despair, but the self-destructive behavior is very costly to the child.

Some of the rebellious behavior is like the old expression "cutting off your nose to spite your face." A child might not become flagrantly self-destructive like the boy bicycling down the stairs, but will resolve to do something like "I won't enjoy myself at the birthday party because that would make Mother happy." Later in life the same child may think unconsciously, "I won't have an orgasm because that would please my partner," or "I won't be successful because that would please my parents."

Withdrawal

Another way out the solipsistic relationship is for a child to build a wall around himself, withdraw inside the wall, and become non-responsive, almost like an autistic child. He simply becomes deaf to the mother's demands and may grow up with a psychological inability to hear a woman's voice. The child creates his rigid boundaries with the muscular armoring of his body. It is the only way he can feel a sense of identity in his body, and it protects him from the solipsistic relationship with the parent. But again the cost is high. He loses the ability to love, to be open-hearted, to be close to other people, and to feel in his body.

This often surfaces as a problem in sexuality, when a person complains of impotence, non-orgasmus, or just plain numbness or sexual "deadness." The person can't perform sexually. He has no sense of Self because of the muscular armoring that blocks the connection to his feelings. It is very difficult to solve these problems by working on sex and on current relationships, because these problems developed much earlier in life. Instead, it is the relationship with the parent that must be cleared so the person's sense of identity can be restored.

Compliance

Still another way to survive the solipsistic relationship is simply to comply, to give in and become the "good child." The child splits off from his connection to himself(or, from his true feelings) and spends his life living up the expectations of others (usually the mother). So far removed is he from his own feelings that he never realizes he is performing, not for his sake, but for others. He is an automaton acting as if he were a thinking, feeling entity. This was true of Galina, dancing to please her mother, and of another client, a doctor who realized when he was forty that he had never wanted to be a doctor at all. He always thought he did because he got his sense of identity from his mother, and *she* wanted him to be a doctor. He had lost touch early with any idea of what he, himself, would like to do with his life.

Polarizing

This in an unconscious defense frequently found in the solipsistic relationship. Here the child polarizes the environment into good and bad parts and is incapable of integrating the two parts. It' s like carrying over into real life the symbolism of a movie in which the bad guys wear the black hats and the good guys wear the white hats. The black and white of his world never blend to produce shades of grey. It' s the same with the child. Although he, too, has good and bad parts, he can not integrate them into a whole person. He must be either good or bad, and which he is depends on his mother.

This happens in the solipsistic relationship because the child is a captive part of the mother. He knows that he is an extension of her. He can' t be separate; therefore, he must be the same as she is. Even when she is mean or mistaken or drunk or disinterested, he can' t see her as bad because *he is a part of her* and if she is bad, then he must be bad too. The pain of feeling bad about himself leads to feelings of annihilation and non- existence, so, to avoid them, he has to *make* her good, either by not seeing the bad side or by changing his image of her.

The growth of the Self depends on the positive feelings and caring of the mother, so it is essential to see her as good, loving, caring, supportive and so on. If she is not these things, he fragments and panics. The panic is complete: a body, Self, and soul experience. To survive, the child must mobilize his energy to change the attitude or mood of the "bad" mother from disapproval or withdrawal into a positive, supportive presence.

Mother
(Object)

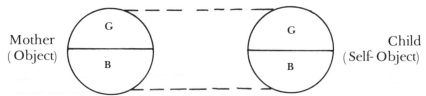

Child
(Self- Object)

The child in a solopsistic relationship learns to feel responsible for his parent' s feelings. If his mother is angry or depressed, that is , if she is "bad," then so is he. He feels that he must be to blame, because he has already constructed her as "good." He is then responsible for her feeling better, so he learns ways of making her "good" again, so he can feel good.

Alan did this with his mother, an alcoholic. When she got depressed, as she often did, he would try to cheer her up. Eventually he learnd that one sure- fire method was to fix her a drink. By the time he was five, he was an accomplished bartender. As he got older, he discovered other ways to cheer his mother up. He learned inadvertently that when he was sick, his mother lost her depression and expended her energies getting him well. He used this technique, too, though not consciously. He had asthma for years, probably because it brought out the best in his mother.

This, incidentally, shows that the polarizing works both ways. The mother splits the child into unintegrated good and bad, and either disowns the bad or feels the same sense of responsibility for it as he does for her bad side. So when Alan got sick, his mother felt that she was to blame and had to make him well again so they could both continue to be good.

Alan also found, when he was considerably older, that he could read poetry or play songs on his ukulele or tell funny stories to cheer her up. Once she cheered up, he could feel good about himself again.

The desperate thing about this relationship is that without separate boundaries, both people are dependent upon the good feelings of others to feel good about themselves. If one member of the pair stomps angrily into a room, the other feels bad, Worse, he feels responsible. When a person has good Self boundaries, he can acknowledge the other person's anger, but not take it upon himself.

In therapy, a person develops his own boundaries and learns to feel good about himself. Eventually he can grow out of the solipsistic relationship, and avoid repeating the pattern. While in therapy, he will tend to split the therapist into good and bad, just as he does with the rest of his relationships. When he projects his good half onto the therapist, it is positive transference, but when it flip-flops due to some injury, it is negative transference. The injury can be something as simple as the therapist being late for an appointment, going on vacation, or being unavailable by phone when he is wanted. Then, instead of all good, he is seen as bad and un-giving. We talk more about transference when we discuss our ther eutic methods.

Other examples of polarizing show up frequently. Joanna, for instance, had been deeply in love with a Marine during the Vietnam War. When he was killed in combat, she despaired of ever loving again. Eventually, she met another man and married him, convinced at the time that she loved him. As time went by, she realized that he could never take the place of her lost lover and the love she thought she felt for him vanished. The realization had caused her to see him as all bad, simply because he could never be "the right one," something that had nothing whatever to do with his very real and desirable qualities.

Another client, Terry, was in the peculiar position of having two "mothers." The extra one was his real mother's sister, who lived with the family throughout Terry's childhood and helped raise him. His real mother was a discontented woman, bitter about what life had dealt her and determined that her son, at least, shouldn't disappoint her. You recognize, of course, another typical solipsistic relationship. What wasn't typical was that, although Terry had the same problems Alan had with *his* mother, his double maternal blessing enabled him to solve them somewhat differently. Whereas Alan had to jump through hoops to make his mother "good," Terry could turn to his aunt to see himself as good. From infancy, Terry had seen his mother as bad and his aunt as good, with not a trace of either quality in the other woman. When he grew up and left home, he continued the same pattern. He always had difficult relationships, so he always managed to have two women, one who was good when the other was bad.

When the sense of Self is poorly established and weak, the only way to protect the valued parts of the Self from the unwanted or "bad" parts is to split them apart and to keep them fenced off. When the bad and good are thus separated, the integrity of the Self is difficult or impossible to maintain. It then becomes impossible to appreciate and respect the integrity of others, and the polarizing process goes on, with the world and its people being forever split into good and bad.

The Solipsistic Relationship: Next Generation

When a child who has had a solipsistic relationship with his parents goes out into the world and forms a relationship, it can only be one of two types, both solipsistic. This is the only kind of relationship he knows, but he can play both parts.

In the first, he plays the well-learned role of the parent and becomes the engulfer, creating a self-object of his partner. Since the partner is the self-object and the solipsistic pattern has been perpetuated, the partner comes to feel unloved, uncared for, unseen. In truth, he *doesn't* exist as a separate human being in his own right in relation to his engulfing mate; he exists only to fulfill the needs of that mate.

In the second type, the person finds a controlling partner just like the mother and perpetuates the pattern by being, again, the passive victim (or self-object). When either relationship is threatened, the partner who has become the self-object loses his identity and fragments. This can happen when the controlling partner dies or finds another person to better fulfill his needs, or when he finds, through therapy, that he can begin to live for himself. In many long-term solipsistic marriages, the death or departure of one may mean the death of the other — either emotional or even the physical death of the other. It can be almost like being a Siamese twin with a connection so strong that one can't live without the other.

Solipsistic injuries exist on a continuum from mild to severe. Although a person in a solipsistic relationship can also suffer from other types of injuries. A solipsistic injury of abandonment is difficult to work with, because there is a diminished sense of Self to reach for within the abandoned person and a flattening of affect. It is an energetic injury — that is, it is felt in the body, like an amputation, because the person feels he has lost part of himself.

Healthy Introversion/Narcissism Stage (1½ to 3 Years) Task: Reinforcing Self

Ideally, the child evolves toward expanded individuality. With adequate bonding and consistent reflection, the third stage of development occurs when the child realizes that he is separate and not a self-object of mother, father, or environment. With enough support, the child can separate and enter the process of life as an individual.

For individuality to grow, a child must develop what we call a healthy narcissism or healthy introversion. The uninjured child already experiences himself as omnipotent, omniscient, and glorified. From his experience of unity with life, through his mother, he has a sense of divinity in his own being (or an awareness of the unity of his soul with the Universal Source). When this divinity is properly reflected by the parents, further development of his individual consciousness is possible.

The child's sense of Self, nurtured thusly, gives him the inner resources to handle failures in his trial-and-error interactions with the environment and to turn them into successes. He has a sense of Self and of identity that have developed on a body level. When there are emotional disturbances in the environment, he can turn to a place within his body for a grounding, supporting feeling of well-being from which he can return, strengthened, to the world. This is healthy narcissism. It allows him to be true to himself, and at the same time, get along in the world outside.

Rosie, a charming three year old, illustrates this quality. She dressed herself for church one Sunday, meeting all her parental standards except for wearing one pink sock and one green one. Her father looked at her and said, "You don't want to wear two different colored socks". She tossed her head indignantly and said, "You can tell me what I *have to* wear, but you can't tell me what I *want* to wear."

It is obvious that each stage is built upon the one before. Through the bonding with the mother, the child gets the physical sense of well-being and the emotional warmth and security. In the mirroring stage he realizes increasingly that he is an individual and his mother reinforces his individuality by letting him see her appreciation and approval. When the reflection is consistent and accurate, he can learn without damage to himself why one action is good and a very similar one is not: that chomping down on a teething ring is fine, for instance, but biting a nipple on Mother is not. It is a process of learning that while some behavior is more acceptable than other kinds of behavior, it's the behavior that's being judged and not the child. A parent who can let a child know that he is good even if some of the things he does are not, helps build a healthy narcissism. So does the parent whose expectations for the child are appropriate to the child's age and abilitites. This allows the child to succeed at the majority of challenges he faces, building his confidence so he can continue to risk failing and thus, learning. He can trust himself, his abilities, and his feelings. When he goes out to test himself against "reality" in the form of peers and other adults, he can also test that outer reality against the truth inside himself, like Rosie with her mixed socks, who could concede to external standards without relinquishing her right to feel another way.

Reinforcing Injuries

Sometimes the healthy introversion doesn't develop even though a person apparently had proper mirroring. The mother may have gone by the book, doing and saying all the right things, but the child could never incorporate these messages. This mirroring injury shows up in this stage as a mind-body split: the child knows in his head that he's okay but knows in his gut that he's not. His mother, probably because she wasn't raised in a Blue Light and didn't get the right affective messages herself, says the right words but gets the feeling tone wrong. Without the right feeling behind the word, the messages are empty and the child can't get the deep, internal belief in himself that he needs.

On an emotional level, children are very aware of what is true and what is not true. The message "Yes, dear, you did very well" from a mother who doesn't look at her crowing child comes, not from the words, but from the fact that she didn't bother to look up. The words aren't important or even necessary. A mother who silently watches and appreciates what her child is doing conveys a positive message with her eyes and her behavior.

A child who gets only empty mirroring can still grow up with some idea of who he is and move out into the world from that idea. This is what we call ego functioning. In place of a strong sense of Self, a person builds an ego, or a personality, like a mask, that allows hims to function without a true sense of Self. These people often function admirably, but are over-achievers in that they operate from their intelligence and not from their connections to the Self and their true abilitites. They appear to be doing fine, but the early injury may show up later in life when they look inside and find emptiness there.

Many successful people reach a point in their lives when they look inside and find themselves emotionally hollow and spiritually empty. Had they been mirrored with empathy instead of vacant words, they would have looked inside and found their connections to the essential Self within.

The work in IBP is especially powerful against injuries in this stage of development because it restores the connection to the feeling of Self in the body, not just to the knowledge in his head. Talk therapy fails because it can't reach the inner awareness that gives the basic nonverbal support a child (or adult) needs.

In IBP, there is an energetic emotional exchange between the therapist and client. Through transference with the therapist, the proper reflection of the client's childhood Self can be reestablished, and he can regain the connection to his Self, in consciousness and in his body.

A therapist cannot give what he didn't get, so it is imperative for the IBP therapist to have had therapy himself. This ensures that the mirroring response has been fully given and received on a body level, with not only the intellectual understanding of what is needed, but with true energetic empathy. In the body work, the client is regressed enough to allow this empathic feeling in. The therapist must be able to convey the affect of this stage, and if he cannot he will duplicate the injury to the client. It is a lack of empathy that stunts development at this stage.

It is important to look at the Primary Scenario for injuries to the parent which explain the origin of this lack of empathy. Then, even if the child thinks he is okay, we can see that the parent could not have possibly given the child anything but the words, and this will explain the client's feeling of emptiness and lack of satisfaction in his accomplishments in later life. One man who went to graduate school for fourteen years knew something *cognitively*, but couldn't really feel good about his knowledge until he had IBP therapy. Then he finally understood— and felt in his body— that he knew what he thought he knew. Now he has an inner connection to his Self, and he can go out into the world feeling truly supported in his knowledge. True separation will not occur unless the reflection that occurs is an empathic one. A person cannot reflect another accurately unless he has a sense of his own identity inside.

Rapprochement Stage (1½ to 3 Years and on) *Task: Reality Testing*

When a child has developed a fair sense of who he is and what he can do, it is time for him to test himself. In his limited environment he has been able to feel omnipotent, and his instincts urge him out into the world to see if his omnipotence holds.

This is the beginning of a lifetime of experimenting with the world and testing himself. It's a process of measuring his skills against the requirements and expectations of other people. It's comparing his attitudes and his views of the world with a reality outside his home and sometimes modifying them based on what he finds.

The process of rapprochement is one of bringing one's sense of Self and one's internal fantasy into harmony with the external reality. To be successful at this stage, the child must have developed a healthy narcissism in the previous stage, because when he takes his internal fantasy into the outside world, it might take a beating. He might not be omnipotent after all. The two year old who has his family on the run when he says "no" will find that most strangers stand their ground and don't give him his way. This is such a shock that he needs that secure sense of well-being inside so he can go in and feel good about himself while he assimilates the lessons learned. There he can adjust his fantasy about himself to fit the outside world. His mother, continuing to mirror him and containing for him his sense of Self, supports him in his reality testing.

Rapprochement takes place every time a person moves into new worlds. The child will go through it when he goes to nursery school, elementary school, high school, and college. At adolescence, he tests himself against the adult world. At graduation he takes on the business and professional world. All along, it is a process of learning and growing confident inside about what he is and what he knows. Then he must go out and verify it. The comedy and pathos of these transitions fill our literature and movies.

The teen-ager, overflowing with self-confidence and disdain for his parents' ways, embarks on his journey into adulthood. His internal fantasy is constantly buffeted by reality. He suffers pain, embarrassment, and humiliation. But it's all for the good, because he also experiences triumph, pleasure, joy, and growth beyond his dreams.

The graduate, too, will be able to look wryly back on the time when he emerged from the ivory tower and began trying to apply his abstract learning to the practical world. We all have our come-uppances, starting when we first leave our mother's side and venture into the world of strangers. But the stumbles and bumbles don't matter so long as there is that inner security to return to, where we can ask, "Am I not who I felt I was?" and know the answer: "Yes, I'm me, and I may have *had* a failure but I'm *not* a failure; I'll try again."

The person who hasn't had a healthy narcissism falls apart during this stage, the teen-ager with a grandiose sense of his own worth who tries to find a summer job and can't, may fragment. A little kid who decides he's ready to play with the big boys and can't even pick up the baseball bat, cries like a baby. And the graduate who knows how the save the world may go into severe depression when his seven-hundredth resume brings no response from the job market.

In therapy, until a client develops a healthy narcissism, he won't be able to carry the feeling of well-being from one session to the next. The therapist's role, like that of the parents (especially the father), is to provide support when it's needed, just as one might stake a young tree. The tree doesn't need the stake to grow, except when the wind blows hard and threatens to break its slender trunk. The client doesn't come to his weekly therapy session to find out who he is, but simply to get a little support against the raging reality outside. In the same way, the child needs to return to the parent for the necessary support in his trial and error experiments in the world. That is what "rapprochement" means.

The more a person tests his capabilities against external standards, the better idea he has about what he can do. When he has a firm sense of identity within, he can afford to take risks because he won't be shattered if he fails. He can never lose that sense of identity, so he is safe taking it out into the world and expressing it. Remember, it's not what you do, but how you do it. You don't go out to find

something that expresses who you are— you find a *way* to express
who you are.

The therapist supports the client in trying new things, in testing
himself in new ways. As people learn to act from their own feelings,
they have to go through the same learning and testing process they
did as kids and young adults. The doctor who realizes at forty that he
didn't want to be a doctor but a potter, has to test out his skills. Even
if he concludes that he'll never be rich and famous from the bowls
and plates he makes, he is still in a win/win situation. He can operate
from his true sense of Self by doing what his feelings urge him to do.
Expressing himself will bring him pleasure. If, in addition, he does
get rich from his potting, it's a bonus. But the point is that he
doesn't need the validation of getting rich to enjoy the potting. The
validation comes from knowing his Self and expressing it in a
medium that brings him satisfaction.

The Constituted Self

The fully constituted Self is the goal and ideal of the preceding
developmental stages. A person who had his needs sufficiently met
in childhood will have a strong sense of Self. The different aspects of
his personality will be integrated into his whole being. The feeling of
well-being in his body will be echoed and augmented by his verbal,
cognitive sense of Self. Both will be continually verified by his
interactions with other people and with the world. He will know who
he is and what he can do, and he can let himself act on his feelings.
He is emotionally free of his parents and self-reliant, so his close
relationships are formed by choice and not by need. Because of his
independence and his deep-down gut feeling of continuity with
some sort of life force, he is able to pursue his own life fearlessly and
joyfully. Because of his firm but resilient sense of identity he can risk
failure, knowing that he can return to his inner core for nurturing
and reinforcement. And from that core, he is able to go beyond the
Self into the spiritual or transpersonal realm.

Although no one emerges from his parental home as perfectly
constitued as our ideal, most people come out able to function in the
world. Some do much better than that. Building on a fair-to-good
foundation of bonding, mirroring, and supported reality-testing,
they find ways to express themselves in the world that allow them to
continue the process of constitution. But for those people who don't
come out very well at all and have trouble functioning, their
compulsively followed paths lead them into repeated failure and
sorrow.

Chapter 7

Hanging Out:
The Therapeutic Process

Even if a person's basic needs are not adequately met in his first few years, he can still complete the interrupted process as an adult with the help of therapy.

The Primary Scenario gives the therapist clues as to what dynamics might have worked on a person during those formative years, which needs were met and which were not met, and what repetitive patterns to expect. Current relationship patterns generally bear out the guesses or predictions we make from the Primary Scenario. The breathing work reveals muscular holding patterns and uncovers the hidden emotions causing them. It is a tool for both diagnosis and treatment, because it puts the client in touch with his body and with the feelings harbored therein.

All these tools work together, augmenting and verifying each other. The diagnostic models in this chapter further expand our ability to understand and to treat the emotional problems predicted, explained, and isolated by the other tools. That is, a person's symptoms as an adult are reflections of his childhood experiences. These experiences, in turn, both reflect and were determined by his Primary Scenario. His current relationship pattern and the Scenario suggest what sort of body work to do.

So, in this chapter, we show how the IBP therapist combines all the tools— the history, the predictions, the symptoms, the patterns, and the breathing work— to help a person retrace his developmental process, to find the place where it was interrupted, and to get him back on the path to the constituted Self.

We start by describing fragmentation. The loss of Self, of one's identity, is a powerful and fundamental fear. All the defensive styles of relating are developed to prevent fragmentation. All the tasks of the various developmental stages ideally establish such a strong sense of Self, of internal well-being, that a person need not fragment nor fear fragmentation. To the extent that these tasks weren't completed properly, an individual will protect himself against the feeling of annihilation, usually at the cost of emotional freedom.

Fragmentation

The sense of Self is slow to develop. At first, the baby's sense of who or what he is is synonymous with his mother. Then he separates into what is actually him, but the process is gradual. For a while, his sense of individuality may be limited to hunger and satisfaction. It expands to sensations involving limbs and eyes, then to physical skills— lifting his head and crawling— and to social skills, such as smiling to get a smile. By the time he's walking, he has a vocabulary for understanding, if not yet for speaking.

This is a lot. The baby has come a long way from oneness with his mother, but his sense of Self is still fairly primitive. What he does know is firm, but most of his sense of Self is still undifferentiated, nonverbal, and fragile. At one moment he may feel good and confident and all together, and the next moment he is in tears. That fragile Self has fallen apart, or fragmented. He has to go back to his mother, who "contains" his sense of Self for him, to be able to put himself back together. Just as she contained nutrients for him during pregnancy, she continues to be an emotional resource for him. As he grows older, if he has enough help from her when he needs it, he develops his own internal resources and can go inside to put himself together.

Unfortunately, not everybody gets the proper bonding and mirroring. For those who did not, when injuries occur the sense of Self fragments. When a person has once achieved a sense of differentiation, it is terrifying to lose it. It is as though he has gradually put together inside himself a jigsaw puzzle mirror with lots of pieces and he has the pieces more or less confined in a frame. Every time he gets proper mirroring, he gets another piece to add to his puzzle. When something happens to shake that developing mirror— his sense of Self— the pieces come unglued, pop out of the frame, and get all mixed up. He is fragmented. It is time for more glue and for sorting and replacing the pieces within the frame.

Fragmentation is so painful that no one can tolerate it for long. It is like being annihilated, wiped out of existence, to look inside and see oneself in a shattered mirror. To protect ourselves from the pain of fragmentation, we develop different defensive styles, just as we armor our bodies to block our feelings.

Fragmentation occurs in adult situations when a person encounters something similar to, parallel to, analogous to, or resembling his Primary Scenario. We use all that redundancy to emphasize that, although a situation seems to have nothing in common with one from the Primary Scenario, if it is remotely like it— if it even *smells* remotely like it— it can send one into fragmentation.

A person may cope well with frustration, fear, or tragedy, but fall apart over a petty squabble. He may surmount enormous technical difficulties only to collapse in a rage over a fellow worker— because somehow the situation resembles something in his past. If it were a new problem, he'd deal with it, but when it's from the Scenario, he fragments. Because he is traveling the patterns learned in his Primary Scenario, a sense of rejection or disapproval can hurl him back to a point at which his fragile childhood Self craved primary nurturance to survive. And when he's at that point, he is fragmented and undifferentiated again. He needs his mother to hold up his Self and say, "don't worry, this is the real You. With a little glue we'll have you back together in a jiffy."

Howard, for instance, went into his bank to get a loan. He had acquired a credit rating he was proud of, just as his mother had always told him to do, and was certain he would get the loan immediately. He strode confidently up to the loan officer, a woman he knew, and made his request. She was friendly and courteous, handed him a loan application, and asked him to sit down with her and fill it out. Instead, he threw it on her desk and stomped out the door, enraged. All day at work it bothered him— not the rage, but her expecting him to fill out the application. By his afternoon therapy session he was able to see that it wasn't her perfectly rational expectation that had upset him, but the fact that she, a woman, a symbolic Mother, hadn't given him instant approval, hadn't trusted him implicitly. It was as if his own mother had insisted he show her his ears when he said he had just washed them. Even if she had said merely, "I'm sure your credit will be approved," he admitted, he would probably have gone into a rage. Had the loan officer been a man, he would have simply filled out the application without incident. Because the loan officer was a woman, he went back in time to a point at which he needed approval from his mother. He interpreted her standard procedure as rejection, and he fragmented.

People do not necessarily recognize that they are fragmented. Like Howard, they may know that they are angry, but attribute their anger to the hostility or thoughtlessness of others. But people do recognize many of the symptoms of acute fragmentation and describe them in such terms as "coming unglued," "falling apart," "seeing the hollow person beneath the shell," "being shattered," "not being together."

We use the term "acute" fragmentation only to differentiate from "chronic" fragmentation, when people are perennially not together. There are degrees of fragmentation, but in order to work with it, one must agree that one is either fragmented or one is not. An episode may be brief or it may last for weeks, but during that episode, the fragmentation is total. It's like an ordinary light switch that is on or off, nothing in between. Like the old nursery rhyme:

> Humpty Dumpty sat on a wall
> Humpty Dumpty had a great fall
> All the king's horses and all the king's men
> Couldn't put Humpty Dumpty together again.

Humpty Dumpty was *on* the wall, then he was *off*. He was a whole egg, then he was a fragmented egg shell.

There are at least two important things to remember about fragmentation. First, one does not fragment a little bit. Briefly, perhaps, but totally. It's like being a little pregnant; one is or one isn't. Second, nothing can be done about the fragmenting event until one gets out of fragmentation. Usually a person's energy goes toward denying that he is fragmented, but it would be better spent in regluing the broken bits of mirror and putting back together his sense of Self. Worse, while he is denying his fragmentation, he is probably trying to work on whatever caused it and is making it worse, especially if it is a relationship. Not only is it better not to work on the fragmenting situation, it is better not to work on anything till one is back together.

A young man learned this the hard way. He had had an upsetting fight with his girlfriend and left her apartment much earlier than he had expected. Realizing that he now had some extra time, he decided to do some minor work on his motorcycle. He started to remove a spark plug, but it wouldn't come out. He tried pliers, then bigger pliers, then vice-grips. The spark plug broke off, flush to the engine. He tried chiseling it out and then he tried cautiously drilling it out. Finally he got out a big drill bit, leaned on his power drill, and went right through the plug into the cylinder wall, utterly destroying the motor. Had he realized that he was fragmented, of course, he never would have started what seemed like an easy task.

The first step, therefore, in dealing with fragmentation, is to recognize that one *is* fragmented. Then— and only then— can he think about solving the problem that led to the fragmentation.

When Humpty Dumpty was in pieces on the ground, all he could see when he looked to the past was tragedy, soles of shoes, and horses' hooves. When he looked to the future, he couldn't seen anything because he was lower than the horizon. There was no point in his wondering whether he fell off the wall or was pushed. If he couldn't get himself back together, it didn't matter. So, whether it's Humpty Dumpty, a client, or yourself, the first thing to do is get out of fragmentation.

To do that, as we said before, one must first accept that he is fragmented. There are many signals that indicate fragmentation. Each of us has a different set of signals, and learning what they are is an important step in therapy. Together, the therapist and client begin to identify the client's own set of symptoms. This might include somatic illness, dreams of illness, or dismemberment, body tremors, defensive behavior, guilt, explaining himself, anxiety, depression, over-eating, memory loss, and many more.

If a person suddenly starts leaving his briefcase in the taxi, his credit cards with the cashiers, and his keys in locked cars, it makes no sense to start working on devices to improve his memory. It would not only be a waste of time, but might exacerbate the symptoms. Instead, he must admit that this uncharacteristic forgetfulness is a symptom of fragmentation. Then he has to realize that he had been fragmented before and gotten back together, so he can do it again. It is as though he has lost his senses. The therapist can teach him to regain them, thus bringing him back to a solid, palpable reality.

"Look around the room," the therapist might say. "What do you see? What color is the sofa? The curtains? Is it warm or cold? How does the arm of the chair feel to your fingers?" People often don't see colors when they are fragmented, nor do they respond much to their other senses, for their sense of aliveness is gone.

The next step is to look at someone else and describe him. "What kind of clothes is he wearing? What color? Can you smell any perfume or after-shave lotion? Look into his eyes." This brings him into contact with the therapist(or another person, if he's trying to get grounded outside of therapy).

Fritz Perls, the founder of Gestalt therapy, said, "lose your mind and come to your senses." We feel that he meant this to describe the process of getting out of fragmentation by using one's senses to come back to awareness.

This step-by-step process of grounding oneself in reality will get a person out of fragmentation. Then it is possible to look for the fragmenting event. He should go back to the moment when he first felt his symptoms. It might be a few seconds before or a few days, and he might get there by asking, "When did I get my feelings hurt? When did I get angry? When was the injury? What was I looking for when it happened? What did I want that I didn't get?"

Knowing when the injury occurred is important because it points out the event that triggered the fragmentation. Once you know what the event is, you can see how it is similar to something from the Primary Scenario. Most of us go through life trying to fulfill un-met needs or longings from the past. We try to get someone outside ourselves to fulfill them, just as a child depends on his mother to make him feel better about himself. From the bonding and mirroring stages, a child gets a lot of tacit or explicit assurances, or messages, from his mother. These are, or should be, the Good Mother messages we talk about later. They tell him that he is loved, that he can feel secure, that he is basically acceptable. To the extent that he doesn't get these messages in childhood, he will try to get them from his adult relationships. If he does get them as a child, they will be incorporated into his Self concept and he won't be subject to fragmentation whenever they are withheld.

When a person finds the injury that fragmented him, he often finds that it was the last of a series of blows. Each may have been inconsequential in itself, but the effect is cumulative and the final one is the last straw. The following sequence of events is typical. Mattie thought she had gotten out on the wrong side of bed that day. She went to breakfast on the way to work and was pleased to find a parking place on the street. Eating out instead of making her own breakfast was a special treat for her, but this morning the waitress forgot her order. This deprived Mattie of the message that she was seen, heard, and special. When she had finally eaten, she went to her car and found a $35 ticket on it for parking during street-sweeping hours. This told her that she wasn't being taken care of and that she was neither special nor acceptable. She was upset, but she was still okay. Then she arrived at work, a little flustered at being late, and found herself locked out. This final message was the last straw, and it led to fragmentation. She knew she not only wasn't special, but she wasn't even wanted, and her day was ruined.

Humpty Dumpty hits the ground again! Under the same circumstances, the person with an intact sense of Self would feel irritated but would not fragment— that is, doubt his self-worth.

The chances of fragmentation are much greater in an intimate relationship than in everyday events. This is partly because we choose partners we hope will fill our needs and give us all the messages we want. We depend more on them than on casual acquaintances, and yet often we deliberately— if unconsciously— choose the people least likely to do so. Since we have a patterned-in compulsion to finish unfinished business, we pick someone like "Mother" in the hopes that "she" (whether it is a man or a woman) will, at least, give us the mirroring or loving we need. And, of course, "she" won't, or can't, and we continue to fragment until we learn how to fill our own needs and supply our own messages of love and assurance. In the meantime, we depend on the defenses we have built up to help us avoid fragmentation and the pain it produces.

Another exercise that we use in healing fragmentation is the House or Foundation Image. The person visualizes a house, imaginary or real, present, past, or future, and goes into the house and down to the basement to look at the foundation. "See if anything is wrong there," we suggest, "and, when you find it, repair it. Feel in your body what it feels like to have repaired those problems in the foundation of your house. Now that the foundation is strong, experience it in your body. How can you handle the current situation differently with a solid foundation?"

Boundaries

The issue of boundaries is central to the therapeutic process because a boundary defines the Self. Some people have what we call *Self* boundaries, which are flexible, some have *defensive* boundaries, which are rigid, and some have few or *vague* boundaries.

By Self-boundary we mean the sense or experience of Self that is separate from the world yet exists in harmonious relationship within it. The Self-boundary defines the constituted Self. It is strengthened by proper reflection and continued interaction with the environment, including the inevitable and necessary failures that lead to new learning and growth.

A defensive boundary is a substitute for a Self-boundary that fails to develop through lack of proper reflection and successful learning. Defensive boundaries are protective of whatever sense of Self the person does have; they keep people out in the same way as one's defensive armor protects the Self hidden within.

The absence or vagueness of boundaries occurs when a person has insufficient sense of Self for him to know where or how to set a boundary.

One expresses oneself through boundaries. When there is little or no connection to the Self— manifested by rigid boundaries or the virtual absence of them — one way to start creating the experience of Self is to establish boundaries. In IBP we want every insight to be a body experience as well as a cognitive one, so we ask a person to draw a boundary around himself, marking his limits physically and energetically. He will eventually feel and understand his own boundaries and their function, but, for the time being, we tell him to think of his boundary line as stating: "This is me and that is you and, for now, we won't cross this line. We will just experience ourselves as separate, and this line is my boundary." By making an implied boundary explicit, he gets a kinesthetic feeling of his energetic limits, of containment, and of safety.

After a client has drawn his boundary, the therapist may push a pillow (representing Mother, Lover, Friend, whatever) across the line. Reactions differ widely. Some sit within their boundaries and do nothing. Some push it out vigorously. And some pull it in and hug it close. What a person does depends on the type of defensive character style he developed as a result of his Primary Scenario.

A person's physical limits are not the whole person; the body is only his most solid representation. His energy field goes beyond the solid physical body; therefore, when a therapist starts to work with a client who has very rigid boundaries, the client gets very uncomfortable if the therapist is too close physically. The client feels it as an invasion. The therapist should sit far enough away, meeting the client at his *energetic* boundary, to let him feel intact. The therapist should not try to press closer. He should "hang out" at the edge of the boundary until the client opens it and lets him in. This will happen when his *constant and consistent* stance in relation to the client is trusted. Insecurity and lack of knowledge of their own boundaries will often cause clients to invite the therapist in too close, too soon. If this happens, the client will very often feel so invaded that he will either leave therapy prematurely or use all his energy to keep the therapist out.

If the therapist invades the client's boundaries, the client will attempt to push the therapist out and to return to a safe distance. The therapist must recognize what has happened and make restitution for the injury that has been caused, for careful honoring of a person's boundaries is an important step in establishing trust. It is imperative that the therapist always take responsibilty for any invasions he makes, whether accidental or intentional. Gradually the client will be able to replace his rigid, un-giving boundaries with flexible ones. The work then is to guide the person to a strong enough sense of Self so that his feelings at the moment of injury can be acknowledged and worked through. The injury, caused by the therapist's invasion, is the point at which learning takes place.

The client must learn to identify the symptoms of fragmentation, to set limits, and to tell others how to be in relation to him. An exercise of moving physically closer and farther apart will allow the client to tell the therapist how close he wants him to be. In this way, the client will learn to become sensitive to his own boundaries. It is important not to do body work for some time, even though the client may be tremendously armored. Although the client may be eager to begin, any minor physical contact before trust is fully established may be seen as invasive and break down any trust already established. To develop the relationship, the therapist must make contact *at the boundary*, and not beyond it.

The therapist may devise exercises to bring the client *to* the boundary in order to make contact, but it is imperative that he wait patiently at the edge for the client to meet him there. This is how the fox taught the Little Prince to tame him in *The Little Prince*, by Antoine de Saint-Exupery. He taught the Prince to establish trust through friendliness and consistent behavior and not to betray that trust by coming close before he, the fox, was ready.

Our approach is somewhat different with a person who has a poor ability to set boundaries. Again, we have him draw a boundary around himself, because it can make a big difference in a person's emotional experience to have the actual boundary drawn. Then the therapist draws a boundary around himself, and the client's relief is often visible. It lets him see that the therapist is doing for him what his parents did not do— that is, stay separate and set limits. Working with this process allows the client to feel safe from engulfment and to learn to set and trust his own boundaries.

An example of building trust through establishing boundaries in this way was a young woman who had had an incestual relationship with her father from the time she was six till she was thirteen. She couldn't get out of it, she couldn't tell anyone, and she couldn't do anything about it. She simply complied and sometimes even enjoyed it, but she "wasn't there" while it went on. She was split-off as well as cut-off.

She came into therapy because she had become acutely conscious of having no feelings below her neck. It would have been easy to demonstrate that she was, indeed, capable of feeling, but her therapist chose not to start body work until she was ready. Although that was what she had come to therapy for, she was clearly relieved. Eventually, the gentle, more sophisticated approach paid off, because the most important thing at the beginning was for the therapist to build a relationship with her so that she felt safe. Even though she knew it was irrational, she was afraid that he would touch her unexpectedly and sexually; that he would grab her breasts or put his hand up her dress. She voiced the belief that "I have to keep my walls up so that no one can get to me. If I keep my barrier up, I don't have to be afraid of invasion." She held the world at bay with her body.

The task here was to find her energetic boundaries and to stay outside of them, even though it meant sitting twenty feet away from her, to keep her feeling safe. Gradually, as she felt more comfortable and less threatened, she allowed the therapist to get closer and was more willing to begin the body work. It took two years of this before the body work could begin. Then things moved faster because the body work softened her defensive armor while simultaneously establishing her confidence and strength in the experience of the Self. Thus, deeper contact became possible. Therapy would have taken even longer without the body experience and would have been impossible without scrupulous observance of her boundaries.

Containment

In chapter 4 we discussed the physical problem of containing the excitement and pleasure in the body. Now we look at the psychological expression of the inability to contain the sense of well-being.

To contain, one must be able to expand. Constricting the body armor makes this impossible physically, while constricting emotional or behavioral patterns make it impossible psychologically.

If people who cannot contain excitement have money, they have to spend it. If they have news, they have to tell somebody. When they get what they want, they have to get rid of it. They'll eat too much after a successful weight loss or consume alcohol to sabotage the good feelings that arose from sobriety. They feel compelled to interrupt the unaccustomed good feelings and return to familiar ones because they know who they are in the old patterns.

For a person who cannot contain, the sense of well-being becomes uncomfortable and he may project it onto someone else and fall in love (this is positive projection). This allows him to maintain the experience of well-being without having to contain it or own it within himself. He projects the overwhelming excitation and then identifies with it, but at a comfortable distance. As the sense of well-being grows within him, though, he may wake up one morning to find that the other person really isn't who he thought, and this may well be "the end of the honeymoon."

Often people leave relationships at this point, but it can become a time for partners' truly getting to know each other. If one completes the process of re-owning the projected qualities of the Self, relationships can become an exciting exploration. As Gregory Bateson once said, "It takes two to know one." For, as one grows more and more able to tolerate the sense of Self within, he begins to take back the projected qualities, to experience them within himself rather than through the projected relationship.

This positive projection may include spiritual qualities, the ability to experience altered states of consciousness, personal power, heightened awareness of one's own sexuality, and excitement, as well as inner peace and sense of well-being.

Sometimes a man will project his un-owned feminine side onto a woman. A woman may do likewise with her masuline side. (These are described further in the chapter 9 as the anima/animus.) When this happens, they may fall very much in love and see the partner as the "knight on the white horse" or the "princess in the tower." Since no one can live up to such idealized expectations, there is much anger and disappointment unless these masculine and feminine projections are reowned. When they are, the individual feels psychologically more complete, and the relationship will undoubtedly go through considerable change.

Defensive Character Styles of Relating

Splitting-Off

We have already described the person who "isn't there." This is a defensive character style of people whose early emotions were so painful that they "split-off" from them. Rather than tolerate the pain, they simply left their bodies, splitting themselves off from the feelings but, also, from the sense of Self, which is inseparable from the body. It is a primitive form of defense, and, if extreme, it can be a withdrawal so severe it is almost autistic. Because the person is removed from his feelings and from his self, he has no need for rigid boundaries to protect him; he has escaped instead.

Splitting-off can be a way to deal temporarily with an overwhelming emotional situation or it can become a true characterological state in which a person lives most of the time.

A person who is split-off is likely not to know it, and depending on the severity of the problem, it might not always be obvious to other people. There are certain types of behaviors characteristic of a person who splits-off. For instance, he may have a lackluster glaze in his eyes. He may not remember much of his childhood or may have frequent loss of memory in the present, such as misplacing keys, packages, or important papers. He may drive on "automatic pilot" and be consciously unaware of signals and traffic. He may daydream excessively, stare blankly into space, or do a lot of thinking that has nothing to do with his feelings. He may not notice colors around him and may even dream in black and white.

People who are split-off can tolerate only a limited amount of stimulation. They may be bruised often from bumping into things without noticing. They are without awareness of their bodies or their surroundings, moving as in a dream, working in the dark. One of the major causes of sexual dysfunction and relationship failure is the inability to remain present and to sustain sexual excitement. Rather than stay in their bodies, people may split-off into the transpersonal and altered states of consciousness where they do not have to deal with the body and emotions.

The As-If Personality and the Sleepwalker

There are different styles of being split-off. For purpose of clarity, we describe the extremes.

At one extreme is the As-If personality. Few people would recognize him as split off because he generally functions well and is liked for his agreeable nature. He does what is expected of him. He tries to do a good job. If he lives in the suburbs, he tries to keep his lawn as nice as his neighbor's. If he has a child, he tries to be a model parent. He dressses appropriately for all occasions, gets his Christmas cards out on time, and roots for what he hopes is the right team.

There doesn't appear to be anything wrong with him unless it is that he is *too* agreeable, *too* in line with social expectations. He himself may not notice anything wrong until he is quite mature. Then his only symptom may be a growing discomfort as he realizes that the activities meant to satisfy him are hollow gestures, not fulfilling engagements. He may begin to feel that he is a phony and suspect that his life is passing him by, bringing him no joy and leaving him no memories.

At the other extreme is the person so split-off that he is almost in a trance. Unlike the As-Iffer, who thinks he knows what he wants (for example, to be a "good boy" and get approval), the Sleep-Walker wanders vaguely through life, unaware of his body and of his needs. He might seek stimulation in drugs, sky-diving, or any idea or activity that arouses in him some semblance of feeling. His lack of commitment and his instability make it impossible for him to maintain relationships for long, and he may drift aimlessly from job to job, partner to partner, town to town.

This is the character style of a person who is pretending to be there. It's hard to ascertain that he's not there because often he doesn't know it himself. He looks real from the outside, but there is nobody behind the facade. He is not in a temporary daze. Rather, he is completely split-off from contact with his true inner feelings and from his true Self. He doesn't ever know what he is feeling, so he depends on cues from the outside. He performs to audience reaction, to Mother's wishes, to anything but his own needs.

After a lifetime of this, a person develops what we call an "as-if" personality. He acts "as-if" he were real, "as-if" he really cared about what he was doing. He is an actor, whether or not he's acting professionally, always looking to the outside for approval and guidance.

The "as-if" personality can often come about as the result of a solipsistic relationship. A child who learns early that he is part of his mother and must feel either as she wants him to or rebel and feel the opposite, splits-off from his own feelings. There is no point in having them. To spare himself the pain of futility, he ignores his feelings and adopts his mother's. When he's not around his mother, he adopts other people's feelings as his own, continuing to act as if they were his.

An example of this is a child who was offered a toy by his uncle. The child looked to the mother, not for permission, but for a clue as to whether he wanted the toy or not.

At first glance, the As-Iffer doesn't seem to have much of a problem if he can please people with no interference from his own feelings. And so it might seem to the As-Iffer himself, until he realizes that he has ordered his whole life, not by *his* feelings, but by those of others. With this realization comes despair. He sees that he has wasted a lifetime of feelings he *could* have, *should* have had. He looks back at everything he has done— going to Sunday school, choosing the "right" college and a "sensible" career, marrying the spouse his parents liked best, panning and praising the right movies and plays, buying a house in a "good" neighborhood— and sees that he never really cared about any of it. It all happened because of other people.

A person who doesn't operate from feelings within is never truly alive. There's no anticipation, no joy in his life. There may also be no dread or sorrow, but relief from these doesn't help. One needs to go through both pain and pleasure to be alive, and by that definition, neither of the split-off types qualifies. The Sleep-Walker can't tolerate any feelings and splits-off from them one way or another. The As-Iffer feels— or, rather, *tries* to feel— as he imagines he should feel. The pain he eventually does feel as a mature adult is for the feelings he ought to have felt and didn't, and for the joys of life that should have made his choices easy.

George is a typical example. He entered therapy when he was nearly fifty. His children were independent at last and he was able to look at his life differently than when he was working to support a family and further his career. Now there was less need to work hard and he could think seriously about retiring in five to fifteen years. His peers talked happily about their plans for travel, for moving to the country, for spending full time on their hobbies, but George had nothing to say. While they were trying to decide on the best ways to spend their declining years, George was trying to think of even one thing that held any interest for him. Finding only emptiness within him was the most painful thing he had done in his life, and it was terrifying, as well, to look inside and discover that "there's no George there." "I'm a phony," he said. "I've been an enthusiastic supporter of everything popular. I've cheered for the local teams and gotten on all the proper bandwagons. I'm a wonderful person to get involved in a cause because I get everybody else enthusiastic, too. But, do you want to know something? When I look back a few years and see some memento of an event or a plaque in honor of my participation, I can hardly ever remember what it was about. I don't think I was ever really involved and I think it must hurt people's feelings. The other day someone said, 'Remember the work we did for the Cranes?' and I said, 'Oh, uh, yeah, they were a great team, weren't they?' and it turned out we had worked together on the 'Save the Whooping Cranes' committee."

Similar to George was Angie, who had also spent her life acting out roles determined by the needs and enthusiasms of others. She was born to heavy-drinkers already in their late forties and fifties, who had started their family in the Depression. Angie was a bit of a surprise when she was born fourteen years after the youngest of her three siblings, and her parents were never quite reconciled to having had her. Her father was a domineering college professor who had retired young and was thus able to be a strong influence on her early years. His pedantic, opinionated nature coupled with the aggressiveness that came out when he drank taught the young Angie to test the way the wind blew before venturing any opinion. Her mother had lost patience with children and weaved erratically between praise for Angie's cleverness and fury at any sign of obstinacy or rebellion.

"When I look back," said Angie, "I remember that I used to get up in the morning, not knowing exactly who or what I would be that day— sort of like not knowing what to wear, Then I'd see Mama or Papa and I'd find out. They would hand me my personality the way they might have handed me the dress I was supposed to wear."

Angie married a playwright, thinking her parents would approve, and moved to New York City. She detested New York and yearned for California, but her husband thrived on the big city and wouldn't consider leaving. She never learned to take advantage of New York. "It was too expensive," she said. "My parents had a real Depression complex and taught me to fear extravagance. But really," she admitted, "it was more that I could never decide what I wanted to do. I went to Jim's productions and those of his friends because he wanted me to and I could get in free, but that was it for entertainment.

"I furnished our apartments with thrift shop furniture to save money, I thought, but again, it was really because I couldn't decide on any basis other than availability. Once Jim gave me money to buy draperies for a new apartment, but the windows were bare for two years because I didn't know how to decide what to buy. Finally *he* bought some and they were horrible. They taught me one thing— that, deep down, I *did* have some taste.

"Our friend were *his* friends, all theatre people, mostly charming, hyper, intellectuals."

One year Angie's sister invited her to bring her children to California for the summer. "It was a terrible summer," she recounted. "I wanted so much to stay, I was thirty-five years old, and it was the first thing I ever knew I wanted. I started seeing my sister's therapist and soon realized I'd never acknowledged my own feelings at all. One day I looked into the mirror and heard this funereal voice intoning, 'there *is* no real Angie,' and I cried for two weeks. In a way it was better when I was vaguely dissatisfied, when I pursed my lips and acted like a martyr and did 'the right thing,' sort of pretending that I would prefer to do it another way and all the time having no idea what I'd do if I weren't being 'forced' to do it that way. My God," she wept, "what do you think my children felt with their mother grimly forcing them to do things she obviously didn't believe in?"

Angie continued in therapy to explore the process by which she had disconnected from her true feelings and her true Self, gradually making the connections in her body. She unearthed old feelings and developed some confidence in her own reactions. It was a long process. She started teaching again to finance her therapy and her summers in California. She met new people and learned to trust her own judgment. She gradually found that New York had redeeming features, though she still preferred her summers. Eventually, when her children were teenagers, she moved them permanently to California.

Treatment Methods. People with split-off personalities enter therapy for different reasons, depending on how close they are to either extreme. A Sleep-Walker may have a real survival problem. His inconsistency and lack of contact make it hard for him to keep jobs and friends. He may have used up his youth and strength and be at the end of his rope when he comes to therapy, but he knows it. The As-Iffer knows only that he's dissatisfied. He wonders what could be wrong— after all, he has done everything right and has everything a person could want, doesn't he? Although he doesn't look split-off because he maintains eye contact and has an intuitive ability to divine other people's wishes, he is just as split-off from his feelings as is the Sleep-Walker, who may not be able to hold eye contact because he just isn't there.

The first thing that must be done in therapy is to make contact with the person who has split-off. Here there is no problem invading boundaries because there are none, and we can literally pull such people into contact. They are the ideal subjects for body work because breathing can bring them so quickly to real feelings in their bodies.

This vigorous approach isn't appropriate for people within rigid boundaries, but is ideal for those who aren't inside at all. The best way to make people be present is to bring them back into their bodies. It is impossible to work with someone who isn't even in the same room with you, so we ground them immediately in their bodies and their feelings. Then it is possible to explore the feelings that led to the initial fragmentation and the splitting-off.

At first they can't stay present and in contact with the therapist, nor can they sustain the excitement of the charge, but as they learn to stay present during the breathing, they can experience for the first time since they were children, their very own feelings and not somebody else's.

The As-If personality, accustomed to doing as he is told, will want to know if he is doing the breathing work right. When he finds that the therapist has no expectations for him to meet and he is confronting genuine, personal feelings, he will tend to split-off. When he manages to stay present, he realizes how much of his life he has missed by responding to external rather than internal cues. A man named Sean said, in describing himself, "I feel as though I've been sealed in plastic wrap all my life. I can see out but the wrap keeps me from feeling what's going on. It's like knowing it's raining because I can see it through the window, not because I can feel or smell it. I feel like a puppet and I don't know who pulls the strings."

It is sometimes the breathing work that first reveals the As-Iffer as being split off, because he has spent his life learning to act like a normally motivated person and may easily get past the therapist's initial scrutiny. In fact, many of our clients have spent considerable time with therapists who don't work with the body without finding the basis for their vague dissatisfaction. The breathing, however, brings the client into direct contact with his feelings, producing a conditioned reflex: he splits-off. Usually the therapist will wait for a few minutes for a verbal response, then ask, "are you there?" Invariably, the client says something like "yes, of course, I was just thinking." To check, the therapist might ask, "What was the last thing I said?" and the client will repeat something. "Fine," says the therapist, "but that was two minutes ago." Most clients need convincing, which is one of the many reasons we use tape recorders. We play back the tape and the client can listen to the two or three minutes of silence, and, most importantly, the emotions that preceded and triggered the silence.

As the client begins to be aware of feelings that were once unacceptable to his mother or intolerable to him, he may seek to hide the feelings and protect himself. Because the body work and breathing make him aware of feelings and the therapist keeps him present and in contact, he can no longer split-off readily. Instead, he commonly develops boundaries where he never needed them before, rigid boundaries hastily defined in over-reaction to his unfamiliar emotions.

This is a critical point. Ideally, the therapist would anticipate it and catch the client before he walled himself in behind the new boundaries. He would teach him how to contain his feelings and how to set flexible boundaries.

Often, though, the client is too quick, and in deference to the new boundaries, the therapist must back off from the intense contact he has made. He can help the client understand that he, the client, is only trying to protect himself from the painful emotions he previously avoided by splitting off. He can empathize with the client's reaction to the flood of powerful emotions and his fear that he is going crazy. He can show him that there *is* an end in sight, that he can run the gamut of all his emotions and survive.

Now that he stays present more and more, his tendency will be to cut off his feelings. Even this cut-off state with the rigid boundaries is an improvement over the split-off state because his being present allows the therapist to make contact with him. As long as the therapist is careful not to invade the new boundaries, he can develop a relationship with him. Through that relationship — the therapeutic alliance — he can work to soften the rigid, defensive boundaries into flexible, Self boundaries.

One way to soften the boundaries is to practice using them. We described this kinesthetic approach before. We can teach a person to know, accept, and respect his boundaries as well as those of others. We also do other exercises to teach him to explore the territory within his boundaries and to stretch them, taking risks occasionally. This helps him learn, not only that he has feelings, but how to recognize and respect them.

Always we emphasize the senses. People who are split-off from or avoid their feelings often simply aren't aware of information that they could receive through their five senses. Some people never know, for instance, when they are hungry. They eat regularly, if other people remind them, but may forget to eat if left to their own devices. This is so common that we use it as an analogy to their unfelt hunger for satisfaction in their lives.

"Here is a menu," the therapist might say, handing a client a marking board or pad of paper. "What do you want for lunch? How are you going to decide what to have? Are you hungry? How do you know what kind of food you'd like to have? Do you decide by price? By what your companions are having? By the Special of the Day?"

This is what many people do — they decide on the basis of their pocketbooks or what others suggest, thus continuing to borrow decisions from other people. We ask them to consider other ways to decide, leading them back to their bodies as a suitable starting point. We suggest that they might see if they *feel* hungry and then to think what amount, taste, and texture of food might satisfy that hunger.

If a client decides that a hot dog would taste good, a typical dialogue might go something like this:

The therapist asks, "where can you feel in your body that a hot dog would taste good?" The client closes his eyes, considering it, and finally says "I can feel it in my cheeks and on my tongue."

"What do you want on the hot dog?"

"Mustard," says the client automatically, then adds with more enthusiasm, "and some sauerkraut."

"Where can you feel the sauerkraut?" asks the therapist.

"On the sides of my tongue pretty far back, just about the place where my mouth starts to water. And I can feel and almost hear my teeth bite into it and I can feel the tangy roughness in my throat as I swallow it."

"Okay," says the therapist, "now you know you have a basis within your body for making choices. It will always be a resource for you. Use it first to get in touch with your feelings. Then, if necesary, you can modify your choices based on considerations other than your desires, such as cost, or social or health reasons. The important thing is to know what you want. You can choose to do something else and still be okay. It's when you don't know what you want that you end up dissatisfied, no matter what you do. Then you will try more of the same thing or variations on it, but it won't ever work unless you know what you want."

Such exercises, simple though they may seem, help a person begin to base his decisions on internal cues. We might follow up this exercise by suggesting that a client go to lunch every day the next week and base every single choice on honest- to- goodness awareness of his hunger and of what appeals to all his senses. This is, of course, to be extended to Life, not just to dinner and breakfast. Instead of a menu of food, he can start thinking of a menu of Life, "trying on" his possible choices just as he did imagining the hot dog.

"What do you like better than anything else?" we might ask. "Where does it make you feel good in your body? What else do you enjoy? Where does *that* make you feel good?"

Often, when a person has functioned with borrowed feelings, it is difficult to get answers with such general questions and we have to get very specific and into details of the distant past. One client couldn't think of anything he liked better than anything else except, perhaps, escape from social situations. We wanted him to ferret out a positive feeling of pleasure from somewhere in his life and, eventually, he did.

"I remember the way I felt standing on the beach the summer my parents took us to the seashore." When questioned further, he was able to give us a vignette of that summer day: the receding waves pulling at his ankles, the sand eroding from under his feet, the warmth of the sun, a pleasant muscular fatigue from playing and swimming all day, and an honest hunger satisfied by watermelon and sandwiches.

"Now that I think about it," he went on, "I've always been drawn to the out-of-doors, but somehow manage to end up indoors all the time. My wife hates bugs and sunburn so we go to air-conditioned resorts for vacations. And I'm an accountant, and how can you do that outdoors?"

That, of course, is what we're getting at when we ask clients to isolate their most positive, most intense feelings — how can they build their lives to honor them instead of ignoring them? The accountant, for instance, once he realized what he had been doing, took a leave of absence from his accountancy firm right before tax season. "It's also ski season," he explained. "I got a temporary job at the ski resort doing, not only the resort's rather complicated taxes, but some of the skiers' taxes as well. I learned how to ski and I made life a little easier for the resort and I felt happier than I've felt since I was a kid."

It is important for a person to realize that he doesn't have to give up what he already has in order to get satisfaction from his life. Just because he acquired the career, for instance, that his mother thought suitable doesn't mean that he can't enjoy it. All he has to do is learn to enjoy it from within himself, so that his pleasure is his own. Perhaps a career itself isn't so bad but the location is. Talents are portable, as the accountant above proved to himself. Families, too, are more or less portable and can be surprisingly adaptable.

What a lot of people don't understand is that other people seldom try to keep them from things they enjoy. Most are quite willing to compromise or even capitulate when something matters very much to a close friend, relative, or co-worker. All they need to know is what the other person wants. And that's all the other person needs to know, too. That's why we go through the body work and the exercises we've described to gain access to a person's authentic personal desires: so he can find where in his body and psyche he knows with absolute certainty that something pleases or displeases him.

Life is both easier and more pleasant when it is lived by honest inner motivation. Decisions are fairly straightforward when one knows what he wants. The boy who decides at fourteen that he wants to be an engineer simply heads for that goal, sorting through the academic requirements and ambiguities, working when he can, and not letting anything interfere. Just as valid is the engineering student in his junior year who drops engineering in favor of his first love, biology, never mind the almost total loss of credits, because now he knows for sure what he wants to do. In contrast to them are the various "undeclared" majors who shuttle back and forth between classes their friends recommend, classes their parents and counselors urge, and classes reputed to be easy, never quite certain what they are looking for.

The trick is to know what you want. Dozens of everyday examples come to mind. Say someone is in a grocery store with a friend's shopping list and it says "Handi-Wipes" and he isn't familiar with Handi-Wipes, so he has to ask what aisle they're on. Then, because he doesn't know what they are, he doesn't know what kind, size, or color of container to look for. Up and down the counter he goes, painstakingly reading all the labels, convinced that it's not there. Finally he asks another customer, who reaches out and picks up the product from directly in front of him, right in the spot where he was just looking. The reason the passerby could find it is that he knew what he was looking for.

To carry this pedestrian analogy a little further, if he knew what he was looking for on the shelves, he would know right away if it weren't there and could stop looking. If he really wanted it, he could ask somebody to search the storeroom or, if necessary, to order it.

The same is true of Life. If one knows for certain, from deep within himself, what he wants, he can get it. Or he may already have it but be unaware he has it, continuing to search on the shelves instead of looking in his shopping cart.

The Double Bind. A potential problem in dealing with an As-If personality is that a therapist could get attached to the idea of the client's improvement. That is, the therapist would be pleased at all signs of his getting better (counter-transference). The As-Iffer will want to please the therapist and, by so doing, he may have to betray his own newly discovered feelings.

To avoid re-injuring the client, the therapist must be very cautious in his reflection of the client's behavior. Too much approval might elicit approval-seeking behavior instead of self-oriented behavior. This is obviously a double-bind for the therapist, too, for no matter how thoughtful and cautious he is, he runs the risk of doing the wrong thing. The person accustomed to being a perennial "good boy" or "good girl" will tend to start performing again for approval, ignoring his internal cues. Or, he may react contrary to the therapist's approval and attempt to sabotage him in some way.

It is very much a matter of building a Self for the client from the ground up, using raw materials from within that the client may never have been aware of. It takes great patience, and there can be a temptation to make the client over in the therapist's image. Seeking the person's true Self is the goal, however, not substituting another solipsistic relationship or using the client as a self-object for the therapist.

Trance State. This is a variation of the split-off state. It is a more prolonged or extreme state than that of the As-Iffer.

People who deal with their emotions by splitting-off are often attracted to therapies and practices that perpetuate this state, such as self-hypnosis, meditation, and so on. These practices are useful in themselves and become a problem only when someone uses them to avoid being present in his life.

Once the therapist realizes that the person is not simply split-off but is truly in a trance, he can treat him by further inducing the trance state through hypnosis. Then he can give a post-hypnotic suggestion that he will no longer *unconsciously* go into the trance state but will, in the future, have a *choice* to stay present. In this way, the client takes responsibility and the therapist has not taken away his defense, just given him a choice. When the client comes out of the trance state, the suggestion to see colors and to experience life vividly often reinforces the choice to stay present. He still has the option to enjoy the trance state, but when he does, it will be by conscious choice.

The Super-Trouper

The Super-Trouper also finds his feeling intolerable, but he doesn't split-off from them, Instead, he seals them inside with rigid armoring so he needn't be aware of them. He sets rigid boundaries around himself and speaks (and thinks) in terms of "always" and "never," being unable to set flexible boundaries that would let him say "sometimes." He can't say "yes" one time and "no" another time, so must live a life of absolutes, no matter how uncomfortable and limiting.

Super-Troupers are often attractive, seemingly desirable people. They are strong and capable, independent and bright. They are often successful in cerebral professions such as engineering, law, medicine, business. They are self-sufficient islands unto themselves, tend to see the world in black and white, and have fairly rigid behavior patterns. Because these are culturally approved characteristics, a Super-Trouper seldom shows up for therapy until he meets with a personal crisis and his defenses crumble.

The crisis is usually a relationship problem. Their general attractiveness gets them eager partners who soon find that Super-Troupers don't need or want them close, despite what they say and despite what they think. They are cold and distant in relationships, keeping people away behind thick, inflexible boundaries. Their defensive muscular armoring is visible, for the Super-Trouper's body may be hard, lean, muscular, wiry, or even very fat— to a person intent on keeping other people from invading him, "Anything will do," says one therapist. "They'll muscle 'em out, fat 'em out, or lean 'em out." In the body work of therapy they often show splits or separations between the body segments: head/torso, bottom/top, front/back, and so on.

Harry is a fairly typical Super-Trouper. His mother was a demanding woman who felt that the worth of those about her was a reflection of hers, and she criticized, praised, or directed every actions of her young son accordingly. She did the same with her husband, but he died shortly after Harry turned three, depriving his hapless child of the one person who could have saved him from her control.

Harry and his mother were very close— as always in the early solipsistic relationship— but in order to grow as an individual, he had to armor his developing Self against her invasion. She talked to him continuously, either controlling his behavior or pouring out her emotions. Harry learned to *appear* to listen while not hearing a word and went about his own business regardless of what she urged upon him. The boundaries he set to keep his mother from overwhelming him were so rigid that they also prevented inundation— or even visitation— by other people, particularly women.

Now, at thirty-six, Harry lives alone. He works out at a gym every weekday, jogs three mornings a week, and plays a swift, aggressive game of racquetball every other day. On Tuesday nights he plays poker with "the boys" and on Saturday nights he goes out with Debbie, the girlfriend he has kept at arm's length for nine years. Debbie is good-natured and accepts that their relationship is limited to Saturday nights and Sundays but, every once in a while, she says, "Harry, I feel so close to you but we hardly ever see each other. Wouldn't it be wonderful if we lived together!"

Hearing this, Harry promptly fragments. The very thought of living with her incapacitates him for days. He can't work, sleep, concentrate on a poker hand, or even lift weights at the gym, and all because of Debbie's gentle push at his boundaries.

Once a Super-Trouper like Harry *does* let someone within his boundaries — either inadvertantly or in the throes of romance and sex — he goes crazy till he can get the invader out again, because he can't set or negotiate boundaries that keep other people at a comfortable distance. As soon as the invader is ejected, he shores up his boundaries lest it happen again. A partner can be shut out only so many times before he stops trying to get in and leaves. This departure may be upsetting to the Super-Trouper, despite his having done all he could to accomplish it, but his fragmentation is soon eased by the relief of having the invader out of his territory. As he settles down behind his walls, he again has a sense of who he is.

Even though the Super-Trouper's whole process is to avoid fragmentation, the pattern laid out by his Primary Scenario drives him to choose relationships that will invariably repeat that pattern. He compulsively picks the same sort of person time after time, unconsciously striving to fulfill, through each new relationship, the unsatisfied longing of his first relationship (with his mother). The Super-Trouper is not alone in his magical belief that "if you do a thing over and over the same way, it will eventually turn out differently." So he continually seeks people whom he thinks will give the warmth and closeness he needs without extracting the painful price of invasion and control that he paid as a young child. Over and over, though, he finds himself suffocated by the close attachment he sought and severs it, retreating behind his protective boundaries.

His behavioral stance is that he doesn't need anybody, and it may be years before he realizes that he does. An older Super-Trouper, looking at a past of cold, disappointing relationships, may finally sense the emptiness inside the walls he has created for himself and invite someone inside. When this triggers the inevitable fragmentation, he may enter therapy, unwilling to return to his chilly isolation but unable, by himself, to relax his boundaries enough to tolerate any other person within his territory.

The creation of rigid walls is, as we described earlier, a common survival tactic of a child in a solipsistic relationship. Rigid character armoring could develop in any background, though, in which a young child found it wasn't safe to let people be too close. A child who got teased a lot when he was very small or one who was beaten when he cried might need to retreat from contact and shut off his feelings. A child who was lonely or neglected could have missed the closeness that would have kept his boundaries flexible, and he might find them quite rigid when he grew up.

Ethel set her rigid boundaries in response to both parents. Her mother was a beautiful but insecure and uneducated woman, as heavily dependent on her husband as she had been on her father. Ethel's birth, she felt, was the culmination of her life, her only significant accomplishment, and every sign of Ethel's natural growth and separation from her was so threatening that she was unable to accept and mirror it properly. The more she resisted Ethel's development into a separate person, the more Ethel's body developed armor to protect her besieged Self, and her psyche developed rigid boundaries to keep her mother out.

As her father was an Army officer and away from home a lot, Ethel was unavoidably her mother's constant companion, but kept herself at a distance emotionally. "I remember,' said Ethel, "that Mother would hug me, pulling me real close, then drop her arms in exasperation and say 'what a cold child— can't even give her mum a love.'"

"Dad was gone all the time, it seemed, and my mother was so helpless that I had to make do without either of them. I got my own breakfast before I was two, and Mother told people, 'That child is the most independent kid I ever saw. She doesn't need nothing or nobody. Why she can feed herself better than most grownups I know.' It sounded like praise but I knew she resented it because it showed how little I needed her."

When Ethel's father did come home, she would turn from him and pout, refusing a kiss because she had missed him and was angry. As she grew older, she persisted in her independent ways saying, sometimes truculently, "I can do it myself; I don't need anyone." When she was three she dragged home an eight- foot two- by- twelve for a teeter- totter, never even thinking to ask her father for help. "Why get dependent on someone who would just be gone the next time I needed him?" she asks. "And it would have been equally pointless to ask my mother for help. For one thing, she would have made me do it her way and, for another, she would have been jealous of something that kept me out in the yard instead of indoors with her."

As Ethel grew up, she became as lovely as her mother, but also exceedingly competent and self-reliant. She balanced the family checkbook, got A's in school, figured out the tips in restaurants, and learned how to take advantage of everything the Army system had to offer. "It wasn't that I wanted to help," she explained, "it's just that it was easier to do things before Mother started whining that they needed to be done. I never did anything she wanted unless *I* wanted it, too, like keeping track of the money or doing the laundry. Mother complained all the time: 'Ethel, put up your chores and sit with me. . . you're always so busy with your precious numbers. . . you're such a cold little thing. . . .' "

When Ethel was twenty, she married a young officer. "I'm not sure about this," she told him, "I'll hate having you gone as much as my father was." He had no doubts, though. This tiny elfin creature was as strong and capable as she was adorable to look at. He was sure they would have no trouble with separations, and he was right — it was only when he became a civilian that their real problems started. Ethel wasn't used to having a man around the house so much and his presence was uncomfortably warm and pervasive. It threatened the boundaries she had developed against her mother's constant incursions and she felt compelled to push him out. After their divorce, Ethel settled happily into a solitary existence, saying, "I don't need a husband."

She put herself through school, refusing parental help. She got a degree in business and started working in real estate where she met Stan, a "very married, very harried" broker. When he took time out from his professional activities and family involvements, she found him warm and passionate. "I didn't realize that the only reason he didn't overwhelm me with his love was that he wasn't available. A passionate two-hour lunch left me wanting more. The end of a lovely, stolen evening made me weep, but I was secretly relieved when he had to go home. Even our occasional weekends were wonderful because I knew they'd soon be over, but I didn't understand any of that at the time. I'd plead for more time with him, but was uncomfortable when I got it. He adored me, though, and his adoration wasn't cloying — you know how you practically have to scrape some people off you? Well, not Stan. He gave me just what I needed, or a tiny bit less, so I always wanted more and tried to persuade him to leave his wife and marry me."

When Stan actually did show up at her apartment with a duffle bag in one hand and a coffee pot in the other, she took one horrified look at the answer to her prayers and said, "Wipe the mud off your feet before you come in." Then she asked if he had really thought about what he was doing. Then she insisted he get a separate apartment so his wife wouldn't know he'd left her for another woman. Then she urged him to date other women for a while "just to be sure he knew what he wanted."

When she finally did let him move in, she planted a prickly hedge around him in the form of criticisms, clever jibes, and sarcasm. The perceptivity she had shown in their early days was no longer applied to pleasing him, but to hitting where it hurt. His apparent dependence on her for daily affection was terrifying, and she had to keep him at bay, an effort she disguised with a smile on her face and a sparkle in her big dark eyes. When he fixed her dining room table — something she felt perfectly capable of doing herself — she told visitors, "aren't men cute? They're so function-oriented. Something's broken and they drive a nail in, no matter how it looks, then tell you it's as good as new."

Despite the puzzle of Ethel's sudden bitchiness, Stan insisted they get married when she got pregnant. The ring around her finger and the commitment it implied was such a tangible invasion of her boundaries that she barely got through her pregnancy before she threw him out, screaming, "I can't breathe with you around!"

The baby, of course, was the ultimate invasion. Ethel got live-in help and went back to work before she could zip her skirts, but the baby was always at home waiting for her. Realizing there were limits to how far she could remove herself from her baby, and desperately wanting to tolerate and enjoy its presence, Ethel finally came into therapy, where she began learning how to do so.

When Super-Troupers like Harry and Ethel cut themselves off from their feelings, they are motivated by fear of fragmentation. As Harry said, after a year of therapy, "I finally realized that when I sit down and start doing a meditation, and I go back and look under each one of the emotions I experience, the bottom line is that I'm afraid. I'm afraid I won't exist."

A Super-Trouper gets that fragmenting sense of non-existence when he is inundated, when his boundaries are invaded. He fears closeness because, when he is close to someone, he may inadvertantly or even hopefully open his boundaries, only to be overwhelmed by the resulting inundation.

This is essentially an injury in the early mirroring stage. Although a person may have had adequate bonding, without proper mirroring he could never separate completely from his mother. His sense of Self is entirely cerebral. This may sound adequate, but because it's a cognitive process only and not embedded firmly in his body, his feeling Self is cut off at a much earlier stage of development, along with his body. Instead of the healthy narcissism he should have gotten in the reflection stage, he had to develop compensatory or cognitive supports. He can't go back inside to his sense of Self for support, but must go to his mental construct of who he is. And he must protect that underdeveloped Self by building a wall around it. He can't afford to let anyone near it because his chief fear is of inundation, of losing his sense of identity.

Because the Super-Trouper doesn't make a therapeutic alliance easily and won't admit that he's vulnerable, his defensive character style is the most difficult to treat, When an As-Iffer turns into a Super-Trouper, however, it is an improvement. His boundaries are rigid, but it isn't a chronic condition. He hasn't been maintaining them in his body for as long as a Super-Trouper, so they can be softened more easily. In contrast, the Super-Trouper has been putting down boundary skirmishes all his life and is adept at doing so. Any temptation the therapist feels to assault his boundaries and tear down his armor must be put aside. The Super-Trouper badly needs his defenses to protect the insecure Self inside. An invasion is a real threat and violates any trust the therapist might have built up, so the therapist must proceed slowly and patiently. This means using the least invasive technique — working on a verbal level — as long as necessary to induce the Super-Trouper to trust him enough to get some flexibility into his boundaries. The conscious melting of his armor will come only when the therapist honors his defenses, thereby building his confidence. With sufficient trust, the Super-Trouper may eventually allow body work to begin.

Once the Super-Trouper lets the therapist within his boundaries and gets in touch wtih the feelings inside, he is likely to fragment and may even leave therapy. As he recovers from fragmentation again and again with the help of the therapist, he eventually won't need to rebuild his armor because his sense of Self has grown strong. From a position of never letting anybody close and never admitting that he could possibly need anyone or anything, he might well swing over to the style of the Never-Enougher.

The Never-Enougher

This defensive character style has nebulous boundaries, often borrowed from or enforced by others. In many ways, the Never-Enougher is the flip side or the opposite of the Super-Trouper. Where the Super-Trouper denies that he needs or wants anything or anyone, the Never-Enougher is haunted by his feelings of wanting.

Where the Super-Trouper has thick, rigid boundaries, the Never-Enougher has transitory, open ones. Both however are seeking the same Self-hood and both are attempting to avoid fragmentation. The Super-Trouper, full of feeling deep inside, avoids fragmentation by cutting himself off from it. The Never-Enougher remains painfully aware of his unfulfilled feelings of longing and seeks fulfillment from the outside world. The Super-Trouper never admits to needing anyone; the Never-Enougher, consciously or unconsciously, needs others continually.

The defensive behavior of the Never-Enougher is "constellating." Lacking inner supports for his Self, he seeks his identity elsewhere. A very young child may constellate around his thumb, blanket, sibling, food, pets, toys, even temper tantrums — anything that makes him feel together, secure in any sense of identity. As he grows older, he's rather like a moth fluttering around a porch light. When the light goes out, he seeks another because the senseless fluttering around the light is the only way he knows for sure he is a moth.

The Never-Enougher has a very limited sense of boundaries. As he gets older, he constellates around more adult things that give him a sense of who he is: his job, relationships, sex, drugs, fine wines, sports, anger, bridge games — anything with which he can identify himself. He literally borrows his identity from outside sources, but he isn't an As-Iffer. The As-Iffer adopts the *feelings* of other people and groups. The Never-Enougher is very much in touch with his own feelings but depends on his relationships with others and his involvement with roles and activities to provide his sense of well-being and of identity. He allies himself with people whose characteristics he can adopt, throws himself into a job that will absorb him, joins a religion, or in some way becomes "something" that he can recognize and use as his identity.

Background or Cause. The Never-Enougher's behavior comes from improper or inadequate mirroring. This happens in the stage in which a child might leave his mother and go to another room, then rush back to make sure she's still there. At the same time, he's making sure that *he's* still there, too, because when a child begins to separate from his mother, she, ideally, continues to "contain" his sense of Self. When he returns to reaffirm who he is and that he is okay, she reflects back to him the image he has begun to know as his Self. When a mother is inconsistent either in her availability or in the accuracy of her mirroring, the child fails to get his reaffirmation of this identity.

When his parents didn't provide a proper reflection, one that could help him maintain a connection with his Self, he began to look for anything that would. This is the beginning of his searching outside himself for proper mirroring (and outside the parental mirror, too, which is still an extension of himself). Thus, an early attachment to a blanket might develop because the blanket is constant. A routine might become important because it provides the consistency he lacks in his relationships, and food might provide the missing warmth and emotional satisfaction. A child who is generally given proper, consistent mirroring, and who is thrust into unfamiliar surroundings may take comfort in his teddy bear or blanket, but he doesn't constellate around it. It is a temporary support for a difficult time. But the child whose normal situation is inadequate will attempt to make that temporary support a permanent substitute for a healthy narcissism.

When he grows up he will find other substitutes, as in the following examples.

Jerry constellates around his role as "manager," with his character seeming to hinge upon his ubiquitous appointment books, calendars, status reports, manpower charts, and file cabinets. He has taken over so many functions in his department that he is virtually indispensable. He wears a beeper so he can be reached day and night. He refuses to go on vacations till his wife and boss insist, and then he scarcely relaxes, calling the office twice a day to check on things. His family and social life revolve around his appointment book, and his conversation, though animated and amusing, centers on his job, his company, and his business contacts.

Peggy constellated around cooking. Although she considered her main roles in life to be wife and mother, these were subsumed under her chief role of "cook." Breakfast was a big meal, and her husband and two children gathered around for eggs cooked to order, bacon or sausage, and homemade coffee cake or bread. During breakfast she talked about lunch, and she began preparing it as soon as the morning dishes were done. At lunch there were special sandwiches or souffles, puddings or custards, and a salad, plus a lively conversation about what everybody would like for dinner. In the afternoon she shopped, talked to the butcher and the grocer, and began preparing dinner. At dinner she served tasty stews and roasts, vegetables with sauces, salad, and pie or cake for dessert, along with anecdotes gleaned from the butcher and the grocer. When her daughter went on a diet, she was very disturbed. When her son started missing meals she went all to pieces. When she got sick and couldn't cook, her anxiety outweighed her physical pain, and when her family left home entirely, and she could longer constellate around cooking, she went into a severe depression from which she never recovered.

The Never-Enougher's constellating behavior is a continuous process. It permeates his entire life. He *is* whatever he does, whether he's a manager, cook, lover, drug addict, or an alcoholic. He must continually get reaffirmation about what he is, the reaffirmation he did not get from his mother in the reflection stage. Instead, he depends on an outside source for proof that he is what he thinks he is. Any time that source fails to give him proof, he fragments, just as Jerry couldn't get away from his office even on vacation and Peggy couldn't function without her role as provider of food. A manager who didn't constellate around his job would delegate responsibility regularly, and a mother comfortable in her identity would let her children feed themselves from time to time.

No matter how exhausting or difficult or self-defeating one's constellating behavior might be, a Never-Enougher will cling to it because it stands between him and fragmentation. Nothing is worse than the pain of losing his identity. If a workaholic completes a project, he isn't content until he has started another one. If Peggy hadn't gone into depression — one form of constellating behavior — she might have started constellating around some other form of nurturing activity.

Sometimes this behavior provides a way to switch people from self-destructive behavior, such as drinking, to more healthful, socially acceptable behavior. Ira, for example, was an alcoholic. He lost jobs and wives and friends because of his habit, but he knew who he was. Finally he hit bottom and woke up in the drunk tank at the local jail. Somebody was talking to him, offering real help in the form of Alcoholics Anonymous. Ira started going to meetings nightly. During the days, before he got another job, there was work to be done in setting up the meetings. Eventually he started working with other alcoholics who needed help, invariably introducing himself with the standard AA introduction "Hi! I'm Ira and I'm an alcoholic." Years later, Ira continues to stay dry and he continues to constellate, except that now he constellates around a valuable, socially acceptable program.

As long as a Never-Enougher's identity depends on sources outside himself, he must live in constant fear of change and abandonment. As soon as his well-constructed environment shifts — which it inevitably will — he must face the dreaded fragmentation. For a Never-Enougher in therapy, fragmentation would be a step toward wellness because it is an earlier developmental pattern. However, most people, without the support of a therapeutic relationship, will do anything to avoid the pain, and will find a substitute activity. Some go into depression, as we mentioned above, temporarily or permanently, which feels better than fragmentation because they at least know they are depressed. When fragmented, they don't know themselves at all.

Even when a Never-Enougher finds a new source of identity, there is always a self-doubt that clouds his greatest achievements and his most creative efforts. If people call him a genius, he denies it, appearing humble and, thus, receiving even greater acclaim. His true talents are lost to him for he has no inner connection to their source, no conviction about who or what he is. He continues to strive for success in the world as a means of reflecting back to himself who he would *like* to be, but he is never satisfied with himself. He still has the impossible childhood omnipotence to live up to or he won't get the proper reflection. Without the healthy narcissism well established in a constituted Self, success will always be an empty victory.

> Any effort that has self-glorification as its final endpoint is bound to end in disaster. . . . When you try to climb a mountain to prove how big you are, you almost never make it and even if you do it's a hollow victory. In order to sustain the victory, you have to prove yourself again and again in other ways and again and again and again driven forever to fill a false image, haunted by the fear that the image is not true and someone will find out.
> Robert M. Pirsig
> *Zen and the Art of Motorcycle Maintenance*

The futility of finding a permanently satisfying identity through constellation is further exemplified in Andrew, who constellated around sex. He had to have sex every day, and if he couldn't find a partner or if a regular partner refused, he fragmented. He pursued sex with a vengeance, masturbated compulsively when there wasn't a woman around, was inordinately interested in sexuality in general, and couldn't consider taking a trip without lining up a female sexual companion to accompany him. His life was totally ruled by his sexual activity. Many people constellate around sex because the release through orgasm creates the illusion of unity and wholeness. It works for only a moment, of course, so must be repeated continuously for that illusion to persist.

Georgette used anger to avoid fragmentation. Such a person has a ready response to anything that might attack her. One day she stubbed her toe while crossing the street and cursed the curb with a string of epithets that kept her so busy she didn't seem to notice that her toe was bleeding. Her anger served to protect her from emotional as well as physical pain. In therapy, she discovered that her anger was an expression of an angry inner child who was, in turn, a cover-up for a wounded child still deeper within her. As she developed a trusting relationship with the therapist, she began to feel safe. The "child within" began to grow without fear and without the continual need for defense against an attacking world. It became possible for her to say when she was hurt, rather than to lash out in anger. She also felt hurt less and less as she became more and more identified with the growing sense of her inner Self, belatedly developing a healthy narcissism.

We would like to say at this point that it is possible to work hard, cook well, enjoy lots of sex, and curse curbs without these being signs of fragmentation and constellation. It is when these become the means by which we are identified, when it is not possible to live with oneself without them, that they have become a defensive character style.

Boundaries. The nebulous boundaries of the Never-Enougher lead to another problem he has — or, rather, a problem his friends have. Names describing this aspect include intruder, moocher, kibitzer, interloper. These names define him in terms of other people's boundaries because, since his are so vague, the outside of their boundaries necessarily become the inside of his. We once used an analogy of two apartments sharing one wall in contrast to two separate houses each with its own wall. The close friend of a Never-Enougher objected to that analogy and drew one of her own: "It's more like *I* have a house and he comes along and builds a lean-to up against my house."

In this case, his identity is defined, not by what he is, but by what he isn't. In his eagerness to be close to others in hopes of finally getting "enough," he infringes on their territories, both physically and emotionally. He will move in closer and closer until another person prevents further encroachment by clarifying his boundaries and pushing out the trespasser.

One Never-Enougher drives his wife crazy at every meal. "He doesn't have any notion that we are two separate people, each with a right to a separate plate. If he happens to see something on my plate that looks good, he snags it with his fork, He's not even subtle about it; it's as if it were his food, too, not just mine. Even when I'm on a diet and eating things he dislikes, his little forays onto my plate don't let up. If I don't intercept his fork with my elbow, he'll get my entire 350 calories. Sometimes he'll salt all the food on my plate, or mash butter into my potato, or put sugar in my coffee— all things I don't do myself— and he looks hurt when I yell at him, but also real blank, like he doesn't understand why I'm mad."

A similar inability or unwillingness to accept other people's boundaries was shown in an exchange between a young man and his father. They were sitting on the family room floor, watching TV. They had removed their shoes and the father looked at the two pairs, so very different in size and style, and thought he could use them to illustrate what he had been trying to tell his son about territoriality rights and private property. "Look," he said, holding up his pair of shoes, "whose shoes are these?" His son looked at them uncritically and said, "Well, if they would fit me, I'd say they were ours."

The father's illustration didn't make his point, but it helps us show how a Never-Enougher readily adopts the identifying features of another, whether they be shoes, foods, friends, or opinions.

A distraught client said one day, "I feel as though I've been invaded. My girlfriend has all but moved into my apartment. She wears my T-shirts and jeans. She looks at my mail and asks who the letters are from. She's not jealous, just interested, and feels that my friends are her friends, even ones she has never met. When I'm on the phone she can always guess who I'm talking to and makes it into a three way conversation. She's started going to my night school class with me and jogging in the morning even though she hates getting up early. She's a wonderful lover, always eager and excited, and she snuggles up real close at night, but it's starting to be oppressive and I feel used. Somehow I've got to get her back at arm's length or I'll go crazy."

Never-Enoughers are the people who inspired such phrases as "don't let him get a foot in the door" and "give him an inch and he'll take a mile." They require constant curtailment because they never get enough of what they think they want, and they keep trying to get more.

Treatment. If the Never-Enougher's attachment to an outer identity around which he constellates is broken, he fragments. The baby whose blanket is in the wash is unglued until he retrieves it. The adult who loses a job, can't drink at happy hour, or breaks up with a lover fragments till he gets another job, drink, or lover. He is in a continual cycle of constellation-fragmentation-constellation.

Constellation almost always fails to work over a long period of time because of its ultimately unsatisfying and unfulfilling nature. Never-Enoughers seek in their current relationships and activities the reflection they craved in early childhood. Since they can't attain that, no matter how intense their current involvements, they try again— another lover, another job, another hobby or cause— but they will never get enough, because they are looking for retroactive loving and mirroring; they want their mothers to *have loved* them. When the futile search ends once again in hopelessness, they may come to therapy to find what is missing in their lives.

The first step in therapy, as with fragmentation, is for a person to acknowledge that he is constellated. Then the work is to identify the constellating behavior and the objects around which he is constellated, and to see how they create the illusion of identity. It is difficult for a person to see and to admit that he is constellated, but it is a necessary step. If, for instance, someone constellates around work for his sense of well-being, the pattern *must* become conscious before he can deal with it. If he comes to therapy depressed after losing a job or completing a project, the therapist has to distinguish between a natural response and an extreme one. The natural response might include a certain amount of anxiety and/or loss of energy, but the extreme response to the disintegration of a constellating pattern would be characterized more by a loss of identity and the pain of fragmentation.

The Never-Enougher may look more emotionally disturbed than the Super-Trouper and the As-Iffer but, in truth, he is much closer to re-establishing his sense of Self than they are. Because of his ceaseless borrowing of boundaries from other people, he readily constellates around the therapist (positive transference). Because he is far more accessible than the split-off As-Iffer or the barricaded Super-Trouper, he forms a therapeutic alliance much more quickly than either. His nature is such that transference (discussed in a few pages) is the primary mode of interaction, and setting boundaries is the primary mode of treatment.

He is also an excellent candidate for body work, which helps him build a healthy narcissism and learn to contain his feelings. The Super-Trouper, on the other hand, is easily injured by premature body work because it breaks through his boundaries before he is ready.

The characteristics of the Super-Trouper and the Never-Enougher can flip back and forth in the same person or between two people. If we look at this in terms of relationships, we often see that the Never-

Figure 22
Comparison of Defensive Styles of Relating

Characteristics	The Split-Off Personality		Never-Enougher	Super-Trouper
	As-Iffer	Sleepwalker		
Boundaries	None (or, if any, flimsy ones) due to lack of awareness of needs, feelings		Nebulous; borrowed from others; transitory; flimsy	Inflexible; closed; rigid
Sexual Symptoms	Lack of interest; boredom; no excitement	Not "in" body; numb or anesthetized; impotent or retarded ejaculation	Can't contain or build excitement; premature ejaculation; diminished orgastic response	Can't release (retarded ejaculation); pre-orgasmic; lack of interest
Relationship Symptoms	Lack of contact; fear of both abandonment and inundation		Abundant contact; fear of abandonment (separation anxiety)	Fear of inundation; distant; cold
Feelings	Split-off early (too painful to stay)		Constant awareness of feelings of longing	Deeply buried under rigid body armor for protection
	Adopts others' as own	Unaware of any		
Type of Transference	Difficult to make connection		Easy to make connection; magic stage	Difficult to make connection
Treatment	Breathing to make contact with body and feelings, other people; keep present		Breathing; setting of boundaries; sense of well-being (healthy narcissism)	Non-invasive (verbal) till boundaries relaxed; eventual body work to melt armor
Origin of Injury (Stage)	Late bonding		Mirroring	Late bonding; early mirroring
Body Structure	Whatever he's "pretending" to be	Toneless, dead quality	Soft outside; armoring at core	Tightly muscled, lean, or fat
Personality Styles	Seeks approval; performer; spiteful	Trance-like spacy	Clingy, dependent, constellates around roles, people, activities for identity	Strong; self-reliant; needs nothing and nobody; spiteful
Recreational Drug	Marijuana		Amphetamines; alcohol; cocaine	Tranquilizers

Enougher and the Super-Trouper tend to attract one another. Each imagines that he sees those qualities of his own Self-hood in the other: the Never-Enougher looks at the Super-Trouper and sees someone strong who can fulfill his needs, and the Super-Trouper sees in the Never-Enougher someone with the feelings and sensitivity that he lacks.

Sometimes, if one changes, so does the other. Thus the system remains unchanged even though the individuals have switched roles. Both show signs of defective Self-formation and working on the problem in terms of the relationship won't help. It is necessary to look into the Primary Scenario of each one to find the source of the difficulty.

Treatment Methods

Releasing and Replacing the Negative Introject

In the Primary Scenario, when one or both parents provide improper mirroring, the "negative introject" develops. This means that a person has incorporated an attitude that is destructive to himself. Psychologically, one has "swallowed whole" his critical parent, judge, or persecutor. The process of maturation involves releasing this negative introject and incorporating, instead, the positive introject.

There are four steps in releasing the negative introject. One must recognize that:

1. He is separate from his parents.
2. His parents did the best they could (and that was good enough).
3. He is probably already injuring others in the same way he himself was injured by his parents (that is, he is repeating the injury).
4. There is pain in life and he must accept it as a part of the growth process. The early longings will not go away, but they can be attenuated and he can learn to live with them.

To achieve the first insight, one can work with resentments and appreciations. He writes in his journal all his resentments towards his parents, plus all the appreciations. Then he turns each resentment into an appreciation. For instance, "I resent that you never recognized my achievements, only my failures!" can be turned into the appreciation, "I appreciate you because I have learned to be strong and to work hard without your approval," or "I appreciate you because you showed me how *not* to be a parent." Holding onto anger and resentment is a way of remaining connected to the parents. Turning the resentments into appreciations is a way to separate. The focus of this work is to define boundaries and to create separate boundaries between the individual and his parents. This will undo the solipsistic relationship, as illustrated in Figure 23.

Figure 23

MOTHER   CHILD   MOTHER   ADULT

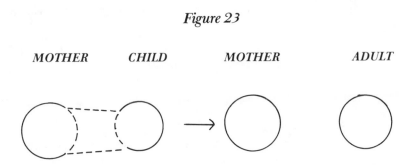

The second insight leads to forgiveness of one's parents. It is not possible to let go of them until they have been forgiven. When both appreciations and resentments have been discharged, then forgiveness is possible. One integral part of forgiveness is acknowledging that the parent may never let go of the child, that the individual must release himself.

Even if a person's parenting wasn't of the quality he would have liked, for most of us— especially anybody capable of reading this book— it was good enough. We know from the work of Harlow and Spitz and others (see chapter 6) that if the parenting wasn't good enough, a child would either have died by wasting away or been institutionalized. Sometimes an injury is so deep that forgiveness doesn't seem possible, but holding onto it by blaming the parents is just another way for a person not to take responsibility for his own life.

Once these two steps are taken, it is possible to take the next two. It is important to realize that one's parents were human and so is he. Each of us is capable of repeating his parents' mistakes and is probably doing so even now. With this understanding comes the realization that the painful aspects of growth are often a necessary part of life. Although the early longings and yearnings will be more tolerable as an adult than as an infant, they won't go away. No person, no magic can release one from that very human condition.

Releasing the negative introject and separating from the parents is best marked by a ritual. In other cultures, the separation of child from his parents is celebrated by rituals formally acknowledging that separation and his passage into maturity. Although we don't have such rituals in our society, we can carry them out for ourselves and invoke the spirit of the archetypical ritual.

The ritual should be chosen by the person marking the separation and, thereby, his maturity. It could be climbing a mountain, burning or burying something symbolic of the change, or completing a task appropriate to this important developmental stage— equivalent, perhaps, to an aborigine's hunting his first lion. It can be as ornate or as simple as he likes. The elemental stuff of ancient ritual— purification by fire and water— may appeal to his basic nature. Just as the bonding with his mother tied him into the continuity of life, so may an elaborate, primitive ritual ease his transition into independence by tying him into the inevitable pattern of birth, growth, and death that his ancestors went through.

The ritual should be performed with a seriousness appropriate to a funeral for, indeed, releasing the negative introject is like losing part of oneself through amputation or losing a close relative through death. It has been an energetic part of the person for most of his life, and its loss is to be mourned even as it is celebrated.

Removing or excising the negative introject leaves a void and this void must be filled in with something. In IBP, we fill it with the positive introject— the Good Mother archetype.

The Good Mother Messages

Most therapies reveal the negative introject but they provide nothing with which to replace it. In Gestalt Therapy there will be the judge and the judged, the top dog and the underdog, the mother and the child. This perpetuates a dualistic pattern of a truce between opposites. In IBP we have a way out of this dualism, a way that eliminates the power of both opposing voices by going behind the duality to find and recognize the Self. We work with the negative introject and replace it with the positive introject, all the while teaching the body to contain the energy of well-being.

The "Good Mother Messages" originated while Dr. Rosenberg was working with cancer patients. He was teaching them to use visualization techniques to change the physical manifestations of the disease in their bodies. He found, as he worked, that there was a range of success, and that success seemed to be correlated with a strong sense of Self. The sense of Self, he knew, depended on early bonding and mirroring. Since he was already having the patients visualize their own cures, he began having them visualize as well their own retroactive "mothering."

You had a glimpse of how this was done in Chapter 4 when the therapist told her client she could go back and give the little girl inside all the loving she needed, any time she wanted to. Gradually Dr. Rosenberg worked out a series of feeling tones or messages, which he called "The Good Mother," and the patients added them to the visualization techniques. Meanwhile, they memorized and wrote the "Good Mother Messages" in their journals every day and acknowledged the attendant feelings in their bodies.

⌐ In visualization, or imagery, one re-creates the injured child. He then brings in the Good Mother image by substituting *himself* as he is today (instead of the actual parent) and giving the comfort that wasn't available in the past. In this way, the person *becomes* his own Good Mother.

The Good Mother work is introduced in therapy when the body work has peeled away the layers protecting the injured child inside. As he identifies this injured child and learns that, as an adult, he has been looking in the outside world for the Good Mother, a person can begin to go inside himself to build — and then to use — the support he needs.

When introducing the Good Mother work, we ask clients to take these thirteen feeling tones or messages and write them in their journals every day. Even if they don't mean anything to them at the time, they are to learn them by rote and write them down once a day, every day. Eventually feelings begin to fill the words and clients start to recognize the ways in which they are seeking these Good Mother messages from everything in their lives. As they begin to take over the mothering voice for themselves and love themselves in these specific ways, the needy, dependent, helpless aspect falls out of their relationships. The searching for love, often with a desperate quality, disappears from their lives.

Another way of working with the Good Mother messages is through imagery, just as the cancer patients worked with them. A client imagines the Good Mother saying these thirteen things to him until the deep feeling of being loved in these ways fills him complete-ly. Then he, as the sympathetic adult, takes over the role of the Good Mother, and gives his own child within the special loving he needs. The exercise can be done while breathing deeply and holding himself with compassion. Repeating the exercise daily or as an adjunct to the process of getting out of fragmentation will help establish the Good Mother as a permanent inhabitant of his inner world.

The Good Mother archetype includes an infinite number of messages, more or less summarized in the thirteen listed in Figure 24. Ideally, they are communicated to the child in infancy. Because this early communication is nonverbal, we try to stress that, although we call them "messages," they are really *feeling tones*, which are never fully translatable into words. They are, in essence, the feelings of love, security, and acceptability conveyed by the mother during the bonding and mirroring stages of development. They are the feelings that contribute to the sense of well-being that is the basis of a person's sense of Self.

The Good Mother exercise works through repetition to re-establish the sense of these loving qualities or feeling, and it is done in conjunction with the body work so the messages are felt in the body. Even though the exercise is effective using the journal or imagery alone, its value is greatly increased when the nurturing and soothing feelings are experienced simultaneously in the body and in the mind. When a client does the exercise during a therapy session, he does it within the ambient compassion, acceptance, and nurturance of the therapist. When he is alone, he may recall that feeling or summon up one from any compassionate relationship he has had, even one with a favorite pet. It is the *feeling*— not where it comes from— that a person needs to experience within himself while repeating the Good Mother exercise.

Often when a client works with the Good Mother imagery, there will be one feeling tone that he cannot really experience and this is the missing message, the one he has been seeking vainly in all of his relationships.

Figure 24

The Good Mother Messages

1. I want you
2. I love you.
3. I'll take care of you.
4. You can trust me.
5. I'll be there for you; I'll be there even when you die.
6. It is not what you do but who you are that I love.
7. You are special to me.
8. I love you, and I give you permission to be different from me.
9. Sometimes I will tell you "no" and that's because I love you.
10. My love will make you well.
11. I see you and I hear you.
12. You can trust your inner voice.
13. You don't have to be afraid anymore.

Each of the thirteen Good Mother messages can be said in other ways. The words themselves aren't important; it is the feeling tone that counts. Each person can choose a way of saying it that works for him, but even before he sees what each one means to him, he should write it in his journal and memorize it. After he can repeat them from memory, we begin to work with the feeling aspects of each.

1. **I want you.** Some people never feel wanted, and it may indicate a reality of the parents' inner state when the child was conceived. The child knows if he is wanted while still in utero. This message is part of the bonded relationship. When a person never feels included or welcomed into a group, it is often this "I want you" message that was missing in his childhood.

2. **I love you.** This is the proper mirroring, bonding, and nonverbal sense of well-being that the child requires in infancy from the mother. This is duplicated by the body work — that is, the sense of well-being that results from the breathing is the same feeling that the infant feels in the bonded relationship. This message, when internalized, provides support for the sense of well-being.

3. **I'll take care of you.** This reflects the mother's physical nurturance at a time of the child's helplessness (the bonding stage). It also reflects consistency in contact and relatedness with the child. The absence of this message can be seen in the way people physically and emotionally abuse themselves, for example, sleep disturbances, substance abuse, sexual abuse, and so on.

4. **You can trust me.** When the parent was not consistently available to the child, this message will be missing from the Self experience, and the adult will find it difficult to trust himself or anyone else in a relationship. Inconsistent parenting and improper mirroring (intermittent reinforcement) are antecedents of the Never-Enough constellating behavior. The child never knew what the parent would do or whether he would be there or not. Integrating this message will assure the person that someone (himself) will always be there and can be counted upon.

Identity deals with consistency and continuity: "I know who I am by what happens again and again." Without this, there can be no trust in the self-object (parent) or, later, in the sense of Self.

This issue of trust touches upon the concept of containment. People who can't contain can't trust that something they have today will still be here tomorrow. They have no sense of continuity in their centers, no faith in themselves, and must seek it outside.

5. **I'll be there for you.** This message means that there is

someone there even when the child is not. A young child may leave the room, then return immediately to see if his mother is still there. He needs to know that the mother, or self-object, is always there in order to develop his healthy narcissism. He needs to know that she was there before, is still there, and will continue to be. Because his own sense of Self is still connected to hers, this fosters his own feeling of continuity. People who are terribly insecure never got this feeling in their bodies.

I'll be there even when you die. Many people spend their lives fearing death, but they avoid facing that fear, so they can never really live. This message, because it expands the first part of the message to include one's death, allows a person to be fully involved in life without worrying about losing his Self in death. It attenuates the anxiety and feelings of aloneness about death by dealing with the transpersonal or spiritual aspect of a person as well as the psychological.

6. **It is not what you do but who you are that I love.** This is unconditional positive regard. Many people live their lives *doing* something in order to get approval and love rather than just being. People often expect to receive this unconditional love from spouses or friends. This unreal expectation creates an inability to have relationships because *no one* loves *anyone* unconditionally past the stage of helplessness in infancy. The meaning of this message, then, is that the only true source of such a love is *oneself*, and it cannot come from an external source.

An example is Susie, a client whose mother and father both told her, "You're not real smart, honey, but you'll get by on your good looks." The Good Mother removed the stigma of both parental messages by saying, "it doesn't matter what you do; it is who you are that I love." When this message was introjected completely— that is, she internalized it, making it part of herself— Susie was able to experience herself as whole, including a fine intelligence her parents hadn't recognized.

Alice Miller says in *Prisoners of Childhood: The Drama of the Gifted Child*, "One is free from depression when self-expression is based on the authenticity of one's own feelings and not on the possession of certain qualities."[1]

7. **You are special to me** (seen as the demand "pay attention to me"). At a certain stage of development, as the child's Self begins to constitute, it is essential that his feeling of omnipotence and divinity be properly mirrored. If it isn't, the child won't have the confidence to carry himself through the difficult period of trial and error, failure

and learning, that follows. If this special treatment isn't received when needed, it will be sought very often through one's whole life. It is a primary motivating force in actors, performers, movie stars, and others(therapists, trial attorneys, stuntmen, and so on) who seem to be performing constantly in order to get their sense of well- being.

8. **I love you and I give you permission to be different from me.** Many people are stuck with rebellious attitudes because they never got a parental message that their being different from the parents was acceptable. Because it was unacceptable, they didn't express it, and this inability to express differences gets acted out in subsequent relationships. Often they feel they must leave relationships in order to be themselves, just as they may have had to rebel and leave their parents in order to be different from them. When this Good Mother message is internalized, they find that they no longer need approval from the outer world and can begin to express their own identities within relationships.

The mother of one client said to her one day in some amazement, "You really *don't* want the same things I did, do you? I wanted children and a family and these aren't primary to you. You want to travel and have a career and the independence of a different kind of relationship. I'm only just realizing how different you are. I really like you and what you are doing with your life, yet I'm glad that I've done the things I've done!"

This acceptance from her mother came only after the daughter had managed to rid herself of her fear of expressing differences. She had finally been able to acknowledge to herself that it was okay for her to do what she wanted to do and that she wasn't a failure for not doing it her mother's way. When doing the Good Mother exercise, she found that this message was a hard one to internalize. This told her that she hadn't gotten it from her mother and that, furthermore, her mother hadn't felt it, so couldn't give it to her daughter. Not until the daughter was grown up and had learned to give it to herself and act on it, was the mother able to accept the differences and, finally, give her the message that it was okay.

9. **Sometimes I will tell you "no" and that's because I love you.** Many parents don't set limits that protect the child and help him grow. Thus the child feels uncared for. Later in life, hearing "no" will reactivate the Primary Scenario and the parents' failure to teach him that certain prohibitions demonstrate loving concern, and the person will fragment.

Setting limits for a child teaches him to set his own boundaries, a lesson that is essential if the child is to become independent of the mother. If he is accustomed to such admonitions as "No, you can't ride your trike in the street because I love you and don't want you to get hurt," then he can grow up with such related introjects as "I won't eat or drink things that aren't healthy for me." People who abuse drugs, alcohol, sex, food, themselves, and others have never learned to set limits and tell themselves "no." Because they don't limit themselves, they find it difficult to set or accept healthy Self-boundaries.

10. **My love will make you well.** If the shift from Mother's magic healing kiss to self-care isn't made, when people get sick they won't be able to assist in their own healing. They will still want Mother to do it. This is apparent in people with life-threatening illnesses who work with self-healing methods. When they discover how they have participated in their own illnesses, they learn to take responsibility for getting well again. This is the essence of the holistic health philosophy.

Sometimes being ill is a way— perhaps the only way— of getting Mother's attention and love. One client, who suffered from arthritis after the breakup of her marriage, reported that all of her siblings had been ill throughout their childhoods. She had been the only healthy one. In therapy, she discovered her belief that "the only way to be taken care of was to get sick!" so, without a husband, and feeling the need to be cared for, she did just that.

At first, in therapy, the client believes that the therapist will take care of him and cure him. Gradually, as he begins to take more responsibility for his own growth and increases his sense of well-being, he integrates this message and begins to cure himself through his own love.

11. **I see you and I hear you.** This message will be missing in the child raised in a solipsistic relationship. He feels neither seen nor heard, and he feels powerless, as though he has no effect on others. Incorporating this message will allow him to get in touch with his power and with his ability to affect Self and others. If a child had appropriate mirroring, he does feel seen and heard because he was at the time he needed it. If a person doesn't incorporate this message, he will go though life trying to get others to see and hear him. No matter how much he actually is validated, though, it will never seem real to him without the incorporation of this message.

12. **You don't have to be afraid anymore.** When a child has a nightmare, the parent comes into his room and comforts him until he falls back to sleep in peace. When this soothing message is present, a person can relieve his own anxieties. Since fear is one of

the most debilitating emotions one can experience, we use this message to help release some of the holding patterns in the chest that are created to repress fear.

13. **You can trust your inner voice.** When a positive introject has been incorporated, one may know it as an "inner voice" as well as a feeling tone. This is a reinforcement of the Good Mother messages and says, essentially, that everything you need to know is within you. The person learns to listen to internal messages as well as external ones and to make the appropriate choices.

People aren't aware that they are looking for Good Mother messages. They know they go all to pieces sometimes, but would never attribute the fragmentation to their not getting one of these loving, accepting messages from some external source. Instead, they rationalize their anger or hurt. In the beginning of this chapter we described Howard's reaction in the bank when he didn't receive immediate approval of his loan request. He thought that all he wanted was approval of the loan, but what he really wanted was approval of Howard.

When one doesn't get one or more of the Good Mother messages that he is unconsciously seeking, he fragments as Howard did. As a person starts to recognize consciously what he needed in the past and didn't get, he can learn to see what is happening in the present and to provide himself with the needed messages. Thus he begins to heal the old injury that has been repeated so often in his life.

Ray, an attorney, would believe neither that he needed nor was he looking for the Good Mother's love in his life. However, as he memorized the Good Mother messages, it became clear that he was constantly seeking at least one of them in relationships with his clients, his girlfriend, and his partner. He began to see that almost everything he did in his life was, in some way, designed to make somebody in his outer world into his mother. He was overwhelmed to see himself in this process.

You can experiment with it yourself in your life. We all can. See what price you pay to get those needs filled. . . is it worth it? Does it work?

It may be that many of the messages were received in the mother-child relationship and only a few or even one is missing. For instance, a thirty- eight- year- old client felt totally loved in all the ways listed except when expressing differences from her mother. She had moved to another town in order to express herself in her own way, and she maintained her relationship with her mother by hiding the differences. This was fine until she decided to live with a man and realized that she would never be able to hide that departure from her maternal standards. By living with a man she wasn't married to, she risked losing her mother's love; at least she *felt* she did. She had different ideas and beliefs than her mother, but because she had never separated emotionally from her, she was unable to set boundaries (to do what *she* wanted to do) for fear of losing her mother's acceptance. She had never been in a relationship with her mother and had her mother say, "I love you and I give you permission to be different from me." As long as her mother didn't know how different she was, the daughter could pretend that the acceptance was complete. In examining her childhood, it became clear that she had always been a good girl, aligning herself with her mother's expectations at the expense of independent actions and expressions and of setting her own boundaries, separate from those of her mother.

The Good Father Work

While the Good Mother work deals mostly with the stages of bonding and mirroring, the Good Father work deals with the stage of rapprochement. Once a person has a sense of well-being in the body (a healthy narcissism), the Good Father messages help him go out into the world with confidence, to practice what he thinks he has learned, and to experience the world more clearly.

It doesn't matter whether the therapist is a man or a woman; he can carry both the Good Mother and the Good Father voices during the course of therapy. The role of the therapist as the Good Father voice becomes that of the person who introduces the child to the realities of the world.

Figure 25

The Good Father Messsages

1. I love you.
2. I have confidence in you. I am sure you can do it.
3. I will set limits and I will enforce them. ("You *do* have to go to school.")
4. If you fall down, I will pick you up. (Learning to ride a bicycle is a common example of this experience with father.)
5. You are special to me. I am proud of you.
6. (Especially for women) You are beautiful, and I give you permission to be a sexual being.
7. (Especially for men) I give you permission to be the same as I am AND permission to be *more* than I am AND permission to be *less* than I am.

As successes in the world accumulate, as confidence increases, as differences are acknowledged and honored, and as the body experience of well-being and wholeness grows, the client's idealized emulation of the therapist ends. His own way of doing things, his own interests, his own qualities of being are finally acknowledged and appreciated.

During this period of therapy, recognition of one's spiritual Self may occur. The IBP approach to the transpersonal experiences that may develop is discussed in chapter 9.

Transference and Counter-Transference

In IBP there are a number of tracks we work with — different aspects of the same person — and that we can look at separately. The central track, the one we always work with, is the body. Others are the Primary Scenario (the past), the current events situation in the person's life (the present), and the sense of well-being (the transpersonal or spiritual process). We also work with the transference relationship (how the client feels about, sees, and deals with the therapist) and with counter-transference (how the therapist deals with the client).

Figure 26

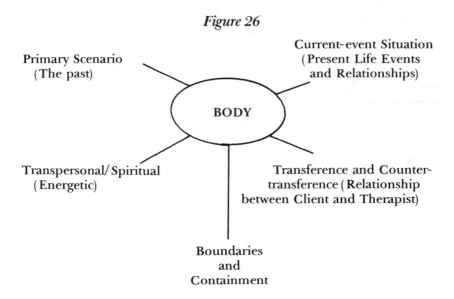

Primary Scenario
(The past)

Current-event Situation
(Present Life Events
and Relationships)

BODY

Transpersonal/Spiritual
(Energetic)

Transference and Counter-
transference (Relationship
between Client and Therapist)

Boundaries
and
Containment

We can work on all these tracks more or less concurrently, juggling them like so many balls, always coming back to the body. The same dynamic occurs within each track, so when we see them all together, we see the patterns of the Primary Scenario emerging. We've already given many examples of how we go back and forth between the body's holding patterns, the early childhood basis of those holding patterns, and the client's problems in the present. Now we are going to talk about transference and how we use it to track and modify the patterns occurring in the other areas.

By knowing a person's Primary Scenario, the therapist can predict fairly well what will happen in the client-therapist relationship. He will expect the same kind of relationship that the client formed with the parent and the same attempt to satisfy needs that he makes in his current relationships. He can guess what types of resistance he will meet, as well as what kind of defensive character style. Through the Scenario, he has a good idea of the client's potential for injury and of which Good Mother messages he might need. He must be able to anticipate what will happen with the client's emotions and body when a close relationship develops between them. He does this both by learning the client's Primary Scenario and through his familiarity with the stages of the transference relationship.

Stages of the Transference Relationship

The relationship between client and therapist is an integral part of the therapeutic process and is of paramount importance. The success of therapy depends, not soly on breathing techniques, on the Primary Scenario, or on awareness of repetitive patterns, but also on the close relationship between the client and therapist while the therapist guides the client through the relearning process towards the constituted Self.

It is a re-parenting process and is similar to the stages of the Ideal Development of the Self (chapter 6). As such, it forms an important part of the treatment of a person's early childhood injuries. The therapeutic relationship itself serves to reconnect him to the experience of the Self continuous within himself.

The Self is injured in infancy when the symbiotic relationship between mother and child is damaged. The therapeutic relationship becomes a replacement symbiosis within which the Self can be healed. The transference, then, is not of the Freudian sort— a projection of the parental relationship that focuses on Oedipal problems and ego function. Instead, we are working with a much earlier developmental stage that requires re-establishing the early symbiotic unity of mother and child. As we do this we can then learn what the dynamics of that earlier relationship were and how the damage to the child's Self came to be. The early injury will manifest itself in the relationship with the therapist.

It is imperative that the therapist be the primary therapist to the client and not see other members of the family in individual treatment. The client needs to feel that he has someone just for himself.

The stages of transference, as we see them, are on a continuum relating to the child's developmental stages of bonding, mirroring, and rapprochement, with corresponding degrees of dependency on the therapist. We see maturation as Perls did, as a gradual shift from external support to internal, self-support. The three stages of transference, in order of decreasing dependency, are the magic stage, the leaning stage, and the self-reliant stage.

Not all clients go through all the stages. If a person's injury occurred during the rapprochement stage of development, for instance, he will probably not form the earlier stages of transference. That is, he won't go back developmentally, so to speak, any further than needed to start repairing his injury.

The Magic Stage. We don't do a lot of work on this level because it is difficult to work with the unrealistic expectations of a client in the magic stage. It corresponds to the bonding stage of childhood development, and the client's behavior with the therapist may be very primitive and regressed. His expectations for an immediate and lasting cure and his response to not having that happen is rage. When a child falls down, mommy kisses his wound and makes it well. When he is very ill, he depends on the doctor to make him well. In the same way, the client on this level expects a magical, immediate, and everlasting cure of all his problems. It must happen *right now*, for he has no realistic awareness of time in relation to change or healing.

A person at this stage might expect to get well in two sessions and become enraged when he doesn't. His perceptions are primitive, just as those of an infant are. The infant can't project into the future, so he hasn't the patience to wait for his needs to be met. This reaction is an excellent clue that a client is in this very early stage of transference.

For example, a new client came in on a Thursday for a problem with secondary impotence. Monday he called to say that during the weekend he hadn't had an erection with his girlfriend, and he thought he ought to quit therapy because it wasn't working. At this stage, the client has blind confidence in the magical therapist, and the unfortunate weekend meant that the therapist had failed.

The client at the magic stage expects miracles. Just as an infant probably sees adults as all-powerful, capable of doing anything if they only will, so the client thinks the therapist can do anything. In fact, there is very little the therapist *can* do until he can get him into the next stage.

He can do that by feeding back to the client his unreal expectations and pointing out the repetitive patterns he is acting out with the therapist. He can give empathy, support, and understanding. He can focus continually on the primitive longings the client has and show how he is always trying to get them met, especially by magic solutions that don't involve time, effort, or reality testing. Placebos, hypnosis, and positive suggestion may work at this time, but being temporary, these methods are injurious to the client. When the effect is gone, he will respond with rage.

People with injuries in the bonding stage of development may need to become temporarily dependent before they can form enough of a relationship with the therapist to move, eventually, to the next level of development. When the injured child underneath is uncovered, the therapist can start the Good Mother work.

In each stage of transference there is a trap for the therapist, and it comes out of the developing relationship. The therapist's role is to guide the client into maturity(in terms of the Self, that is). The client accepts him as guide and has certain feelings about him and expectations of him in that role. He projects these unreal expectations onto him and reacts to him as if he were, indeed, a magician(transference). When the therapist starts to believe that he can, indeed, meet the client's unreal expectations and fulfill his needs, that is *counter-transference*. Faced with the client's belief in his magic, the therapist may begin to think that he *is* magic.

This is the trap. If the therapist has an unresolved sense of Self, he may allow this divine reflection of himself go unchecked. One thing every therapist must remember is: for every positive belief in his greatness, there will be a negative one following not long after. This is because of the process of polarizing that we discussed earlier, in which someone cannot integrate the good and bad parts of another's nature. It is very easy to injure a client at this stage, because the therapist's magic cannot help but fail. The primitive belief in magic shifts to another primitive pattern— polarizing— and the client sees the therapist suddenly as all bad. If the therapist has been trapped in the counter-transference, that is, if the therapist believes that he's magic, then he will be unable to deal with the rage resulting from his fall from grace and it may propel the client out of therapy altogether.

The primitive medicine men had rituals and beliefs to protect the magic and its human instrument when they failed to heal, but the therapist doesn't have any such built-in protection. When he has unwittingly accepted the magician's role and injures or fails to heal a client immediately, he often puts the blame on the client rather than acknowledging that he has failed as magician. This does nothing to mollify the enraged client. If the therapist hasn't gotten caught in the counter-transference trap, he deals with the rage as he deals with the unrealistic expectations, by pointing out to him that no one (outside of the client himself) can ever satisfy his needs.

When the client can be made to understand that he cannot create with the therapist the relationship that he wanted with his parent and that this is not a realistic expectation of therapy, he will move on to the next stage.

The Leaning Stage. This stage corresponds to the mirroring stage, the first of the separation stages. The therapist's role is to give the client accurate reflection, to be the approving mirror. He continually refers back to the client's Primary Scenario where he didn't get the proper mirroring from his mother. Just as in the infant's corresponding stage, the sense of Self is fragile. People literally forget the work they have done, and it is necessary to remind them over and over who they are, and to bring them back to the sense of well-being, the sense of Self. The body work is exceedingly important at this time because the client can be reminded each time of the sense of Self by experiencing it again in his body. Feeling it concurrently with the psychological work makes it much more likely to be fully integrated.

In mirroring the client, the therapist has to see through the facade or the armor laid over the Self, and reflect the true self. In the same way a mother "contains" the feeling of the Self for the child, so does the therapist for the client. This helps the client develop the healthy narcissism that he was never able to get with his mother.

At this stage, the healthy narcissism can't last from one session to another and the tape recorder is a useful adjunct. By listening to a tape of the previous session, the client's healthy narcissism can be reinforced between sessions. The tape recorder becomes a transitional object to reinforce the good feelings of the therapy session. Recording the sessions is useful, also, in making material available to the client that he has either forgotten or missed entirely due to splitting-off from painful emotions.

In the leaning stage, in contrast to the magic stage, the client exhibits a childlike quality, but not an infantile one. He knows he has to take responsibility for himself, but he leans on the therapist for support until he's able to do so. He will test the therapist and his consistency. He might want to know, "Are you available to me?" and "Do you go away when I do or are you still there?"

The client will have successes in his life and report them for mirroring. The therapist needs to be a consistent and accurate reflection for these successes. The client's stance is, "I'll depend on you to tell me what to do. I don't know the answers; I'll do what you say." The belief in magic is gone, but the reliance on the therapist is still like that of a child with a parent.

If there is a misunderstanding between client and therapist in this stage, the client's feelings will be hurt and the trust between them will break down. The rage of the first stage will not occur, though. The therapist must use the mistake of improper mirroring to good advantage, for it is in these moments of injury that true intimacy develops between client and therapist as they both work to repair the damage and restore the trust.

In doing this repair work, they work first with the relationship, not with the content of the injury. *They have to track the process when an injury occurs.* That is, the therapist might ask "How are you feeling about me now?" and the client might answer "I don't trust you now. I want to move away from you." The therapist can point out how the client is withdrawing, and how he can see this withdrawal in his body and in his energy field. By observing the process, they can see how the pattern follows the same repetitive pattern from the Primary Scenario and how it is the same in his current relationships as it is in the therapeutic relationship. Eventually the client will recognize that he is still acting out the unfulfilled expectations of the Primary Scenario, that he is still engaged in a futile search for Good Mother messages.

The therapist can facilitate this recognition by stopping when the client is angling for a Good Mother message and saying, "Let's explore what you were looking for when you told me that. What response would you like from me?" For example, one client told his therapist that he had gotten drunk the night before, a habit he was trying to break. When the therapist asked why he had told him that and what response he wanted, the client said, "I guess I wanted you to see that I was bad, and I wanted you to tell me that it was okay, you liked me anyway." In this way, the client can see repeatedly how he is trying to get from the therapist what he needed from his mother. This understanding will lead to the third level — how to be a separate person within a relationship.

In the magic stage, the client wants closeness, and his initial response to an injury— before the rage sets in— is to get closer. In the leaning stage, the client is more likely to react to an injury by withdrawing enough to reform his boundaries so he can feel his separateness.

The counter-transference trap of this stage is when the therapist feels indispensable and constellates around the client's need for him. He forgets that his role as guide merely parallels and heals the past parenting relationship. He begins to feel like a real parent, but not one who supports the child's need to separate. Instead, he turns the client into a self-object and supports his own sense of well-being that he gains from his feelings of being indispensable.

The Self-Reliant Stage. At this stage, the body work and the psychological work come together in their effect on the client's sense of Self. The client feels a sense of well-being, which he experiences in his body. "I know I have problems," he can say. "I know I will have ups and downs in life, but I know I can solve the problems. I can find help when I need it. I am okay and I can take care of myself."

The client enters the self-reliant stage when, just as in the mirroring developmental stage, he has achieved the comfortable separation that comes to pass when differences between him and his therapist are acknowledged and accepted. In a family, the differences between parent and child can be painful. The child wants the parents to be like him, and they want the child to be like them. Many people have little tolerance for difference, yet it is individual uniqueness that is the sourse of creativity and excitement in one's life and relationships. True relationships can come about only when the differences between those involved are acknowledged and accepted. So, when the client has incorporated the Good Mother message "I love you and I give you permission to be different than me," he may enter this third stage of transference and the beginning of self-support.

If an injury occurs at this stage, the client may regress temporarily to the leaning stage. An injury may come about when a client misses an appointment, for instance, and the therapist insists that he pay for the time anyway. Sometimes the injury will reflect a shaky acceptance of the differences between them, as when a client learns that they have sharply diverging political views.

The counter-transference trap on this level occurs when there is regression in the client's progress. If the therapist has made the client into a self-object, he begins to feel much better as his client moves into this stage. His own sense of well- being is at stake in the client's progress, and when the client falls back to earlier behavior patterns, the therapist might say, "you know better than that." His sense of being a good therapist may depend on the client's getting better and sustaining the new level of behavior. This dependence can cripple and double bind the client who must be prompted by his own feelings and needs, not by those of his therapist.

If the client is thinking about tackling a particular problem in his life, for instance, and the therapist happens to suggest that he work on that problem, the client feels that he has lost the initiative. Now, instead of it's being *his* idea, it's the therapist's idea. Instead of working on the problem because *he* wants to, he will work on it because the therapist wants him to if, indeed, he will work on it at all.

It's similar to what happened to Phil, only it was Phil's wife who managed to supplant his initiative with hers. Phil had been feeling completely non- sexual for some time and had sex with his wife only when she initiated it. After he had been doing the body work for a while, he began to feel like a sexual being again. He was pleased with the change and approached his wife for sex. After an exciting and satisfying evening in bed, his wife said , "There! *That's* what I've been wanting you to do!" It could have been a compliment, expressed differently, but instead, it took all the wind out of his sails. His pleasure in his new vitality vanished. Unwittingly, she had reframed a change he was making from his own needs into one he should make because she had been wanting him to. Once again he would have to sort out whether he was taking the initiative because he felt like it or because his wife wanted him to.

When a therapist pre- empts a client, the client feels that his impulses are not authentically his. If an injury occurs and the client falls back into the previous stage for mirroring, the therapist will become upset and be unable to make the shift. The client will fall back again— this time into the magic stage— and may respond with rage when the therapist doesn't meet him there.

In the transference, the therapist will already have become the Good Mother for the client. Through writing in his journal and doing the Good Mother work, the client begins to take over the responsibility himself. Whereas he relies upon the therapist at the beginning of the relationship to fulfill his needs, he can now rely increasingly on himself.

Tammy, for example, had anxiety attacks between sessions and would call her therapist in a state of fragmentation. He would listen with empathy and concern, drawing her out to establish the cause the fragmentation. Then he would lead her through the Good Mother work, reminding her to do it in her journal, too. After a number of such calls, all he had to do was remind her of her journal. That went on for a while until the onset of an anxiety attack itself made her reach automatically for her journal instead of the telephone. Eventually, the messages of the Good Mother will be so internalized that she won't even need to write them down.

Negative Transference

In each one of these stages there is the possibility for polarizing to take place, in which the client is unable to integrate the good and bad parts of the therapist. True polarizing actually occurs only in the magic stage, and it's very dramatic here. The therapist goes suddenly from very good to very bad. The worship turns into rage. The degree to which he was loved is now the degree to which he is hated. When a client in the magic stage polarizes, he may leave therapy altogether.

When a client is in the leaning stage, he relies on the therapist for support and may polarize him if he seems to be less supportive and more witholding. If this happens, the therapist mirrors the client's upset and points out the repetitive patterns from his Scenario. If the client continues to polarize, he may leave and find another therapist, to whom he maligns the first as passionately as he might a parent or spouse.

By the self-reliant stage, the client is more able to accept the good and bad sides of the therapist, because he is now able to tolerate differences between them. While he may see distinctly separate, non-integrated good and bad aspects, he can deal directly with what he doesn't like. In this stage, as the client gets closer and closer to separating from the therapist anyway, he may get angry with him. His reaction is similar to a teen-ager or young adult who perceives his parents' habitual behavior as controlling him. He asks himself, "Do I really need this anymore?" and uses his anger to leave the parental home and/or establish himself as emotionally independent of his parents.

So, in each case, polarizing can take place when the client feels that the therapist is not fulfilling his needs. This reaction — this inability or unwillingness to see both the good (approving and supporting) and bad (disapproving and non-supporting) sides of the therapist — is a function of the Primary Scenario. It happens when a person was raised in a solipsistic relationship and characteristically split the parent as well as himself into good and bad halves. The bad half he would either contrive to change to good (as the boy did when he cajoled his mother out of depression) or he would block it out of awareness.

In IBP, the therapeutic process is something of a microcosm of the life process. It is a relationship model in which a client repeats or re-enacts the patterns from his Primary Scenario, just as he has been repeating them throughout his life.

This model centers around the therapeutic relationship. Most of the injuries that cause interruptions in the formation of the Self occur early in life. They occur *within* a relationship and *because of* the dynamics of that relationship and are rarely visible except within other relationships.

So, within the therapeutic relationship, IBP uses its various tools to heal the early injuries, to reconstruct the experience of the Self in the client's body. With a constituted Self, a person becomes truly self-reliant. Furthermore, it is not until he has a constituted Self that he can be a spiritual being, that he can exist on the transpersonal level.

Chapter 8
Getting Off:
Sexuality and Sexual Counseling

In sexuality, the body and psychology come together. While some sexual problems are due to physical anomalies, ignorance, or misinformation, most of the sexual problems we see are due to psychological and emotional factors. A sexual problem is just the tip of the iceberg, symptomatic of a more massive disturbance underneath. A person may go through much of his life largely unaware of this basic disturbance, but when an emotional or psychological problem surfaces as a sexual problem, his distress is often sufficient to propel him into therapy.

Many times these sexual presenting problems disappear in the course of the body work or even in the gathering of the Primary Scenario, without ever having been addressed directly. This repeatedly offers us support for our contention that sexual problems are no different from the problems that people have in other areas of their lives in that they stem from the same basic problem: interruptions in the development of the Self.

Nevertheless, to a person suffering acutely because his sex life has become traumatic, it is more useful to focus directly on his sexual problems. And it makes little difference where we start, because one symptom is as good as another to start leading us back to the origins of the basic problem. Sex as a presenting symptom may be better than bad headaches, for instance, or depression from losing a job, because it involves everything— the body, the person's sense of Self, and his relationship patterns.

Therefore, we do treat specifically such sexual dysfunctions as premature ejaculation, impotence, pre-orgasmus, retarded ejaculation, and genital anesthesia. We treat them, not from the usual technical approach, but from an energetic point of view.

Most people think of sex and orgasm as starting and ending with the genitals. By accepting our viewpoint and looking at sexuality as an expression of energy, a person is freed from dependence on technique or luck for successful sex.

The breathing and charging pattern follows so closely a person's sexual response that he can learn from it how he stops himself from building, containing, or releasing his excitement in sex. It is not only a diagnostic tool, however. Because one can easily learn new breathing patterns or techniques, he can change his old patterns. Thus the breathing and body work do two main things: it makes him aware of what he is doing and teaches him how to change. Through awareness, he can alter his sexual response pattern.

Once a person's perspective has been reframed from genital to energetic, he can focus on the idea that orgasm is a release of energy. The more charge or energy he builds, therefore, the greater chance he will have to enjoy the release of that energy. To help understand the energetic point of view, we like to use the analogy of a loaded gun. This is the Big Bang Theory. To get a bigger bang (a more intense orgasm), it won't do any good to squeeze the trigger harder— you load the bullet with more powder (a bigger charge)! Squeezing the trigger harder for a bigger bang would be analogous to stimulating the genitals more for a bigger orgasm. Loading the gun with a larger charge approaches the problem on an energetic level, just as building a higher level of excitation in a person allows a total body/mind response in orgasm.

What we hope to communicate in this chapter is our idea of the full potential of human sexuality. Sexual energy is so powerful that it creates life! There is no image in our culture of what we mean by the potential of our full sexuality, what we see as *ideally* available to all of us. We often settle for less and consider ourselves healthy, because we have no image of our sexual birthright, which goes well beyond the ability to simply achieve orgasm.

In the body sessions people experience what is possible— to be fully expanded and open in one's whole being, in relationships, in one's heart and in one's body, so that the fullness and wholeness of one's total being is experienced in his sexual life. In our view— and this is to be seen as an *ideal*, not to be set up as an expectation for the client— sexuality encompasses the complete experience of one's sexual excitement in a total body involvement, as well as the joining with another human being in a total sexual, sensual, and loving release, with full contact emotionally as well as sexually.

If an orgasm is a person's criterion for sexual health, then someone who experiences orgasm regularly may not see that he hasn't reached his full sexual potential, since it is possible to have an orgasm without a total body release. We see orgasm and full sexual release as two different things. Therefore, the ability to have an orgasm is not our criterion for healthy sexuality.

Often in psychotherapy, particulary in what has been called "sex therapy," sexual counseling has been made a specialty divorced from the emotional and therapeutic process. Even though we devote a separate chapter of this book to sexuality, we see sexual counseling as an integral part of IBP. As you will see in all of our descriptions of problems and their treatment, we always consider the whole person. Whether the acute problem is a sexual one or a relationship one is largely unimportant. We look at a person's *total* energetic process and find that the ways he uses and/or blocks his energy apply to all areas of his life.

When a person is split-off from his body, for instance, his lack of feeling may result in problems that bring him into therapy. One of the most important aspects of IBP is that it allows the individual to integrate his sexuality into the total involvement of his life. We often see people who have no problem in the sexual area, but who have no emotional relationships with their sexual partners, so that sexuality and emotions remain unintegrated in their lives. Although they can perform well physically, their sexual relationships remain unsatisfying.

We also commonly see people who say that their sex lives are just fine, and yet show in their charging process that they have difficulty containing their excitement, are unable to release it, or that they have to push to attain release. The therapeutic process shows that these difficulties are also symptomatic of their total life process. That is, the person who can't contain his sexual excitement might also have trouble containing the excitement of a secret and have to tell it, and someone who pushes himself in sex might push himself through life in general.

IBP ultimately restructures a person's attitude about sex by showing that sex is a way of expressing energy. As he moves away from the limitations of genital expression, he finds a greater total involvement and sensual enjoyment in working on the energetic level.

We spoke of sexual problems as being the tip of the iceberg in terms of the whole person, so we'll continue the analogy in terms of sexual counseling. There are three levels at which we can work. It's not a step by step function — we don't do one, then the next, then finish with the third — but may work on all levels concurrently.

Figure 27

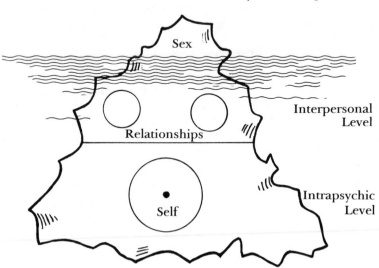

Physical/Energetic Level

Sex

Interpersonal Level

Relationships

Intrapsychic Level

Self

The first level we'll talk about is the tip: sex and sexual problems. This is the physical level; that is, the actual, practical, mechanical ways of improving sexual intercourse and sexual excitation. This level has to do with the technique of increasing, tolerating, and containing excitement *within oneself* to heighten one's orgastic response and sensual pleasure. The second level is the interpersonal or relationship level. Since the sexual problem is often a symptom of the problem in the relationship, we want to also look at the interpersonal relationship, and the individual's difficulty in sustaining it. We know from the Primary Scenario work that the interpersonal problem is a reflection or symptom of the individual's intrapsychic problem and is a continuation and repetition of the Scenario (see chapter 3). This, then, is the third level, the intrapsychic level, the biggest part of the iceberg. It is here that we begin to understand a client's attitudes and beliefs about sex from his past. To do this, we have developed a technique called "The X-Rated Movie," which is really a tracking of the sexual aspect of the Primary Scenario. Just as we begin working on a verbal level at the beginning of the therapy, we begin verbally when working with sexual issues. Creating a support system and trust through the intrapsychic and interpersonal work allows the client to eventually open and release the pelvis, gaining awareness of the holding patterns there.

The Physical/Energetic Level: Methods of Building Excitement

There are many ways to build sexual excitement or charge. Although most people think in terms of genital stimulation, to do so exclusively is to overlook other effective techniques as well as certain conditions requisite for building and using the charge. Everything, however, depends on a person's being present, so we address that first.

Presence and Contact

Splitting Off. A person must be present in his body in order to build excitement and attain orgastic release. One of the places that people most clearly split off and leave their bodies is during sexual excitation. As we said earlier, the breathing work parallels the process of sexual excitation, and just as we must have a person present during the breathing, he must also stay present during sexual excitation. A person who splits off does so because he can't tolerate the feelings of excitement. He may also not be able to tolerate the feelings of warmth and loving intimacy or the unfulfilled longings that arise when the body opens, or expands.

If a person can't stay present, his chances of building and sustaining excitement are nil. He may try to increase the physical stimulation in an attempt to feel something, but it won't work as long as he remains split off from his body. It would be futile, also, to try counseling him or teaching him any techniques, so we make no attempt to do so until we have grounded him in his body.

There are many causes for splitting off during sex. One is that a child may learn in early childhood, depending on the social environment and parental attitudes, to restrict much of his normal expression of energy. When he is boisterous, he is told just to "calm down" instead of to express his rowdiness by going outdoors. To do this, he has to split off from his excitement. When he's older and becomes sexually active, he may continue to leave his body automatically when he gets excited.

Another common cause of splitting off during sex is the use of drugs. Contrary to popular belief, most drugs do not heighten sexual response; they deaden it. Marijuana, for example, may *appear* to heighten sexual response because it releases sexual inhibitions for some people. What is really happening is that the marijuana causes the person to split off so he does not inhibit his sexual response. Because it makes him split off, it actually inhibits the charging process, thus working against a full orgastic release. The use of cocaine is another example of this misconception. Cocaine will give the person a false sense of well-being (Self) and power, and it is because of this feeling that the person experiences intensified orgastic feelings. These drugs really work against a person, because they don't allow him to be fully present and in contact during sex.

People who don't feel anything may go to bizarre lengths trying to do so. One practice is sado-masochism. Whether they are thickly armored or split off, their inability to feel the subtle pleasures of sensuality leads them to seek greater stimulation by inflicting and receiving pain.

In sex, splitting off is like Helen Singer Kaplan's (*The New Sex Therapy*) term "spectatoring," a state in which the person removes himself from the actual experience and watches himself while not being emotionally involved. Sometimes this process can be exaggerated to the point that no relationships at all can be sustained. More commonly, this process is seen as a coming in and out of being present, and splitting off when the situation comes close to the Primary Scenario (that is, when it becomes evocative of painful early longings). These early dilemmas must be resolved before the person can choose to stay present. Once a client can remain present in a state of excitation, it is important that he maintain contact with the therapist (or partner). There is an energetic connection between the eyes and the pelvis in the unblocked body and much energy can be expressed through the eyes. Eye contact will keep a person present in his body, in the "here and now." He must learn to tolerate his own excitement and stay present and in contact.

Breathing

The prime way of building sexual excitation — a way that is often overlooked — is by breathing. Many people hold their breath during sexual excitement, despite that fact that it is a time when increased breathing occurs naturally. This natural phenomenon must then be taught and re-patterned since it is inhibited by fears locked into the body and made unconscious.

Breathing is the major way to develop excitation in the body sessions, and in doing this one learns the development of internal excitment, independent of outside stimulation. One of the key tasks in our work is to introduce the concept of breathing and movement into sex and to teach, especially, how to increase one's breathing. As Dr. Rosenberg describes in *Total Orgasm*:

Breathing is the most basic function of your body. Without it all other systems of the body fail. It is the first internal self-supporting activity your body performs when you enter the world. However, you probably take this important activity entirely for granted. This book assumes you have never thought about breathing and sex together, and have never realized the central role the breath plays in your sex life.

To a certain extent you easily have control of your breath. The relationship between it and other functions and activities of your body is quite complex. I want to talk here only about breathing, movement, and emotion, and what they have to do with sex.

Breathing is directly related to emotion. Any emotional response you have will immediately change your breathing pattern. Conversely, by consciously changing your breathing, you can alter your emotions and feelings. Many relaxation techniques (and yoga exercises) are based on this principle.

Excitement, the opposite of relaxation, is also achieved by altering the breathing pattern. This is what my exercises are designed to do. One result of doing the exercises is that you will have more energy or "charge" available to you during intercourse. This increased charge will result in a more intense orgasm.

Containment and Boundaries

People must be assured that sexual arousal need not inevitably lead to sexual activity. As they become aware of their own boundaries, they can contain their sexual excitation and enjoy it. Many men and women mistakenly believe that if they experience their sexual energy, they must do something about it— they must perform, act it out, discharge it. Since having sexual energy is simply a function of being alive, all they need to *do* with it is *experience* it. They can learn to contain it and to allow it to spread out to the whole body rather than to express it genitally. This concept of containment is especially important for people who are constellated around their sexuality and identified with it and who feel compelled to act it out whenever they feel it. If they can learn to contain the energy by expanding the body (through releasing blocks) and thus allowing the energy to build to even greater levels of charge, they no longer need to feel frustrated by the sensations of increased excitement. This practice of containment is like the Hindu practice of Tantra, which also involves intense eye contact while the energy is circulating from the genitals through the whole body up to the eyes. Again, the intensity is possible because the focus is not in release. A person can generate and build excitement because he has adequate boundaries that allow him to simply experience his energy without having to release it.

One way to conceptualize boundaries during sex is by the diagram below. This allows for contact, but no invasion, since the person keeps his boundaries intact.

Figure 28

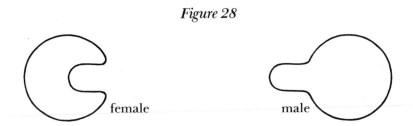

female   male

It is common for us to hear people, especially women, say, "I can't give myself to my husband or lover. . . I'm afraid that if I really let go into an orgasm I will lose myself." They feel strongly that having an orgasm is tantamount to giving themselves away, to abandoning their boundaries completely. This is how a Super-Trouper feels. We've found that these simple diagrams in Figure 28 are often all that's needed to solve that problem. We say, "Now think of yourself as a circle with a perimeter that can bend enough to let someone in for a visit but cannot break and let him move in." They can visualize this way that it is possible to have someone inside them *and* remain an integral being. Keeping one's boundaries intact is what allows the act of surrender. Then boundaries can join for a moment of oneness in orgasm with a loving partner without the loss of identity.

Boundaries are like gates— they can open and close— and they can bend, but a person can't open or bend them until he has them. Without boundaries, a person can't surrender in a sexual situation without a fragmenting loss of identity.

Nancy was typical. In the first couple of years of marriage, everything was wonderful, especially sex. But Nancy gradually got the feeling that she had no separate identity within the marriage and began working on the problem in therapy. She developed a sense of her Self and of her boundaries. While she felt more her own person within the marriage, she began to find sex threatening to her new sense of identity. She still loved Harry and still turned on, but whenever they had intercourse, she wound up fragmented for days. It got so that it was easier if she didn't have an orgasm. She could have intercourse, but so long as she didn't release, she didn't lose the small scraps of identity and Self she had pulled together in therapy.

What Nancy had yet to learn is that there is no one to surrender to except oneself. You give your orgasm to yourself, not to anybody else.

The best way to open the boundaries, to surrender, to release the armoring and the coldness, to allow the excitement of someone coming close emotionally, is in an atmosphere of love and trust. We have emphasized repeatedly the importance of honoring a person's boundaries in the therapeutic situation. We never want to risk losing someone's trust by pushing so hard he feels threatened or by treading where we are not invited. Often we may hold back unnecessarily because we are no more sure of where a person's boundaries are than he is himself. Our point here is that we exercise great caution and sensitivity in honoring a person's boundaries and hope that, by our example, they will learn to honor themselves.

But people don't always do that. Very often we see people having sex with people they don't care about or with partners who have hurt them or made them angry. Having sex when one is angry separates the pelvis and the heart, creates distance, and fortifies the armor. The person who is angry must split off from his emotions in order to separate from the other person and autistically have his own orgastic release with no real contact. One should never try to use sex to solve a problem. Instead, he should deal with the relationship problem and learn to set boundaries. Then he can have the loving feelings that contribute to more intense sexuality.

We believe that it's best not to make love when one partner doesn't really feel like it. People often consent to having sex and then feel forced into it and used. This is one of the primary causes of fragmentation, and many people are chronically fragmented in their relationships because they feel used sexually.

This is common in the woman who becomes less and less

interested in sex but feels she ought to comply to be a "good wife."
The more she complies, the more she loses her sense of identity, the
angrier she gets, the more she feels raped and objectified, and the
more distant she becomes until finally sex becomes a duty, a dreary
chore, a lifeless act.

If, instead of complying, she dealt with her anger, her frustration,
and her unfulfilled longings in the relationship and, thereby, set her
boundaries, she wouldn't have to give up her sexuality.

This happens to men, as well as to women, probably more often
than one would guess. One young husband, feeling it necessary but
exhausting to keep their sex life active despite their frantic schedules,
blurted out to his wife, "I feel so obligated to make love to you!"
whereupon they both fragmented.

It is okay to have sex with someone even if you are not madly,
passionately in love, and it's okay not to make love with your partner
when you don't feel like it. The important thing to remember is that
having sex when you are uncomfortable about the person or the
situation is a violation of your own boundaries as well as an avoidance
of the problem.

Sex, obviously, exaggerates boundary problems. The Super-
Trouper often won't allow himself his sexual feelings because the
intimacy of love making, not to mention the orgasm, may cause him
to open up his boundaries and let someone in. Once that person's
inside, the Super-Trouper goes crazy until he can expel his guest
and lock the gate again. He may be able to sustain a warm, friendly
relationship up the point of having his boundaries threatened, then
he must withdraw and trust to his chilly behavior and armor to
protect him.

The Never-Enougher, on the other hand, *wants* to be close, the
closer the better. He has no boundaries to worry about except those
of his partner and will cozy up as much as he is allowed. If, as often
happens, he has found a Super-Trouper for a partner, he will be
rebuffed long before he starts feeling comfortably close, because his
lack of respect for boundaries will drive the Super-Trouper crazy.

Two graduate students were once bemoaning their lot. One was a
Super-Trouper, and he told his friend how hard it was for him to
accept his feelings. "I warm up really slow," he said, "and it takes me
a long time to find a girl I admire and trust and even longer to go to
bed with her. Then as soon as we go to bed, she turns into a
monster, like a giant octopus. She's all over me from then on and
won't let me go, so I get rid of her and start the search over again. I
envy you— you don't seem to have any problem with women."

"Oh, no?" said the friend, a Never-Enougher. "I find women all the time and they say they like me for my warmth and sensitivity, but as soon as we go to bed, they freeze up and tell me I'm pushy and demanding and — always — that I'm too close. I wish I were more self-contained, like you. Then I wouldn't feel so beat up and rejected all the time."

Thinking and Fantasy

Another way of building excitement is through thinking or fantasizing. There are positive and negative aspects to this. On the positive side, a person can drop into the archetypical level of sexual energy through fantasy. It can be used to heighten that energy and one's awareness and sense of aliveness. On the negative side is the fact that it can be a cul-de-sac of sexual energy, or a dead end street into which one puts his excitement. Feelings he would normally have for his partner are diverted instead to his fantasy.

Some people are so inhibited that they can't fantasize at all. They were taught when young that to think something was as bad as to do it, so to fantasize would be to commit a "thought crime." Other people get stuck in fantasy and can't allow themselves to be present with their real life partners. They are so dependent on the fantasy for stimulation thay they eventually stop relating to their living partners.

The therapist must explore his client's fantasies with an eye to what is missing from his life. He must ask, "What is your fantasy of a lover?" and "what should lovers know and do?" and so on. People often fantasize romantic characters who will fulfill the unmet needs of their early relationships. The romantic fantasy is in this case an extension of the Good Mother imagery projected onto the lover who fills the needs with messages such as: "You can trust me; you're special to me; I love you," and so on. These fantasized messages make a person feel constituted enough to have a release. This is the fantasy of a wife who allows herself to be the little girl whom Daddy (her husband) will take care of and protect for always. When she believes her fantasy firmly, she feels safe enough to have her feelings and her release. By bringing such fantasies into the open, the therapist and client can work with the pain, remorse, disappointment and longing expressed in them.

Lots of people use fantasy to heighten their excitement. They go back and forth between their fantasies and their partners, enjoying the excitement, but often feeling guilty about it. If they're fantasizing, they don't feel as though they're with their partners, but if they don't fantasize, they don't build up enough excitement for a release.

A woman client was once torn by her use of Robert Redford in fantasy to increase her flagging excitement with her husband. Her therapist told her, "Look, you just have to be able to shuttle back and forth between fantasy and reality. If you're making love with Robert Redford and never see Elmer there in bed with you, then you're stuck in the fantasy. But if all you ever see is Elmer, and Elmer turns you off, then what's wrong with a few seconds of Robert Redford?" The therapist was giving her permission to fantasize, not permission to duck her problems with the relationship. She would still have to deal with why Elmer was dull, why he couldn't fulfill her longings, and why he couldn't compare with Robert Redford.

Fantasy can be valuable if a person doesn't lose sight of his partner. If he gets stuck in the fantasy and never sees the person in bed with him, he may maintain the relationship but at the cost of reality. On the other hand, if he's too rigid and guilt ridden about fantasizing, he robs himself of a bit of extra excitement. A little fantasy, then a little reality— without losing track of which is which— can be a creative way of heightening the pleasure of sex.

Sometimes people not only get stuck in fantasy but they impose that fantasy on their partners. June's husband did this. He thought it was terribly alluring and seductive for her to wear black lacy lingerie. In fact, he couldn't get an erection unless she dressed this way. For a while she went along with him and even enjoyed buying erotic underwear from catalogs and playing the tart to excite him. In time, though, she realized that he never saw *her*, just the tart. Angry and hurt, she refused to play along anymore, forcing him to confront the real issue. This was that he was responsible for his own excitement when he was in a relationship with her and it wasn't up to her to play out his fantasy.

From the therapist's point of view— and possibly the client's, too— fantasies can be useful tools for tracking changes in a person's life. One woman had fantasies of totally anonymous and erotic sex when she began therapy. As she began to have a better sense of Self through therapy, the nature of her fantasies changed. She fantasized love and affection with a specific caring partner.

An example of ineffective use of fantasy is when it is used in premature ejaculation to turn off sexual excitement by imagining negative images. For example, some men may imagine rotten garbage, while others may simply think of something else, such as work. This method often allows the man to believe he is sustaining his level of excitement, but he is really splitting off. A major factor in premature ejaculation is that the man is not present and is therefore not able to contain the excitement except in the genitals, and so he has a premature release, rather than spreading the charge out over the entire body. Thus the unpleasant fantasy works against him in two ways — by spoiling his pleasant sensations and by making him split off, which can only make the premature ejaculation worse.

One fantasy in particular is a valuable one and should be relatively guilt free. In this fantasy, one is back in a previous, especially satisfying, real sexual experience. The person doesn't imagine the lover, just himself and his very own, very real feelings. This is better than pure fantasy because it's from a person's own experience and, as such, can be much more convincing than the uncertain attributes of a sexy movie star.

Despite the inhibitions and guilt surrounding fantasy, a client in a good, trusting relationship with a therapist can use his fantasies to learn more about himself.

Sensuality and Pleasure

In referring again to our charge/discharge graph (Figure 29), the reader will note that the process of the orgastic cycle is divided into two sections, sensuality and sexuality. Under sensuality, we focus on excitation and charge; under sexuality, we focus on orgastic release and resolution. Most people focus entirely on sexuality and orgastic release. It is important to emphasize sensuality, which in this context, has to do with stimulation of the entire body: touching, holding, cuddling, and massaging all over. This stimulation is *not* in the genital area. This encourages a person to build a higher charge in the whole body — not just the genitals — much as breathing does.

Earlier in this book we discussed the use of energetic release points to open blocks in the body. This is also a way to spread the excitement. As one is sensually, caringly touching his partner, touching those points (see IBP Release Techniques, p. 325) will help heighten the charge. As we said earlier, the building of a charge of excitation is similar to the practice of Tantra; in fact, this is part of the Tantric ritual.

Genital Stimulation

Energetically speaking, the *last* way of building sexual excitement or charge is by genital stimulation. It is true that increased genital stimulation will trigger an orgasm, but if stimulation has been limited to the genitals the release will be limited to the degree of charge that has been built. That is, it will be a genital release rather

Figure 29
Charge/Discharge Cycle*

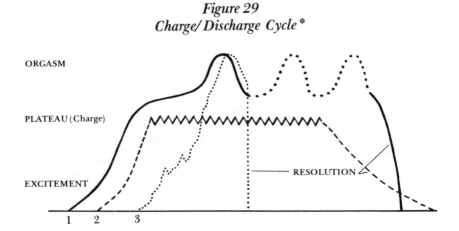

1 A typical rise in excitement until plateau, then orgastic release. If the excitement is high enough and sustained, the plateau or charge state is not diminished and a little stimulation (this can be inner excitement also) will allow a multiple experience of orgasm.

2 In this type cycle (experienced all too frequently) the woman arrives at the plateau phase yet is unable to achieve an orgasm. When this happens there is usually a longer period of resolution, leaving most women quite frustrated.

3 Some women quickly pass through the excitement period and the plateau to an orgasm. Their resolution time is very rapid (they may even fall asleep or pass out from the rapid release of tension).

* This diagram closely typifies female response patterns. See page 101 for the typical male pattern.

than a full body release. According to our Big Bang Theory, a bigger charge in the gun will get a bigger explosion. Thus, building and sustaining a higher charge in the body by spreading the excitement throughout makes the release commensurately greater.

It is an inherent part of the breathing process that a client's perspective is changed, so that the whole body and the body energy field, not only the genitals, become part of the sexual excitation. No longer will he limit his concentration to the genitals once he finds how much more charge he can contain in his entire body.

We would like to address the issue of the use of a vibrator as is recommended by some sex therapists. This is an excellent illustration of our big bang theory. This technique can be useful for preorgasmic people in order to introduce them to the experience of orgasm, but the pitfall is that people often become dependent on the vibrator. The vibrator can be so intense as to actually decrease sensitivity rather than to increase it, so that the emphasis is again on genital stimulation only (pulling the trigger harder).

The problem with this is that the responsibility for building excitement is handed to the electric socket. Because of this, the person does not use the methods we have described to build excitement; he just plugs into the vibrator! People should learn to develop their own excitation. Breathing, as well as sensuality, fantasy, love, presence, and contact (and not just genital stimulation), are ways to take responsibility for building one's own charge. IBP *promotes excitation of the total sensual aspects of the body through breathing.*

We recommend that the therapist *never* touch a client's genitals although it may be useful for a client to touch his own to bring awareness to an area that may be totally blocked. At this stage of the therapy, when the pelvis is being opened, the client may become seductive with the therapist. Besides being professionally unethical, it would be extremely injurious to the client if the therapist succumbed to turning the client on; this would perpetuate the dependency that already prevents the client's growth. It is very important for the client to understand that *no one* can create his excitement but himself. Often what happens is that a person depends on his partner to bring the excitement to their sexual relationsip. That's when the problems begin in their relationship — when one is blaming the other person. One tells the other person he should provide the excitement, and the other person can't possibly do it. When they have a difficulty on the sexual level, this person blames it on the relationship. The problem is *his* inability to bring his own excitation to the sexual situation, which is an intrapsychic problem, not a true problem of the relationship.

The Language of Sex

Before we can begin talking about sex or working with the body, it is important to establish with a client what language he feels comfortable with, because everyone has different attitudes about sexual words. The client is asked what words he would be comfortable using with the therapist to describe his genitals, intercourse, and other sexual activities. The purpose of this is to introduce the language of sex in a non-threatening way. If we use clinical terms, the apparent formality may be inhibiting, and the client may try to "upgrade" his feelings and descriptions to match the language. Once the therapist learns the client's preference, he shifts his own way of speaking to the client's language. This exercise alone may be fraught with anxiety, since talking about sex is often difficult for people. In fact, some people *never* talk about sex beyond saying "harder,' "slower," and "that was great" to their partners. They communicate by pointing and demonstration, and they count on their partners to interpret correctly their sighs and moans. People like this need help just in finding a language.

When we do this exercise in workshops, the reactions range from acute embarrassment to hilarity as we go around the room asking, for instance, "What is your word for 'penis'?" The facial expressions and tones of voice show how much emotion is involved in the language of sex, even while the answers illustrate the great variety: "wee wee," "pecker," "cock," "penis," "Ichabod," "thing," "Me!" and so on.

It is important to be very *detailed* about sexual anatomy, since often people refer to their entire pelvic region as "down there," and we need exact information. For example, can a woman differentiate between her labia, clitoris, vagina, internal and external genitalia? Can a man feel the difference in his scrotum, shaft, and head of his penis? In discussing language, it is important to ask the client to describe *in detail, specifically*, what he means. For example, a client may say she was "playing around" we want to know *exactly and specifically what that means.*

Language is also very important when working with couples because the connotation or flavor of certain words can be arousing to one person and downright repugnant to the other. They may go on for years turning each other off simply because they never considered that their choice of words could have such an effect. One such couple was the Lees. Mr. Lee was a burly, husky, macho-looking man, the epitome of the competent construction worker in a man's world. Mrs. Lee was petite and quiet and feminine. When asked what each said when he wanted to have sexual intercourse, Mr. Lee answered first: "Would you like to make love, Sweetheart?" "Oh, for God's sake!" burst out an exasperated Mrs. Lee, "Why don't you just say, 'let's fuck!'?"

In eleven years of marriage, Mr. Lee had never guessed that the language and behavior that came naturally to him instead of the polite phrases he affected would also have turned on his dainty and refined wife. She, in turn, was reluctant to shock him by appearing coarse when he seemed to value her "refinement."

As we said previously in the discussion about taking personal histories, if you don't *ask*, you won't find out, and this applies here as well.

It is extremely important to ask the person, or couple, *exactly* what they do; you can never *assume* anything! One couple who could not conceive was referred to therapy by their physician. They had been asked if they *slept together*, to which they replied in the affirmative. Since no physical dysfunction was found, the physician *assumed* their problem was psychological. When the therapist asked them to describe *what they actually did* when they slept together, he discovered that the husband never actually penetrated his wife. As a result of this simple question, the "infertility" problem was soon cleared up, with some simple educational information from the therapist.

The Intra-Psychic Level: The X-Rated Movie

After we have discussed language with a client, we ask him to go back to his breathing. Then, when he has built a charge, we begin to ask about his early sexual experiences. This is a regressive technique and is associated with body responses, since it is done while the client is breathing and has a charge, but it is primarily a verbal technique aimed at extracting the themes common to past and present events.

Often, early traumatic sexual events have been so overlaid with emotional fantasy that the actual event has been distorted. For example, a client said that her grandfather had incestual relations with her. When re-experiencing *exactly* what he did, the client realized that her grandfather had rubbed her body all over, but had not actually touched her genitals. She had felt guilty all these years about an event which had never *actually* happened. What *had* occurred was that she had been turned on by his massage and had projected her *own* sexual feelings on to her grandfather. So it is necessary to ask *exactly* what occurred in early sexual memories to help re-frame imagined negative experiences.

This form of sexual history taking is called the "X-rated movie," since we use the same movie metaphor as we did with the Primary Scenario. This movie is directly related to and runs parallel to the first. We use the same techniques of asking the client to picture events as if they were happening on a movie screen in front of him. This makes it more real for him and helps emphasize the fact that he is projecting this history on the world as well.

We begin by asking the client to project onto the screen the *first* scene that emerges from his mental imagery that is related to sexuality, genital feelings, etc. We ask him to recount it to the therapist in the first person, present tense, as if he were narrating a real movie. That is, he would say something like "I am five years old and I am under the front porch with my cousins and my girl cousin dares me to take my pants off. . ."

Using the present tense is very important because it is essential that the client *relive* the experience, rather than just tell the therapist about it. To help him relive it, we ask him to re-experience every detail with *all of his senses*. We ask what he sees, feels, hears, and particularly, what he smells. The olfactory part of the brain is very primitive and many of our sexual responses are patterned in the brain by the sense of smell. Smell can heighten the sexual experience, as is evidenced by the sale of perfumes, scented douches, deodorants, and so on. Often, sexual odors are very stimulating. We ask the person to restimulate the sense of smell because it is often cut off as a means of sexual excitation. A considerable amount of memory can be recovered if the smells of an experience are remembered. An example of this is a man whose alcoholic mother used to hold him affectionately, and this was sexually stimulating to him. When he relived this experience, he associated the smell of alcohol with sexual feelings and was able to understand why going to bars always turned him on.

We ask clients to recover the early, early experiences and have discovered that many people cannot remember very much before they were five or six. Some people can't remember much before adolescence, yet many attitudes and feelings about sex are established *well before the age of five or six*. This means that there is a tremendous amount of unconscious material that people do not remember, although it influences their sexual habits. The purpose of the X-rated movie is to bring these early experiences into consciousness and discover the person's belief system about sex and his body reactions. Once a person has retrieved these unconscious beliefs, he can modify them to fit the current situation.

To get at the belief system through the X-rated movie, the therapist listens to all of a recovered incident. The first thing he asks is, "What is your belief?" or "What do you believe about that?" He wants to keep the client *in* the experience while he answers because he doesn't want a current belief but whatever spontaneously emerges from his old belief system. An example might be: "I am playing doctor and my mother walks into my room and catches us." The belief is "I am doing something wrong; I'm bad."

The second question the therapist asks is, "What is your feeling?"

Most often the feeling is fear, or some form of fear. It may be guilt, shame, or embarrassment instead, but these are all constrictive emotions built on a foundation of fear. Even if the actual original feeling was a positive one, it will almost always have been overlaid and obscured with some form of fear. In our example above, the feeling is, "I'm afraid of being caught, of having my mother know I'm bad."

The next question is, "Where do you feel that in your body?" The client will then experience in his body where he's holding that feeling. He may begin to tighten and hold in exactly the way he did then. Very often the holding is in the pelvis or neck, but it may also be in the chest, belly, or other parts of the body. We can associate the current holding pattern in his body with the early X-rated movie, and that awareness will facilitate some of the releasing.

The X-rated movie process continues to the next scene that the client can remember and the next and the next, from the earliest stage up to his current sexual situation, ideas, and fantasies.

Critical Stages of Sexual Development

The X-rated movie is really an extension of the Primary Scenario. We look at it not just as a sexual history, but to see how it is related to the Primary Scenario, because many people try, through sex, to meet the unfulfilled longings of the early developmental stages of bonding and mirroring.

There are critical stages during sexual development, and these are the times in which one is more subject to and more vulnerable to sexual trauma. These also are the times when sexual attitudes and belief systems become fixed in the body. So it's most important to follow each of these critical times and see that they are thoroughly explored in therapy.

First we look at a person's overall development at a specific time in his life. We grow in different ways: chronologically, physically, socially, emotionally, and intellectually. The problem is that we often grow unevenly. The environment may spur or hinder growth in one area while Mother Nature may put us ahead or behind our chronological age. These disparities among our different areas of growth can cause trauma and holding in the body. A person's relative development in different areas has an emotional impact, and the attitudes arising from that impact become his sexual identity for life. It is the sum of his total development that becomes his fixed sexual identity, not just one aspect of him, because the balance is important. It makes a big difference whether or not one develops apace with his peers. Acceptance of being far ahead or behind depends on his emotional maturity.

For example, the girl whose development is charted in Figure 30 is chronologically ten years old. She is physically thirteen years old and could soon begin to develop breasts, menstruate, and bear a child. She is eight years old socially, and intellectually she is sixteen. Such physical and intellectual maturity would be very difficult for her because she is only six years old emotionally. If she did develop breasts, it could be traumatic for her, whereas if she didn't develop till she was thirteen, she would be maturing along with her classmates, and would take it as a matter of course.

Figure 30
Diagnosing Fixed Sexual Identity

Chronological Age	Physical Age	Social Age	Intellectual Age	Emotional Age	Fixed Sexual Identity
10	13	8	16	6	This individual may see herself as socially inept, emotionally immature, intellectually bright, and sexually retarded.

One of our clients started her period when she was chronologically eleven but so young emotionally— about seven or eight— that she wasn't ready to become a woman. She literally shut off her hormones and stopped the process. When she was fourteen and ready, she had to be given hormones to re-awaken the interrupted process. Only as an adult was she able to understand why she had cut off her own growth. This was an impressive demonstration of the power of one facet of a person over another facet. Had she not been able to turn off her hormones, then her psychological facet would have had a powerful effect on her emotions and on her social development, and it would be reflected in her sexual identity.

If, for instance, the ten-year-old girl of Figure 30 grew to be a poised forty-five-year old woman with a slender figure, she might well still think of herself as a socially inept little girl with big breasts. Her fixed sexual identity would come not from objective reality, but from her subjective experience of herself at age ten. It is possible to separate out one's feelings about sex, and go right on developing normally in all the other facets. No one, even a lover, really can know someone's deepest attitudes about sex. So people often do not look at their sexual identity in therapy, and it remains split off from the rest of their identity.

We can begin to understand such happenings by looking at a person's development in terms of Figure 31. If he doesn't get proper bonding as an infant and proper mirroring (see chapter 6), he may, as an adult, be able to perform sexually on a physical level, but may not be able to sustain relationships and intimacy. Or he might have the opposite problem and be desperate to get close to people for the bonding he missed. Feelings of being unwanted get carried over into one's sexual life. Relationships are disturbed by a lack of trust and fear of abandonment, which then interfere with one's sexuality. People who have experienced problems in this stage may be very active sexually, but it is all genital (erotic), and they may have difficulty with heart connection or intimacy.

Figure 31
Critical Stages of Sexual Development

Chronological Age	Developmental Task	Possible Trauma	Possible Related Dysfunction
0 to 1 year	Proper bonding and mirroring. Formation of a sense of Self.	Desertion, lack of touching, isolation, physical abuse.	Lack of ability to form intimate relationships — fear of abandonment or desperate seeking of closeness.
1 to 3 years	Toilet training, separation.	Early intrusions, enemas, catheterizations; solipsistic relationships;	Chronic cystitis, bladder infections, anal fixation.
3 to 5 years	Sex play, curiosity masturbation	Rape, incest, molestation, punishment for masturbation	Voyeurism, exhibitionism
5 to 7 years	Playing doctor, normal homosexual explorations, masturbation	Punishment, interrupted sex play	Difficulty in later same-sex relationships; guilt associated with sex play.
7 to 12 years	Puberty, menstruation, ejaculation, nocturnal emissions, breast development, secondary sexual characteristics	Unhealthy attitudes, fear of loss of control, teasing, embarrassment	Painful menstruation, pelvic disease, ejaculatory dysfunctions, chest blocks
12 to 25 years	First sexual explorations, petting, first intercourse (any time between 10 and 25 years).	Childbirth, gynecological exams, pregnancy, abortion, miscarriage	Sexual dysfunctions, guilt, shame, rage — unexpressed fear

Toilet training is extremely important in terms of sexual development, and many sexual traumas are associated with too-early toilet
training. As Ellsworth Baker, M. D., explains in *Man in the Trap: Causes
of Blocked Sexual Energy*, before the age of about eighteen months the
cortical-thalamic track is not completely formed, and in order for
someone to contain his feces, he has to pull up the floor of the pelvis
and tighten and hold. [1] That's so painful he has to learn to turn off
the feeling in the pelvis. He learns to turn off the feelings of the urge
to urinate and defecate, and he learns it very early in life. In working
with the body, it is possible to see that people with release problems
are often not holding in the *genital* area, but in the *anal* area, which
still shuts off the feelings to and from the genitals.

Another trauma during this stage can come from excessive enemas
and catheterization of young children. These are not uncommon
practices and can create a trauma that is often a source of feelings of
rape and invasion, causing holding in the pelvis. As the pain is
turned off, so is normal, useful awareness such as the urge to urinate.
This sets up a whole cycle of reactions and can create chronic
problems in later years. An adult may have chronic cystitis or
recurrent infections as a result.

The next critical period is around ages three to five years. During
this stage, the child is extremely curious and wants to see and
touch everything and know what it is. This often leads to perfectly
normal sex play, exploration of the child's own genitals and those of
his friends, and masturbation. A person doesn't have to have an
obvious sexual trauma such as molestation, rape, or incest in his life
to be sexually traumatized. *All he needs is to have had a normal sexual
activity interfered with during a critical time!*

All infants touch and fondle their genitals, but social and parental
pressures are introjected so early that most people's early memories
of it are repressed. Masturbation is usually remembered as occurring
later, even though it is a much earlier development. By the time a
child is three to five years old, he already has a belief about
masturbation. During this critical period, most sexual traumas are
associated with *punishment* for masturbation.

For example, a woman client started to masturbate a great deal
when she was five, just after her baby brother was born. The practice
provided some comfort for the loss of her mother's undivided love,
but her parents considered her masturbation a problem and were
terribly upset about it. The family doctor sympathized with their
concern, did a pelvic exam to insure that there was no infection, and
recommended that they tie her hands to the bed at night. In the eyes

of the adults, the treatment was successful for she never masturbated again. However, at the age of thirty-five, she is very inhibited about her genitals. She has no language for them, no understanding of their anatomy, and no appreciation for their potential worth. She washes perfunctorily and ignores them otherwise, having no interest in sex whatsoever.

This example shows how severe traumas can happen. It is common to find many women whose genitals are a mystery to them because of the inhibitions from this critical stage. Other possible traumas at this stage are molestation and incest.

One of the values of the X-rated movie is that it can be used in conjunction with the Primary Scenario, shedding new light on recovered experiences. For instance, a young woman named Cathy suffered badly from asthma. It had developed while her mother was in the hospital giving birth to Cathy's brother. Cathy had always assumed that the asthma was connected to her brother's birth and the "abandonment" by her mother, but something about it never rang quite true. It was only during the taking of her X-rated movie that a related incident emerged. When her mother went to the hospital, a family friend picked Cathy up and took her to stay at her house. The friend's husband, ostensibly getting Cathy ready for bed that first night, exposed his penis to her. She was terrified and had her first asthma attack. Recovering this incident significantly changed the flavor of this period. In trying to make her asthma better, she had approached it with the assumption that the birth of her baby brother was the primary trauma. Now she was able to see that the severe trauma of her mother's absence was due, not to a terrible sense of abandonment, but to a sexual fright that occurred during that absence.

Incest

This is actually a very common occurrence, yet it has often been a prohibited subject even for therapy. Jeffrey M. Masson suggests in *The Assault on Truth: Freud's Suppression of the Seduction Theory*, that Freud's later theories of incest fantasy were, in fact, a denial of what he knew to be true: that incest was both traumatic and fearfully common. His later insistence that incest was fantasy may have been prompted by the fierce resistance he met from his colleagues when he presented his original and heart-felt opinions about incestuous relations between girls and their fathers.[3] Whether or not Freud's notion of the incest fantasy was a reversal of his earlier finding or opinions, it nevertheless thwarted generations of victims who sought help and comfort in therapy.

An incestuous incident may have been a one-time event only but can still be traumatizing. For one thing, the child is often identified or bonded with the molesting figure and doesn't yet experience him as completely separate from his own Self. For another thing, when an older sibling or adult approaches the child with strong sexual energy, it overwhelms the child. It's not so much the sight of the penis or the sexual act itself, but the energy that comes with the molester's excitation that the child cannot contain. Its very force can be terrifying.

Incest is an invasion of a child's energetic boundaries, as well as his physical boundaries. It is overwhelming because he has no way of dealing with the external encroachment of his energy field by the adult sexual energy. The parent or older sibling is caught up in the sexual excitation and is split off from his normal pattern of relating to the child. This means that the child is not only overwhelmed by the encroaching energy but is also cut off from a nurturing support figure. This makes it a lonely experience as well as a frightening one. It isolates the child because he cannot tell anyone. If any ordinary craziness were going on, he could tell a parent or sibling about it, but when his normal confidant is part of the craziness, there's nowhere to turn. The child lives in his private fear, a fear expressible only by the body, which closes up and cuts off his feelings.

Often the reason that people will not talk about the incest incident is that they have split off from it. Besides being traumatic, the incident may have been enjoyable, which is so guilt-producing that, either way, the incident is repressed and held in the body. The child gets the parent or older sibling close in one way, but cannot tolerate the degree of excitement although he may be drawn to it. When this happens, the child loses his own boundaries, promoting guilt and fear. In our work with incest victims, we've found that the incest may actually have occurred only once or twice and have been a minor episode. The problem, though, is that the child's forced containment of his fear and the secret causes a fixed holding pattern in the body for many, many years.

As the client breathes in therapy, we point out the holding pattern and go back to the incident. It's fairly easy to recover major incidents, which stand out in memory, but not the subtle invasions that are energetic in nature. There may not even have been an actual physical molestation, just an energetic one, but the child still shuts off around it. It doesn't matter if the incident is real or imagined — the sense of invasion and the holding in the body *are* real. For instance, a physical examination may frighten a child and be traumatic. Although the physician doesn't molest the child, he may not conduct the examination with the proper sensitivity, and, therefore, it may be *recalled* as a molestation.

For example, a client with a history of problems in the pelvic segment had been in IBP therapy for about a year and a half, when she recovered a memory of her father coming into her room when she was three years old and touching her genitals. She had earlier recovered childhood memories of having to take vinegar baths for vaginal irritation. She also remembered being catheterized because the doctor didn't know what was irritating her. When she remembered this incident with her father, she came out of the repressed state, saying, "I don't really know if I'm imagining this or if it really happened." The reality of it is irrelevant. The guilt, fear, and muscular holding in the body over the incident are the source of her pelvic symptoms. The fear arose from the real or the imagined invasion by her father from whom she had not emotionally separated, and the guilt could come from her possible enjoyment of the act or the fantasy.

One client remembers that she sucked on her father's penis in the shower and that it was a terrifying experience. As she relived the incident in a regressed state, she realized that, as she stood next to her father in the shower, her head came to exactly the same height as his penis. The *perspective* was what was really frightening, and she isn't sure to this day if she really sucked his penis at all. Again that's irrelevant, since the memory itself is traumatic, regardless of what really happened. In fact, she may actually have thought of sucking on his penis and projected that as being forced to do so. By projecting the volition away from herself, she could fantasize what it would be like. If this had happened, the unpleasantness of the memory could have stemmed from her guilt at thinking of such a thing, and the terror could have come from her fear at the time of what would happen if she followed her impulse.

The next critical stage is between ages five and seven. During this stage there is an increase in homosexual behavior, sexual curiosity, and playing "doctor," which, if interfered with at this stage, can cause difficulties in relating to members of the same sex in later life. Same-sex relationships ("best friends") are very prevalent at this time, which often leads to sexual experimentation with the same sex. If an eight-year-old boy is caught and severely punished for having sex play with another boy, he may have trouble forming close adult relationships with men due to the trauma of the early experience and the resulting *fear* of homosexuality. The fear might never have developed if the early explorations had been allowed to go on without interruption. Girls also exhibit homosexual sex play during this stage. This is less likely to lead to trauma for a girl, since close female relationships are more readily condoned by society than are close male relationships. Therefore, girls are much less likely either to be caught or to be punished.

An early homosexual experience such as a boy playing with his best friend may often the only non-maternal source of nurturing and caring that many boys ever feel. Later in life, under stress perhaps, they may return to the male for a renewal of those nurturing feelings. These men may not be homosexual, but like to be around the energy of men caring for men, since it re-enacts the good feeling of the past. When they get lonely, or something in a current relationship goes wrong, they might revert to the early homosexual experience. This can be devastating to the man who fears being a homosexual and who doesn't understand the true nature of his longings: the warmth, security, and love he felt with his childhood friend.

These incidents will appear very clearly as one watches his X-rated movie. And these experiences are important because many times they are enjoyable parts of one's sexual life. Since memories of these events have been cut off from one's awareness, it is important to explore how that happened. If, for instance, a person *didn't* act out his normal homosexual interests for fear of being caught, or if he were traumatized by the interruption or prevention of the activity, that fear will stay with him. He may have forgotten that a natural curiosity was nipped in the bud, but he remembers the fear, which is likely to surge up and overwhelm him whenever he gets friendly with another man. His panic at the possibility of being a homosexual precludes any relationships with men other than business or very casual ones.

The next critical stage is puberty. Between the ages of eight and twelve, menstruation, nocturnal emission, and first ejaculation are likely to occur. With a woman we explore the subject of her first menstruation, her parents' attitudes, what information she was given prior to its onset, and actual incident of her first period. In one culture, there is an obscure tradition of slapping a girl when she starts to menstruate. Originally this was done to bring color to the girl's cheek. The meaning has been lost today and all that's left is the slapping. In other cultures, a menstruating woman is "unclean" and mustn't be touched.

There are all kinds of attitudes about menstruation that are never talked about directly, but are nonetheless, taught through assumptions. If a girl is told that she should go to bed as soon as her period starts because she is going to have cramps, she will go to bed and have cramps. If she's told that she won't want to swim, dance, or have sex during her period, then she probably won't.

Kelly's mother, for example, put her to bed when her period started, gave her a hot water bottle, set a bottle of aspirin on the night stand, and conveyed the unmistakable message that Kelly was "sick." The mother had always had cramps and her mother had had cramps, so she assumed that Kelly would have cramps. Kelly obligingly did for the next five years. Then she went away to college and her belief system underwent a sudden change. When her period started two weeks into the semester, she went to bed and asked her roommate to take class notes for her. Her roommate was incredulous. "What are you doing?" she asked, "you don't look sick!" "But I'm going to be," said Kelly, "my period just started." "Don't be dumb," said the roommate, dragging her out of bed and throwing her clothes at her. So Kelly stayed up during her periods for the next four years. She played intramural volleyball, swam, danced, and made love regardless of her periods, and she never had cramps. But a week after graduation, home again for the summer, Kelly automatically went to bed when her period started, her old belief system fully reinstated.

It is important to acknowledge that with the great hormonal changes during puberty and the onset of menstruation, there may very well be some cramping when a girl first starts to menstruate, but if not reinforced, these cramps often stop. There may also be emotional and physical reactions to these hormonal changes, but they need not be so traumatic as to cause fragmentation. They may do so, but only because it is a *taught* fragmentation that has been repeated over generations. Many women tolerate some cramping during menstruation but never fragment over it. We want to say emphatically that there can be a very real hormonal imbalance called Premenstrual Syndrom (PMS), which is a medical condition. This is *not* what we are referring to when we say that many women's menstrual difficulties are learned. We are saying that adolescents are especially vulnerable during this time of physical and hormonal changes. Attitudes they learn then are tenacious, affecting their sexuality throughout their lives.

We had a very athletic twenty-five-year-old client in IBP who ceased menstruating when she stepped up her already vigorous exercise program. Her therapist referred her to an endocrinologist to rule out physiological dysfunction. It turned out that her hormone levels *were* somewhat low, but the doctors dismissed the connection with an off-the-cuff opinion that "you just don't want to bleed every month, honey." This psychologically unsophisticated approach merely placed blame on the client, who already had conflicts over her sexuality.

After intense body work for a few months, she regressed to the time when she first began to menstruate. She was twelve, and her period started the day before her father went to the hospital. The trauma of his death a week later got associated with her sexuality and she lost her sense of female identity before she ever really had it. The loss of her father was especially traumatic because it was he who could have mirrored her budding sexuality, made her feel desirable, and given her permission to be a sexual being and enjoy it.

After that work in therapy, she began to emerge as a woman again. One day she called her therapist excitedly, saying , "I got my period! I got my period!" and "I feel just like I am twelve years old!"

For a boy, first ejaculation and/or nocturnal emission may happen at adolescence. Boys may have previously had erections, but usually will not have ejaculated yet. Nocturnal emission or ejaculations can be frightening, and the boy sometimes thinks he has wet the bed or lost control of his bladder. This belief can be the basis for later ejaculatory dysfunctions. If the first ejaculation is traumatic, such as a mother finding his wet sheets and embarrassing him, he learns how to cut off by holding in his pelvis. When this become chronic, he may have later problems in sexual functioning.

Other traumas to boys and girls in this stage come from too-early or too-late development of secondary sexual characteristics, such as breasts and pubic hair. Embarrassment over large or small breasts, developed early or late often cause holding in the chest. If secondary sexual characteristics develop late in a boy, he may compare himself to other boys and believe that his penis is too small. Although he eventually develops pubic hair and perfectly normal sized genitals, he may always *feel* as though his genitals are too small. One problem in our society is that our sexuality often becomes disproportionately identified with our secondary sexual characteristics. One middle-aged woman with very large breasts needed a bra by the time she was eleven. Her mother, possibly unwilling to accept competition from her suddenly sexual daughter, gave her a bra several sizes too small. The woman still wears a flattening-type bra, trying to suppress the unwelcome symbols of her sexuality. Rejecting parts of oneself is sad in terms of the sense of Self, but we believe that it also leaves the body open to disease because the flow of energy is restricted in the rejected parts.

The next critical stage is from twelve years to the twenties. Usually it is during this time that the person begins dating and petting and has intercourse for the first time. It is important to learn what the early sexual explorations were like, to ask about the first kiss, the first petting, the first intercourse, the second and the third. As the person *relives each experience* and explores the *belief* and the *fear* involved, we begin to trace a thread through each experience from the very first sexual action. We find that the *belief*, and the *fear*, and the *holding patterns in the body* are still prevalent in the current relationship, even though they were set up many years before. These early beliefs become part of the person's fixed identity for the rest of his life.

We track someone's X-rated movie up into his twenties, and discuss pregnancy, childbirth, and the feelings about these events and the traumas associated with them. We also discuss miscarriages, abortion, rape, and molestation, all of which are extremely important for *both* men and women.

Traumatic Sexual Experiences

A great deal of pain accompanies the re-experiencing of traumatic sexual experiences. The stories must be heard with warmth, compassion, support, and great empathy. If someone has been raped, for example, we listen to the story, then ask what the belief and the fear were, and point out the holding patterns in the body. This alone won't dissolve the holding, because the unfinished situation has to be resolved. Until it is, the feelings of invasion and helplessness are expressed in the body by shrinking and contraction.

We also see unexpressed feelings of rage at the invasion and at her impotence. These feelings are often retroflected (turned back on the Self) in the form of guilt. The logic of this can be seen when a child, doing something wrong (or even nothing) in perfect innocence, gets a spanking. He doesn't know what he did wrong, but he does know that he gets spanked when he is naughty. Therefore, if he gets spanked, he *must* have done something bad. Even some adults, when they suffer inconvenience or some calamity, are inclined to ask, "what have I done to deserve this?" They interpret the calamity as a punishment, then look to see what they might have done to incur it. People also find it hard to express their anger, even against violence directed toward them, because they were often punished as children for expressing it. So, instead of directing their anger outward where it belongs, they turn it back on themselves.

Therefore, there are complicated and contradictory emotions resulting from an invasive physical attack like rape, and all of these emotions need to be expressed in order to finish the unfinished situation. We encourage the person to do this in a Gestalt manner by imagining the rapist on a pillow, and directing the expression of rage *outward* at the rapist. This is often a very painful, sensitive, and emotional experience, and it is with great respect and care for the client that we support this work in therapy.

After there has been some kind of resolution of the anger surrounding the rape situation, it is necessary to work on retribution. Even if the rapist is caught and prosecuted, that alone does not settle the matter for the victim. One way we work with this is to ask the client, "What did the rapist really want?"

For example, a man broke into Tonia's apartment and hid behind a folding screen until she came home. Six months after he raped her, Tonia was still angry and afraid. She was reluctant to enter her apartment alone, and she never left it without folding up the screen and opening closet doors to eliminate hiding places. When the therapist asked "what did the rapist want?" Tonia answered, "He must have wanted to make me afraid, to live like a hunted animal instead of a human being. And he must have wanted me to hate him, so I would hate all men and be afraid of them."

The therapist said, "So, when you are afraid of going alone into your apartment, and when you feel less than human, and when you transfer your anger to all men. . . then the rapist has won, hasn't he?"

Tonia answered, "Yes!" emphatically. Then, slowly, as she realized the truth in her answer, she said, "but I don't want him to win. He won once and that's enough; I won't let him win anymore! I don't have to feel bad, because *I* didn't cause the attack and I couldn't prevent it. And I'm not going to look at every man I see as if he's a rapist, not any more."

For Tonia, this was a way of re-framing her experience so that she could re-own the power she had given to the rapist.

One interesting thing about rape or molestation is that sometimes it is not the incident itself that is traumatic, but what happens after the event: the police interrogation, the doctor's examination, the parents' or lover's attitude. Many important things surrounding the situation can inflict great psychic and physical trauma. These related events have to be exposed.

An example is a story about Jenny, who, at thirteen, slipped away from a family picnic with an eighteen-year-old cousin. She had such a crush on him and they had been flirting so long that he easily persuaded her to have intercourse with him. Up to that point, the experience was delightful. Then their fathers, suspicious of their long absence, tracked them down. Enraged at finding them happily wrapped in a blanket with their clothes strewn around, Jenny's father bellowed, "You've raped my daughter!" The boy's father pulled the boy to his feet and started beating him. With Jenny hysterically pleading that it wasn't his fault, the two men bloodied his face and broke a couple of his ribs.

The injustice of the beating, her fear, and her guilt stayed with her for many years, making it impossible for her to enjoy sexual relations. This example *by no means implies* that we think women enjoy or are responsible for a rape situation (which this *wasn't* except in the eyes of the fathers and the law, although it was treated as such). We merely want to show how related incidents can be as traumatic or more traumatic than the actual rape itself. Until recently, in fact, it was almost axiomatic that a woman reporting a rape to the police met with more emotional brutality than she suffered from the rape. Children, too, finally admitting that they are being sexually abused, often meet with disbelief when they tell parents or authorities. They find they have exchanged the pain of containing their fear for the humiliation of being thought liars and are no closer to escaping the situation than they were before.

Besides a person's anger, guilt, and fear, there is often shame and the fear that he is ruined, that no one will ever want him again. We have to look for and at *all* of the feelings associated with the event. Even though the person may feel that he has already worked through the situation, we often find that what people have actually done is split off from the situation without ever really connecting with their feelings about it. This splitting off from the event causes it to remain as an unfinished situation, which is *held in the body*, usually the pelvis.

Another important issue that causes a holding pattern in the body is abortion. An abortion is almost always a very traumatic, emotional experience for a woman *and her partner*, even though they may not acknowledge this. Emotionally, a second abortion is no easier than the first. Unlike some other experiences, repeated abortions cause greater physical and psychological trauma. Holding patterns in the pelvis associated with abortion may restrict orgastic release, and the woman may be totally unaware of this connecton. Part of the work of therapy at this time is to make the conscious connection between the holding pattern and the abortion. The trauma of abortion is one of the most common causes of closing off the pelvis.

In therapy, the work to be done is releasing the pelvis. This is done through an energetic process. This process, like actual childbirth, completes the process in the body that was interrupted by the abortion. This is usually started in a breathing session that stimulates the muscular holding pattern in the pelvis. The therapist asks about the woman's abortion and the repressed emotion of the unfinished situation is released. The pelvis, however, may not release with the emotions because the interrupted energetic process of pregnancy and delivery has yet to be completed. The therapist then has her brace her feet on the wall and says something like "Can you imagine that your body is giving birth. . . ? Now bear down and push to help it."

With the pushing, while she imagines she is giving birth, aliveness comes back into the pelvis and causes a body release. It's a simple, natural physical process she is trying to complete, and the "phantom delivery" helps resolve the unfinished situation in the body.

In the same session or a later one, the psychological part of the work is done. Again, the woman uses imagery to put herself back into the childbirth she stimulated and to feel herself there. We might suggest that she talk to the fetus in a Gestalt dialogue, and when she does, she very likely apologizes for aborting it. Taking the role of the fetus, she forgives herself, maybe saying something like, "that's okay, maybe next time you'll be ready." This Gestalt dialogue is important. Because she is *in* the situation and really feeling it, the things she says *to* and *for* the baby are right from the heart, and because they are, they have the capacity to heal her psychic wounds. This and the "phantom delivery" help to resolve the unfinished situation.

The feelings aroused by an abortion are usually ambivalent. Even though a couple anticipates only relief, there is often sorrow, regret, and a sense of loss to be worked out. A woman also frequently holds a lot of anger — anger at the doctor, at herself, and at her partner.

Men often split off from their feelings about abortion, since it's not something that actually happens to their bodies. But often in therapy, they examine their feelings about the creation of life and their role in the life-giving process. It is then that they confront their guilt feelings about participating in the abortion process, feelings which may have not been previously expressed. Many men feel very left out and powerless at the time of an abortion, since the decisions and the act essentially belong to the woman and the men are stuck with their anger at being excluded. Their feelings must be worked out in the relationship or in therapy, because a wide range of responses can occur when the feelings are unexpressed. They remain unconscious and are expressed somatically by certain dysfunctions such as premature or retarded ejaculation and temporary but recurrent episodes of impotence. The man never connects the impotence to the earlier abortion experience, but often in therapy he discovers that although he may feel loving toward his partner, he has unconscious fears of impregnating her again, possibly setting her up for another abortion. When these connections are made clear, the sexual symptoms are often relieved.

A common result of releasing the pelvis in men is the ability to sustain erections and to stay present during sex. In women, it is the ability to have orgasm and conceive.

Cheryl had been trying in vain to get pregnant for two years. "Why is it so hard to get pregnant now that I'm married, and it was so easy when I was sixteen?" she asked her doctor. "It's not at all uncommon," he said, and referred her to an IBP therapist.

In therapy, Cheryl denied that she had any residual emotions connected with her early pregnancy and abortion. "It's been ten years," she said. "so what could possibly be left over?"

She called it her "teenage melodrama." Her boyfriend was two years older and had declared undying love and devotion. When she missed her period, though, his declarations got weaker. When her father visited the boy's parents with a proposal akin to a shotgun wedding, the boy got a job in a distant town and vanished. Cheryl's parents were mortified and said they would never be able to hold their heads up again.

"Oh, it was dramatic!" she laughed. "They're good people so they got me decent care. They held their heads up so straight they both got stiff necks, but it all blew over in a few weeks."

However, for Cheryl, it didn't blow over. When she did the body work and released her pelvis, she released a tremendous amount of anger she had held for ten years. She had felt betrayed by her boyfriend, of course, and by her parents who hadn't attended at all to her feelings of sorrow, anger, and fear. But the big realization was that she had made a decision at the time of the abortion that she would *never* get pregnant again. Just a month after realizing this, she became pregnant, another successful case of releasing old emotions and resolving unfinished business in order to get on with one's life.

We can't emphasize enough that the way— maybe the only way— to resolve these unfinished situations is through the body, but the resolution can also include the use of the Gestalt dialogue we mentioned earlier. The woman can use this in her journal at home and also in the therapy sessions. The dialogue consist of one part of oneself talking to another part. For instance a woman might ask her uterus how it felt about the abortion and then answer herself from the point of view of the uterus: "I feel cheated. I started out trying to do a really good job because that's what *I'm* made for— and you are, *too* — to have babies, and you jerked the rug right out from under me. I don't think you have the proper respect for me, or you wouldn't have subjected me to that pain and humiliation." Or she might say to her unborn infant, "I'm sorry little baby. . . I'd love to have you, but *not now*. I'll welcome you when I can really take care of you." And the baby's answer would convey understanding and forgiveness, perhaps saying, "That's okay, there's a time for everything and we're both better off this way."

We mentioned the use of ritual to celebrate one's maturity at the point of final separation from the parents, and we often suggest it here. Emotions are powerful anyway, and those connected with profound human experiences like birth, marriage and death are especially suited to rituals that acknowledge them. There can be primitive or archetypical satisfaction in the personal, private ritual held to create an inner sense of resolution of the anger, guilt, or fear stemming from an abortion.

Summary of the X-Rated Movie

It is important to note that the taking of the X-rated movie is *not* a simple history taking. It is an actual *re-entering* and reliving of these personal historical events and putting them into a proper perspective in terms of these critical stages and in terms of the individual's Primary Scenario.

The theme most often emerging from the X-rated movie is that of blaming the parents for one's sexual way of being. In order for a person to take responsibility for his own sexuality, he must take the same steps we described in the previous chapter for releasing the negative introject and achieving emotional maturity. He must separate from his parents, forgive them, know that they did the best they could, and realize that he too can inflict the same kind of pain. These steps represent the stages of emotional maturity that we pointed out earlier, and we apply them to the area of sexuality, too.

The first step is to realize that one's attitudes and beliefs *are separate from those of his parents*. He doesn't have to do anything the same way they did it. The second step is to forgive them and stop blaming them for the way he is. Most people are stuck at this blaming stage. They often realize that they're different from their parents, but they continue to repeat: "If it weren't for my mother and her attitude about sex, I would be able to have orgasms and be free to do anything I wanted to do! If it weren't for my father's attitude about sex, my sex life would be entirely different." This is an excuse that perpetuates their lack of sexual freedom and pleasure.

One way to separate from parents is to use Gestalt methods either during the session or in the journal. The person should list all his resentments about his sexual way of being and address them to whomever is being blamed (mother, father, society, the church, and so on). He should then see how many resentments can be turned into appreciations. For example, "I resent having had to sneak out on dates behind your back. I appreciate your teaching me to really listen to my children, to notice if I'm imposing my values on them, and to be fair." If this is done, the person can then move out of the blaming phase into the forgiving phase, leading up to his separation from parental approval and the setting of his own boundaries.

Both parents participate in the inculcation of rules and attitudes about sex. The mother has more effect in the early years of development, conveying attitudes of approval and disapproval with subtlety and persistence. In cases requiring discipline, the father is usually called in. Traditionally, the father would balance the mother's strict morality, wink at the son he's supposed to whip, and caution him to sow his wild oats discreetly. He would be stricter with his daughter, but cuddle her affectionately to counter the mother's disapproval. He might lay down some firm rules for her behavior and give her some idea what to look out for in the way of predatory males. Thus, in a traditional family the father's role as disciplinarian was tempered by his role as teacher and as the person who gave, by implication, permission to his children to follow their instincts along with certain rules.

Unfortunately, tradition isn't what it used to be. Not only are there many more fatherless families, but the male and female roles have changed. Furthermore, this important function of the father to introduce his children to the adult world of sex was never formalized in our society. In other cultures (usually the primitive ones that really understood the rites of passage), ceremonies celebrating adulthood included initiation into that adulthood, with all the secrets thereof being imparted by older members of the community. It wasn't usually the boy's father that taught him how to be a man, but it might be an uncle, cousin, or brother. Similarly, though seldom with as spectacular ceremonies, girls were initiated into womanhood by older women and told, explicitly, all the secrets and rules of adult sexual behavior.

In the primitive (or aboriginal or traditional) societies, the secrets imparted to the adolescents weren't entirely new to them. Boys were familiar from infancy what a man's role was and aspired, early, to do what their fathers did. The girls did the same with their mothers. They could see, every hour of the day, what it meant to be an adult, even if they didn't understand some of the mysteries of maturity.

Needless to say, that's a far cry from our society. A boy, learning how to be a man from his father, learns that, to be a man, one disappears every morning at 7:30 and returns at 5:30. Maybe someday he disappears and reappears only on weekends. It's very mysterious. And to be a woman is increasingly ambiguous. Some disappear just like the men and some stay at home. Of those who stay at home, some mutter and some sing. The roles are confused and confusing. Possibly it is easier for a girl to see herself in what her mother does because mothers are usually more consistently present in the home, whereas fathers are more likely to be absent for reasons of business or divorce.

At any rate, ever since men began working in offices instead of on the farm, boys have had a harder time learning what it means to be a male. His mother takes it for granted that he will simply grow up masculine. She can't teach him to be, because she doesn't know herself. So the boy does the best he can piecing together his masculine identity. If he's not totally alienated from his father— if, indeed, his father even lives with them— he adopts what he can from him. He uses what he sees in movies and on TV. He responds to the expectations of the women around him.

By this process, he usually ends up at one extreme or the other. Either he will express his masculinity by being macho— all tough and all male— or he will own his feminine aspects instead and be gentle, tender, and sensitive. Both of these are one-sided and neither is a true masculine identity.

The Good Father. When the client is in the process of separating his sexual attitudes and behavior from those of his parents, we do the Good Father work (see chapter 7) to help him re-frame some of his sexual assumptions and beliefs. We see many people whose inhibitions came from their fathers' not giving them permission to be sexual beings. When a man's daughter begins to menstruate, he may regard her as potentially fertile, a mature sexual woman, and stop treating her as his little girl. He may stop touching her affectionately because of his own unconscious sexual attraction for her or his fear that it would be interpreted that way. He may suddenly prohibit her wearing a bikini or be harshly restrictive of her friends and activities in an unspoken attempt to protect her from her sexuality. So, in addition to any possible trauma of getting her period, the girl may also have the trauma of losing her father emotionally. The same thing can happen between mother and son. One client said that when he was fifteen, his mother stopped hugging him and began shaking his hand instead. Naturally, he felt rejected. He had no way of knowing that his mother couldn't handle her own excitement at hugging her grown-up son and *had* to stop hugging him to make herself feel comfortable. People have to understand this sort of parental reaction so they can begin to forgive their parents.

The Interpersonal Level: Relationships

Once we've taken the X-rated movie (the intrapsychic level), we can address the relationship level. The X-rated movie and its reliving technique bring a person to awareness of the holding patterns in his pelvis. This awareness is requisite to the relationship work because a person must understand his own intrapsychic sexual patterns before he can begin to understand the interpersonal patterns in his relationships. Just as he must learn to take responsibility for his own sexual excitement, he must learn how his own repetitive patterns cause him to make unfair or unrealistic demands on his relationships.

Before we discuss some of the conditions that cause problems in sexual relationships, we want to mention boundaries again and talk about projections.

One aspect of the relationship work is done within the therapeutic process between the client and the therapist. As the client and the therapist develop a relationship of trusting, then the client may take that openness and compassionate caring with the therapist to support the release of the pelvis. So, in other words, *the path to sexual release may not start with the pelvis but with the heart!* Many people experience the inability to have complete orgastic release unless they have a feeling of love and affection. It is extremely important that there be an atmosphere of trust and compassion between therapist and client before we move into the body. This is working with boundaries as we discussed in Chapter 4. Often people cannot have an orgastic release unless they are consciously aware of their boundaries.

It is important, too, that the *therapist* makes sure that he has set *his* boundaries so that the client feels safe. This has to be done at the very beginning. The implied "no sexual involvement" must be made explicit verbally. The therapist must say, "I am here to do body therapy with you. We are not going to do anything sexual. We are not going to have any sexual contact now or at any time in the future." He must be absolutely sincere and must reinforce this boundary consistently. Without this consistent reassurance from the therapist, the client will not feel safe enough to discuss his deepest sexual feelings and may be uncomfortable doing the body work.

Projection (Projective Identification)

In our work we often see people who say that they are just not interested in sex; that they rarely experience sexual feelings or excitation. We believe that they have not allowed themselves to have these feelings for fear of having to experience again the early childhood pain of not having their longings met. The frustration of being reminded of how isolated he is, for instance, makes it risky for the Super-Trouper to let himself feel sexual excitation.

Often a client doesn't consider this lack of interest and feeling a symptom. He comes to therapy for depression or relationship problems or any of a multitude of reasons other than sex, and his disinterest emerges in the course of therapy. Even if he isn't particularly concerned about it, we want to help him awaken his sexuality. Then he has the *choice* of acting or not acting upon his feelings. The problem is learning to *contain* sexual excitement rather than acting upon it.

The danger in not experiencing one's sexual energy is that the unacknowledged feelings become projected outside of oneself. Some people who claim that they have little or no sexual energy find that they are pursued by others. We insist that, if a person is alive, he has sexual energy, whether he feels it inside himself or projects it outside, onto others. The question is not whether he *has* sexual energy but whether he is aware of it.

Many people deny their own sexuality and externalize it onto others. There they can safely reject it and never take responsibility for their own feelings. Their projective process is very subtle and usually not within their awareness, but will be evident throughout a person's interactions. More than one politician has vehemently condemned "deviant" sex behavior only to "come out of the closet" later and be arrested for the same behavior he sought laws to curb. Closer to home, it can be seen when prudish Aunt Matilda calls two affectionate teenagers "disgusting" and goes on to call him a "young sex maniac" and her a "hussy." Such people are denying their own sexuality, shrinking from it, and projecting it onto people they can condemn. This is not just psychological shrinking, but physical contraction in the body as well.

Another person might not react so negatively but still be bewildered by what happens when his sexuality is projected. One woman we know is very seductive. She fairly glows with clues that she is available, yet isn't in the least aware that she does so. On the contrary, she is constantly annoyed by people closing in on her sexually. "I go out for a nice intellectual or business discussion," she says, "and I'm immediately propositioned. All I ever want is talk and all they ever want is sex. . . I just don't understand it."

Re- Owning Projections

Opening the pelvis depends on a state of well- being that will come from working through the current relationship. The client does this by "re- owning" his projections, those qualities or needs in himself that he has given away or projected onto another person. The state of well- being comes as he becomes more whole, as he brings back into himself what has been missing.

As he re- owns his projections, he comes to understand that he is (as are most people) trying to get his inner needs met by his partner or therapist. He projects onto that person the unfinished parts of his Primary Scenario, trying, as he has been trying all his life, to get the messages that only the Good Mother can give. Intimate, sexual relationships are the most common place for people to look for these messages. The warmth and closeness are not unlike the early warmth and closeness we had — or wanted to have — with our mothers. So people project their unfulfilled longings from that first relationship onto their sexual partners. This projection leads to problems in the relationship because their partners cannot fulfill those needs. Their attempts to do so will probably be on the physical, technical level. Even if they become virtual sexual acrobats, though, they still cannot fill those needs because they are not sexual needs. Only the individual himself, by incorporating or internalizing the Good Mother messages, can do so. In failing to recognize or acknowledge his own ability to satisfy his inner needs, he projects or gives this ability to his partner. Then he expects satisfaction to come from without instead of within.

For example, if we ask a client what he expects or hopes for from his spouse or lover, he is very likely to say, "I want someone who's always there for me," or "I want love," or "I want to feel that I'm special to my partner, that I was chosen for *me*, not for my money, my beauty, or what I can do in return." It's almost always one of the Good Mother message that he wants.

We point out that he's expecting from another person something that the person can't give, that he must work, instead, on being able to give it to himself. As he learns that he can do this, he re-owns his projections, a lesson that has far-reaching effects. For one thing, when he no longer depends on others to make him happy, he is no longer vulnerable to the inevitable and chronic disappointment that comes from such dependence. As he discards his vulnerability, he frees his partner from responsibility, which may ease the tensions between them. And, as he becomes more complete, more self-reliant, he comes closer to having a constituted Self.

There's another reason for re-owning one's projections. After a client starts seeing what he's doing, he might be horrified to realize that he, in effect, has mated with a parent. The incestuous aspect to this relationship is seldom sexually appealing. If his projection of the Good Mother isn't re-owned, the relationship may suffer badly.

Another part of himself that a person might project onto a partner is his male or female side (his animus or anima), because it is uncomfortable for him to be conscious of the opposite side of his nature. He may feel that it weakens his male/female image, that it indicates or implies that he is homosexual. He may reject it because he thinks it is counter to what people expect of men and women. So, instead of acknowledging and accepting his male or female component, he projects it onto a member of the opposite sex. Once it's safely away from him, he might fall in love with it, unconsciously honoring an aspect of himself.

In not owning his opposite side, a person deprives himself of the pleasure it would bring him, as well as the sense of completeness it would bring to the Self. In projecting it, he attributes romantic and exciting qualities to a person who might not have them at all. In fact, the recipient probably *doesn't* have those qualities; projection, with people as well as movies, works best on a blank screen. When he finally re-owns his projected male or female qualities, he is very likely to find that his partner has nothing that he needs or wants. He may leave the relationship, saying, "That person's not at all who I thought," while his bewildered partner wonders, "How could I be the answer to a dream one day and *nothing* the next?"

Dorothy is an example of a woman who projected her masculine side onto her husband. She saw him as strong, capable, and powerful. He could fix things and manage people. He had both moral and physical stamina. He was a man to be counted upon, and she, in turn, was a woman who truly needed to count on him. Or was she? After ten years of marriage, three exuberant children, and a multitude of emergencies, she began to realize that *she* was strong, capable, and powerful. Furthermore, she had been all along. She had taken the role of a weak, dependent woman because she had been taught from childhood that she mustn't come on too strong or she would frighten men away. So she married and became the power behind the throne, so to speak, until the day she took back her power, looked around at the throne, and found it empty. The effect on Dorothy, despite her problems in reconstructing her marriage, was a feeling of joy and peace. "All my life I've been afraid of what would happen to me without a man. How could I take care of myself, little ol' me? Now I know I *can* take care of myself, and the kids, too. I think it has helped Louie, too. I've pretty much let him off the hook. . . . I used to be very demanding, always pushing him to be strong and wise. . . ."

A similar peace and joy came to Leonard when his twins were born. He had married a wonderful woman, a paragon of femininity. She kept a clean, lovely home. She baked bread and cookies. She knit and crocheted and sewed her own clothes. And she had beautiful babies, whom she kept clean and happy and well-fed. Everything she did, she did so pefectly that Leonard never considered interfering. He held the children briefly and awkwardly and never changed diapers. When they bled or cried he sent them to their mother. He was a very masculine person — everybody said so — and he would have felt effeminate had anyone seen him dandling a child overlong on his knee.

Then the twins were born and his wife fragmented. "I've had it up to here," she moaned, and turned her face to the wall. Leonard quickly became Mother *and* Daddy while his wife tried to pull herself together. In the frenzy of trying to cope with newborn twins as well as the pre-schoolers, it was a while before he realized how much fun he was having. Bathing the children, combing their hair, reading to them at night, holding the babies close as he fed them — it all gave him a wondrous pleasure he had denied himself by projecting his feminine side onto his wife.

When a person re-owns his projections, the effects on a relationship will be as varied as there are kinds of relationships. The effects on the person, though, are more predictable. As he completes his Self and becomes more self-contained and self-reliant, he gives up fears and gains satisfaction. He can look at his relationships more clearly and address some of the sexual problems he may have blamed on them.

Sexually Expressed Energetic Blocks

Once a client has gotten in touch with his feelings through the body work, released the holding patterns in the pelvis, and relived his X-rated movie, he will have worked through most of his sexual problems. Some that a client and his therapist may want or need to address specifically are premature ejaculation, retarded ejaculation, impotence, and related orgastic dysfunctions. In general, most symptoms of sexual dysfunction can best be described from an energetic point of view; that is, they are problems of not being able to build a charge, contain a charge, or release a charge.

Premature Ejaculation. Premature ejaculation, for example, as seen from the energetic viewpoint, is an inability to contain excitement, to spread the energy out and to stay present with it. One of the characteristic ways of not staying present is to *split off emotionally from the body, so the person is not aware of how much charge he is building up.* The treatment for this is to teach the person how to tolerate and spread out his excitement. A homework exercise would be to *breathe and build a charge and stay present while masturbating.* We begin by asking the person to work alone rather than to work with a partner because it releases him from the duty or responsibility of pleasing his partner. *Premature ejaculation is usually a performance problem as well as a containment problem,* so we teach him to stimulate himself by the methods we have described (breathing, fantasy, and so on) and to sustain his excitement for fifteen minutes to half an hour before he ejaculates.

Sometimes we have to re-define premature ejaculation for a client who is confused by some of the prevailing definitions. One of these states that one's ejaculation is premature if he fails to satisfy his partner half the time. This would be a ridiculous criterion if, for instance, his partner were non-orgasmic. *We define premature ejaculation simply as ejaculation before reaching a high enough level of excitement to allow for a true orgastic release.* The ejaculatory release, occurring before sufficient charge builds up, is a genital release and may leave the man unsatisfied and unfulfilled. In our work, we strive for the orgastic release, which involves the entire body. To solve the problem of premature ejaculation, we have to look at the difference between the two kinds of release. As the client does the breathing work and learns to tolerate and contain the charge until he has a true orgastic release, he will automatically solve his problem of premature ejaculation.

The next step is to move into relationship. Once he is able to do his homework satisfactorily and consistently, he will have the foundation of confidence he needs to attempt intercourse. One way to facilitate learning the orgastic release, as opposed to the genital release, is to have an ejaculatory release, and *then* have intercourse. This way, he can last longer during intercourse. Instead of fighting his first ejaculation, he simply goes with it, and when he does make love, he has built up a sense of well-being and can spread the excitement out. He can ejaculate the first time either by his own stimulation or by his partner's stimulating him.

During the training period, his partner should have her orgasm by some means other than intercourse. This removes any performance expectations from the man and assures the woman of satisfaction. The man must not release into orgasm until he has built up a high level of charge and must be able to concentrate on doing so without worrying about his partner's satisfaction. He also mustn't measure his level of excitement against any criterion but himself. He must remember that his charge must be adequate before he releases or his ejaculation will still be premature. This is why he must first learn to reach and maintain a high level of charge alone before he tries intercourse.

It is important for both partners to understand that premature ejaculation is the man's problem to solve, not the woman's. There are certain techniques for a woman to use to halt the man's ejaculation (for example, the "squeeze" technique, in which she squeezes his penis firmly at the onset of ejaculation so he may learn ejaculatory control), but these overlook the basic problem— that the man must learn to build and contain his own excitement. It's an intrapsychic problem, not an interpersonal one. Furthermore, such participation by a woman makes it a performance problem again. His ejaculation is being controlled *by* and *for* a woman. When he works at it from an energetic level, he puts the responsibility where it belongs. Even better, he learns the greater pleasure of maintaining a high level of excitement and having a true orgastic release.

Retarded Ejaculation. The opposite of premature ejaculation is retarded ejaculation. This may reflect two quite different conditions depending on the defensive character style of the man. In the Super Trouper, it is an inability to release a charge due to muscular contraction and blocking in the pelvis. In the Split-Off man, it is an inability to stay present long enough to build a charge to the point of release. Although the symptom is the same in both cases, the means by which the man creates the symptom is different and the treatment must suit his particular defensive character style.

One sign of holding in the male pelvis that reveals blocking is retraction of the scrotum. Another sign of retarded ejaculation is a *semi-erect penis due to unreleased vasal engorgement.* This is due to a state of chronic arousal, often stemming from inadequate discharge. Instead of releasing and having an orgasm, the person is too split off to build up enough excitement to release. He uses both cutting off of feeling and splitting off from feeling, so he neither builds a charge nor releases it. The treatment for this person is to learn to *stay present and in contact with his excitement.* On the physical level, we recommend some movement/release positions for intercourse that stress the large muscles in the legs and back in order to cause a release. These positions can be found in the IBP Release Technique Chart on page 334. These positions are used to release the pelvis.

Impotence. First we have to rule out any medical causes of a man's impotence. If none are found, the problem is probably a form of performance anxiety or, possibly, a tendency towards spitefullness carried over from a solipsistic relationship. Whatever the particular cause, we view the disorder as a problem in the person's *life,* of which the inability to have an erection is only a symptom. We focus on the fragmentation of the Self, which is the true cause of impotence. In treating it, we work with the Primary Scenario to see how the injury in the relationship, the performance anxiety, and the spitefulness are being repeated in the sexual arena. At the same time, we work with the body so the person, through building up a charge, can begin to experience the feelings in his body that have been shut off.

It is important, too, that clients understand that impotence is the man's problem, not the woman's. Many women assume that it's their fault— they're not attractive enough, they're too aggressive or too passive, they're too much like their partner's mother, they're not accomplished enough in the art of lovemaking. While a man may be impotent with one woman and not another, it is more a reflection of the repetitive patterns from his Primary Scenario than of anything the woman has control over.

Orgastic Dysfunctions. In preorgasmic women we see either an inability to build up or an *inability to release a charge*— that is, a blocking of energy in the pelvis. All the things we've already discussed about releasing the pelvis and building excitation are applicable to preorgasmic women. To work with preorgasmus, we usually have the women masturbate at home so she can learn to shift the responsibility for her orgasm to herself— not only responsibility for her *orgasm*, but for her *excitement* as well.

We have to find out if the disorder is primary, secondary, or situational. That is, it's primary if she has never had an orgasm. It's secondary if she can have orgasms while masturbating, but not with a partner during intercourse.. And it's situational, of course, if there are distractions that keep her from being present.

If the disorder is primary, we rule out physical problems (which are rare) by medical referral. Then we instruct her in masturbation as a way to build up and release her excitement *all by herself.*

Remember that we have previously discussed six ways to build excitement, and stimulating the genitals is the *last* of these and is seen solely as a releasing technique. As already stated, we do not recommend the use of a vibrator since the woman would still be depending on something outside of herself to provide her excitement and release. We feel that vibrators are ultimately destructive to sexual excitation, since they are too intense to allow a woman to feel her *own* excitation (this is also true for men). Only the most chronically blocked person needs this intense stimulation. It actually desensitizes the woman to subtle feelings in the genitals. If you rubbed your finger on sandpaper for a long time, the finger would become calloused, and its exquisite sense of fine touch would be lost to feeling. There's a similar loss of feeling if you rub your genitals with a vibrator.

Breathing would actually resolve this problem of pelvic and sexual deadness far better than the use of a vibrator. Once we begin to teach a woman to develop her excitement through breathing, the work then moves to the relationship level.

The real problem is not in teaching a woman to experience orgasm, but to experience it with a sexual partner. So, in secondary orgastic dysfunction, we have to work with the ability to sustain excitement and to *be in contact* at the same time. Pre orgasmic women often split off during sex and aren't aware enough of their bodies to feel any excitement.

Another practical reason the woman may not have an orgasm with a partner may be her anatomy. There is a large variation in female genitalia. If a woman's clitoris is too far from the vaginal opening, the chances of its being stimulated by vaginal penetration alone, even with a high charge, are very limited This can be determined by the Rosenberg Thumb and Finger Test. Using the thumb and the middle or index finger as calipers, insert one into the vagina and place the other on the clitoris. Withdraw and measure the distance between the two. One and a half to two inches is okay. Further apart and the clitoris won't be stretched enough during intercourse and the woman and/or her partner should see that she has some clitoral stimulation during intercourse. There are a number of sexual positions that easily allow this.

Remember the "Big Bang Theory": as long as you build enough excitement, it doesn't really matter what part of the body you stimulate. It doesn't matter what you do to the trigger, or even what trigger you use— if you don't have a sufficient charge built up, you won't get an orgasic release.

All the while the verbal work is occurring the client has been breathing and is charged. The therapist will constantly connect emotional insight to the holding patterns in the body. The finishing of the unfinished business is done in the context of a body session, so as the situations are resolved, there is a simultaneous release in the body. This, of course, is pointed out to the client, so that the body and the emotional release are joined.

What is important here is that even if practical physical techniques are never used, *if the foundation work has been done in IBP, the sexual symptoms may resolve themselves as a result of the breathing work. It is impossible NOT to treat sexual symptoms while addressing the body, and the treatment of such is inherent in IBP.* The sexual therapy is really an expression of our total work and not a separate function at all. We talk about it separately in this chapter because sexuality is often treated as a function unrelated to all others. But the sexual and life processes are one, and the goal of our work is to bring them together.

Chapter 9
Turning On:
The Transpersonal Experience

The Night My Mother Died

My mother told me the secret— she died before she could live it, but she did tell me on the phone that night before she passed. Of course you're waiting for the secret aren't you? Well, she found it at the bottom of illness and depression in the back corner amid a worn out bunch of shoulds and can'ts.

Funny, one of the major things I remember of our last meeting was her fear, not of dying, but whether she would do it correctly. My God, the last moments of being concerned with what is the proper way to die.

Well, let me examine that question more thoroughly — maybe she wasn't so far off; after all, she did find the secret, you know. What is the proper, the right way to die— I wonder? To me the question is not what is the proper way to die, but to whom shall I put the question. As far as I can see, that communication is so personal, so unique to each of us, that only at the level of the soul can it be asked or answered.

Well, my answer is that one dies the way that one lives. Some softly, some carefully, some like a skyrocket at a July celebration. Perhaps another answer is the way one dies is like the way one makes love — sometimes with force and lovingly, angrily, sacredly, delicately, savoring the last moment of ecstasy or— but living, that's the secret legacy she gave me.

"Jack Lee," she said on the phone, "I really know I'm going to be OK. I'm going to get well and go to the beach and ride in an inner tube and play in the sand. I'll sit in the sun, and *I'll be there every moment, I'll enjoy every second.* Oh, I've wasted so much time worrying about how I look or what people think. Yes, I'm sure I'll be fine now, I'll talk to you later, remember, I love you. Goodbye."

The next day she was gone in body, but never in spirit.

Jack Rosenberg
Excerpt from his journal

The transpersonal experience is one in which a person gains an awareness of his Self as something extending beyond his limits as an individual. It usually involves a realization or an insight or an understanding that he perceives as undeniably true. These truths come from within the individual and are verified intuitively (subjective validity).

We use the term "transpersonal" more or less synonymously with spiritual, although many people who have transpersonal experiences would object to the term "spiritual" because of the religious connotations. Nevertheless, the concept is common throughout history and all over the world. The scientist who finds a universal truth in his lab may have had a transpersonal experience, just as the mystic meditating in the desert or an art student lost in the wonders of an intricate shell.

We also speak of the transformative process, in which a person frees himself from his obsolete constraints and energy-blocking patterns, and starts to realize his Self. As his Self-awareness increases, he can expand further to include whatever's beyond, to merge with the universal source.

Some insights about the transformational process are found in the following article written by Dr. Rosenberg for "The Journey" (of the Center for the Healing Arts, Los Angeles, California):

> To me the *transformational process* is really seeing anew (in a sense being born again). I define transpersonal experience as a nonverbal experience of recognizing an inner energy or core of knowing and being. This core has subjective validity. It is the essence of knowing one's Self from the inside, and feeling a connection to a greater flow of consciousness or Being or Tao or God.
>
> When this experience first happens we begin the journey inward. Strangely, we often look to the outside, to someone, some technique, some place, to something outside ourselves. Yet, inside our being is where the experience takes place. The path is unique for each of us.
>
> Each person carries his own personal light for seeing the final summit. Guides from the outside for that reason can only point the way and shine their lights along the path. There is always darkness, though, when their light cannot stretch far enough, for the final step is always alone.
>
> And, strange as it seems, the most difficult task is to know you are guiding the guide.

While traveling the path, change begins to take place inside our being and also in our bodies. We begin to see and experience life from a greater vantage point, from a greater depth of meaning, from an inner place of belonging. There is an inner surrendering to the beauty of the Tao or "the plan," divine wisdom, or cosmos. This inner surrender has its counterpart in the relaxing, surrendering, and healing of the body. We have a body we cherish and care for, and yet we are more than our body.

Life's journey is now traveled differently. The road is the same, but the path is more encompassing. Our deep attachment to the drama of this reality, to the belief of how it should be or is, becomes clearer and clearer, and we are able to let go of attachment and surrender a little more to the Tao.

The paradox is that as we surrender to the Tao we become the Tao. We gain a greater and greater perspective of life yet we have to become the knowledge in order to know the knowledge. This transformation takes place in our total being. Body, Self, and soul are one. Still we experience this overview becoming more exquisitely complete, and always we stay in the moment of the flow or Tao. The understanding frees us from imposing our trip, our shoulds, on others. There is only compassion for our collective being.

The content of life's movie is then the same, but we experience it in a different context. "There is no ending, only new beginnings," and "I am my brother's keeper," now have different meanings.

The definition of spirituality adopted by the California State Psychological Association (CSPA) Task Force on Spirituality and Psychotherapy also defines the transpersonal:

It has been said that spirituality is the "courage to look within and to trust." What is seen and what is trusted appears to be a deep sense of belonging, of wholeness, of connectedness, and of openness to the infinite. [1]

Perhaps this means that spirituality has become more acceptable to Western psychology.

IBP graduate student Lynne Saltzman described in her unpublished doctoral dissertation [2] some of the coming-together of modern science and spirituality:

Ken Wilber (1980) [3] asserts that although orthodox Western psychology does not recognize levels beyond the existential, the great mystic-sages of East and West are in accord about the nature of higher consciousness (or the transpersonal experience). With meditative practices breaking rigid and repetitive cognitive patterns of. . . . thinking, and introducing higher states of consciousness, the individual enters the transpersonal level. It becomes possible to transcend body and mind and to experience out-of-body and psychic phenomena that seem incredible. Wilber says that in the stage of the transpersonal realm, one may have meditative experiences of high intuition and literal inspiration. . . of symbolic visions; of blue, gold, and white light; of audible illuminations and brightness upon brightness; it is the realm of higher presences, guides, angelic beings. . . *all of which are simply high archetypical forms of one's own being.* (italics ours)

Intensified awareness and comprehension of the underlying order of the universe continue to evolve. Fritjof Capra in *The Turning Point* says many leading scientists consider the mystical view of the universe to be relevant to and consistent with the findings of modern physics. For two and a half centuries, Capra says, scientific thought in the West was dominated by the Cartesian-Newtonian paradigm:

"Matter was thought to be the basis of all existence, and the material world was seen as a multitude of separate objects assembled into a huge machine. Like human-made machines, the cosmic machine was thought to consist of elementary parts. Consequently, it was believed that complex phenomena could always be understood by reducing them to their basic building blocks and by looking for the mechanisms through which these interacted."

Capra explains that the theory of evolution developed by Lamarck and Darwin in the nineteenth century led biologists to view the universe as a dynamic system in which simple structures evolved into more complex ones. The Cartesian-Newtonian model was shattered for phycisists by two theories introduced by Albert Einstein in 1905. According to Capra, quantum theory demonstrated that the particles within the atom were not isolated units but were "wave-like patterns of probabilities" interconnecting a cosmic network. Relativity theory, which radically changed concepts of time and space, emphasized that the activity of the cosmic network was more important than its components. In modern physics, says Capra, the universe is seen as "one dynamic whole whose parts are essentially interrelated and can be understood only as patterns of a cosmic process" (p. 92). [4]

The concept of human consciousness evolving to higher levels within a dynamically interconnected universe has implications for the thrust of psychotherapy. The work of therapy can move beyond symptom relief, beyond autonomy, to an integrated Self, composed of body, mind, emotions, and spirit.

The shift in experience from personal to transpersonal can be triggered by a number of things. It might happen to a person having a crisis — his own life-threatening illness, for instance, or the loss of someone very close to him. A crisis makes even the least questioning of people ask, "Why?" or "Why me?" or "Why my child?" A person driven to ask "why" has already gone beyond himself toward the transpersonal realm. By his very asking, he implies the possibility of an answer. In his pain or desperation, he is receptive to it. And, being receptive, he may well receive an answer.

The answer itself isn't important, nor is the question, nor is the event that prompts the question. It is the awareness and understanding and clarity that come when one seeks beyond himself that are important.

It may not be a crisis that provokes the movement into the transpersonal. It can come about in the therapeutic process as one resolves his intra- and inter-personal conflicts. It can come gradually as one grows older, sees change, sees death, and begins to consider his own death. It can happen in psychedelic experiences. And it can happen spontaneously, perhaps in a moment of wonder or happiness, or during meditation.

These brushes with what is often called the spiritual world can catapult a person into a serious examination of the meaning of his life and into a process of change — the transformation of the Self. In this process of change, one frees himself of the constraints limiting both the awareness of his soul and the expression of it. In terms we've already used, transformation of the Self is the shedding of learned patterns and defensive character armor that keeps one locked into ways of seeing and behaving in the world, ways that don't support the expression of his inner essence (his Self, or his soul).

We have described Integrative Body Therapy as a transpersonal model because it can lead to this transformation of the Self. In the journal entry at the beginning of this chapter, Dr. Rosenberg described his mother's deathbed realization that she had let her enjoyment of life be limited by unimportant things outside of herself. With the realization came the determination to rectify it immediately by living life fully, by getting well and by savoring the here and now. But the realization came too late.

Through our therapeutic method, people reach the point of clarity and readiness for the transpersonal *before it is too late.* As therapists, we help people eliminate obsolete patterns, introduce them to meditation and altered states of consciousness, and virtually create a crisis of confrontation with the inner Self that leads to the transpersonal experience. We lead people through a process of self-healing, of changing belief systems, of releasing fixed muscular patterns, and of finishing unfinished business of the past. This leaves them open to the experience of the Self, unadorned and unfettered.

We see life as a journey of the soul, an inquiry, and a learning experience. From the moment of birth to the moment of death, we are on this journey. In the first part of our lives we seek outwardly for learning, but in the second part, we seek inwardly. As we journey inward we begin to see the possibility of transforming our identity from small egocentric self to large universal Self. This is the transpersonal experience and the beginning of the transformational process. It is the direction toward which IBP points and is inherent in its methods.

In the physical work, when a client releases the tensions of old traumas, the blockages to the energy flow in his body are dissolved. Then, through the breathing, he can attain altered states of consciousness not unlike those encountered with psychedelic drugs. The purpose of emotional release is not for the release *per se,* but that he may experience the sense of Self. We explore the archetypes less as fascinating aspects of the Self to be understood than as guides for him to use in his journey to the Self. We examine the past to clear up old misunderstandings that led to the repetitive patterns of his Primary Scenario and prevented his experience of the Self. As Jung understood, this is a time in life when one's emphasis changes from the personal to the universal perspective.

We said that the transformational process was inherent in IBP because we have observed this consistently. When someone has done the groundwork of physical and psychological self-exploration, he will begin to explore the meaning of life and to ponder his individual journey of the soul. Even if this doesn't occur in therapy, a readiness has been created. It's like a seed planted in well-tilled soil; when the time is right, it will germinate.

In this chapter we describe the archetypical transpersonal insights that occur to people and how these insights help people reframe their experience of Self. Then we describe the body changes that come with the changes in consciousness, and finally, the "transpersonal traps" that often interfere with the inner journey.

Archetypical Transpersonal Insights

Numerous insights typically emerge from transpersonal experiences. The ones we describe here include our own as well as those gleaned again and again from clients going through the transformational process. We think of them as archetypical experiences because they occur independently and unsolicited to individuals journeying inward. In addition, they parallel the ancient spiritual paths from the world over.

We call them insights, but sometimes prefer to think of them as "recognitions" in the sense of "re-cognitions," to stress the idea that we are "knowing again" something that we knew before, something that has lain hidden from us while we sought knowledge in the outer world. When we turn from that world to the inner world of the Self, we find certain truths, and we know they are truths because we *recognize* them. All the things we *felt* as babies are felt and known again— the energy flowing freely in our bodies, the sense of connectedness with Mother, and through her, the sense of continuity with all life. Coming back to our bodies, we find that the knowledge harbored there validates what we have learned on the outside, while our acquired knowledge allows us to appreciate and express the internal truths.

These insights, or recognitions, are like road markers or milestones. When a person tells us about them, we know he is going through a change in perspective, and we can track the progress in his search.

1. **There is a soul or essence that continues beyond physical existence.**

This essence exists outside the time/space continuum and the body work will often lead a client to experience it. We have spoken of the sense of continuity with all Life that we get from our mothers even before we're born. This sense of continuity stays with us as a part of our sense of Self. As we grow older, we may begin to feel not only continuous with the flow of Life that *brought* us, but that we can also continue on with that flow. At the same time, we may come to feel that, while we harbor this sense of continuity along with our other senses in our bodies, we are more than our bodies, that we are individual energy fields that will go on even when our bodies are no more. We may feel, increasingly, that our bodies' prime function is to be a vehicle for the soul in a journey that will, or can, take us into relationship with the Tao or with God. And we come to feel that the purpose of the soul's journey is learning and, by learning, to further the collective human experience.

2. **Being the purest expression of his soul (or essence or vibration of energy) is the most important experience a person can have.**

"All else in accomplishment is shallow and of little lasting significance." [5] There is nothing more important than honoring one's essence by expressing it in his life because one must honor what is essential to that life. By working to expand the person's sense of identity, IBP as a psychology of the Self is closely aligned with some of the oldest eastern traditions and methods of moving into the spiritual and transpersonal aspects of life. Ramana Maharshi used the "Who am I" exercise as a way to lead people into very deep levels of consciousness. This self-inquiry is the basis of many yogic and mystical systems, and a whole lifetime could be spent in its pursuit. In IBP we continually guide people into asking "Who am I?" and examining their sense of identity and seeking its source.

3. **Physical energy must be marshalled, channeled, mastered, and grounded in order for the spiritual energy to move in one's life.**

Most lasting mystical and/or metaphysical systems work with the body— the Sufis, for example, with trance dancing, and Yogis with Hatha Yoga and Pranayama, and the Taoists wtih Tai Ch'i and forms of martial arts.

In Chapter 2 we mentioned the value of physical exercise for both body maintenance and emotional stabilization. In therapy we use the breathing work to direct and control the flow of energy in the body and to free up the blocks that inhibit the flow. Through breathing, we make our bodies the channels for energetic expression. We have such respect and awe for the energy in the body that we are inclined to agree with Teilhard de Chardin that physical energy transforms or evolves into spirit.

4. **Through body work, the individual moves into an experience of Self that is nonverbal and uniquely personal.**

The profound sense of well-being that marks this experience is very difficult to articulate. Rather than letting a client get bogged down in trying to find the right words, we say, "When you feel a purely physical, energetic sense of identity or Self in your body, just say 'I am.'" This simple phrase is the verbal expression of the feeling tone of the Self and the essence of well-being in the body.

A similar phrase is found in the Hebrew "Yahweh" or "Jehovah," which is the unutterable name of God and means "I am that which I am." In the Indian tradition of Kundalini Yoga the mantra of the Self— "Hamsa" — means "I am that." The name "Hamsa" comes from the ancient sound of the breath. When repeated for a long time, in rhythm with the breath, it is said to reveal the secret of life that lies there, hidden in the space between the exhale and the inhale.

Since the transpersonal experience *is* unique and nonverbal, often the most effective way of communicating it is through poetry, music, art, movement, metaphor, or ritual. Some of Dr. Rosenberg's poems were written as a result of trying to convey the feeling and meaning of that experience in his journal.

> Who am I? — what shall I do now?
> What is there to accomplish?
> What more have I to learn from my life?
> Shall I ever learn? Is what I am ok?
> What? Where? How? When? Why?
> I ask questions that I have not answers for
> so I ask inside some more
> Who am I?
> I am a man and more
> I am a center of energy and more
> I am an influence that extends far
> beyond my body and this moment and yet I am more
> Who am I?
> I'm Popeye the sailor man on a
>   journey to an endless sea
> God bless me and my fellow sailors
>   we journey to a place unknown to each
>
> Yet a place known to all who earnestly seek
>   within
>
> What do I want of this life, this moment
> in history, will I ever stop seeking?
> Who am I?
> I am a seeker lost in seeking
> who wouldn't know if he found the sought secret
>
> Who am I?
> I am seeking
> Who am I?
> I am trying
> Who am I?
> I am surrender
> Who am I?
> I am forward
> Who am I?
> I am home
> Who am I?
> I am
>
>   Jack Rosenberg
>   From his journal

And the short poem quoted at the end of Chapter 1 will have even more meaning here:

To come from the core of essence
the center of being and significance

And to share that inner Light and Joy
with my fellow man by my own
expression in form

All else in accomplishment
is shallow and of little lasting significance

Jack Rosenberg

5. As a person begins to experience his essence, his Being becomes more important than doing or having.

One loses the emphasis on his attachment to the outer world. As his sense of Self expands within, he will naturally abandon any activity that doesn't assist in the ever-increasing outward expression of one's essence. One of the fears of surrendering to the transpersonal experience is that one's activities in the outer world will have to be given up or left behind. This is a misunderstanding of surrender and attachment. It is only that one's *emotional attachment* to these experiences and relationships diminishes. The situation may or may not change. People develop strong emotional attachments when they bond to self-objects in the environment. Many people experience their own identity mainly through their relationships. That is, their identity is attached to an outer situation as in Constellation (chapter 7). When one begins to experience the Self directly from within, the objects, activities, and relationships in his environment no longer serve to provide his identity so he gives up his attachments to them. This movement from the outer to the inner support and expression is what we called "healthy introversion" or healthy narcissism in chapter 6.

Without going outside, you may know the whole world.
Without looking through the window, you may see the ways
of heaven.
The farther you go, the less you know.

Thus the sage knows without traveling
He sees without looking
He works without going

Chapter 47
Tao Te Ching[6]

6. There is no place to go in seeking the Self except inside. There are no answers except those within.

One doesn't need gurus or temples or pilgrimages because the experience of God or Tao or Self is immediate. From the transpersonal perspective, there is only Self. There is no Other. All separations are artificial. "You are what you seek," as in the Hindu phrase. As one begins to understand this and directs his seeking inward, a tremendous amount of creative energy is released. This powerful expression of inner awareness and energy can cause people to shrink away out of fear and not allow its release. It is essential that people develop outlets for expression of this flow of creative energy in their lives. The journal becomes an even more important tool for reporting, studying, and capturing this energy. To allow a person to become more famiiar with the exploding inner experience of Self, we introduce him to the practice of meditation.

> One can never race toward oneself, only away
> For the dazzling essence of Self is stillness
> And to experience this stillness one must stay and listen
> Rev. Daniel Panger
> *Thoughts and Benedictions* [7]

Poetry, painting, drawing, sculpting, music, dance — any of the creative and expressive arts serve well as outlets for this rush of creative energy. It can, however, be put to use just as well in sports, politics, or business. The form of expression isn't important. What *is* important is the fostering and support of a person's expression of his essence in a pursuit of excellence, as the therapist does in the following example with a client named Joan.

Joan was an attractive forty- five- year- old suburban housewife who had spent about fourteen years in conventional analysis. She had done a lot of the psychological work, but her sense of identity was somewhat limited. When she came to IBP and began the breathing work, she saw clearly that she had no way at all for expressing who she was creatively. All she knew was how to be a good wife and a support system for other people. Somehow there didn't seem to be room in those roles to express the intuitive essential Self she was growing more aware of. "Maybe I'll go back to school," she mused, "or take up real estate. . . or court reporting. . . .," but nothing appealed to her.

"Think of something you like to do now," the therapist said, "something you do a lot. . . anything, no matter how trivial, just so long as you enjoy it. I don't care if it's polishing faucets; let's just find something that makes you feel good doing it."

"That's easy," laughed Joan. "It's only a step above polishing the faucets, too. My favorite thing is puttering in my herb garden. I come in on a warm day reeking of basil, thyme, oregano, and tarragon, and fancy that I've spent the day on a Greek hillside."

"What do you do with the herbs?" pursued the therapist.

"I cure them and give a lot away as gifts. And I make wonderful vinegars for salads." She paused, her face aglow.

"Why not sell them?" suggested the therapist.

"Sell them? " she repeated blankly, but the idea appealed to her as nothing had in years. She quickly found a source for bottles, brushed up on her calligraphy, bottled up some of her favorite vinegars, and labeled them with her beautiful hand-made labels. She marketed them herself in fancy foods and housewares shops. Her trivial pleasure turned into an overnight success. The operation outgrew her kitchen and moved into a factory where she continued to oversee it with the same enthusiasm she had bottling gifts for her friends.

This just happened to be a success story in monetary terms, but the real success was that Joan found an outlet for her creative energy.

7. The most universally consistent experience that marks the shift to the transpersonal is a sense of profound aloneness.

To some people this awareness will give strength. To others, the experience of aloneness may be so devastating that they rush back into constellating behavior and/or into relationships to avoid feeling it further. Before a person can get past this stumbling block, he must acknowledge the essential aloneness of each of us. Without acknowledging and accepting this, one is driven by fear to deny it or fight it. One such case was a thirty-five-year-old woman who had spent half her life in an unsatisfactory relationship just to avoid being alone. During a breathing session she had what she called a revelation. "I *am* alone," she said. "No wonder I always feel that way. But the funny thing is that now it doesn't bother me. I'll never get over the feeling; it'll always be there because I *am* alone."

So, it's not that the sense of aloneness occurs only at a certain point in one's life; it's that one discovers that it has always been there.

In the screenplay for "My Dinner With Andre," by Wallace Shawn and Andre Gregory, the characters talk about being alone and about death:

Andre: ". . . to confront the fact that you're completely alone, and to accept that you're alone is to accept death."

Wally: "You mean that somehow when you are alone you're
    alone *with death.* Nothing's obstructing your view of it,
    or something like that."
Andre: "Right."
Wally: "If I understand it correctly, I think Heidegger said that
    if you were to experience your own being to the full,
    you would be experiencing the decay of that being
    toward death as part of your experience."
Andre: "Yes. . . " [8]

> If you are alone, then I am also alone;
> If I am alone, then we are both alone;
> We are together in our aloneness.
>   Jack Rosenberg

Within every human being there is a core whose perfect center
is a dazzling galaxy of energy, whose perfect center connects
with the ultimate source of being. To reach this center you
must risk going through and· beyond fear. You must journey
past magic, past method, past mentors however great; you
must journey to the place to face yourself, naked, and alone.
Only in that place, only there will you know with certainty that
mocks despair, that laughs at death, that you are not alone.
                            Rev. Daniel Panger [9]

A person who has a healthy narcissism can tolerate the sense of
aloneness because he has that secure base of Self inside to which he
has always returned for sustenance. To him, the awareness of his
essential aloneness will not be a surprise nor will it be particularly
frightening. A person without a healthy narcissism has almost no
chance of overcoming the fear of being alone without more work.
The work at this point— though it may seem paradoxical when
working at a transpersonal level — is to complete his separation from
his mother. It is the incomplete separation from the parent that
causes the inability to tolerate being alone. Only by incorporating
the sense of security and safety one should have gotten from his
mother, and by coming to feel truly safe when separate and alone,
can he ever sustain the aloneness in the transpersonal.

As a person begins to experience and to express his true identity
or Self, he also begins to go beyond that (thus, *trans*personal). The
Good Mother he has integrated also goes beyond. Her image
transcends the personal and draws him into relationship with the

universal, with the Divine Mother. The Good Mother messages have been deeply embedded in his self-awareness:

"I am loved perfectly, totally, and for all time";
"I am safe to explore, to grow, to be exactly who I am";
"I am nurtured; my needs are met perfectly";
"My specialness is acknowledged and nurtured in my life."

Now these messages— this love— seems to come from every tree, every bird, every star, and every breath. The love that was given by the physical mother became part of the person's Self as the Good Mother. That love, still a part of the Self, is now transcendent, and the Divine Mother moves in his heart to expand his bonded relationship and his self-identity to include the universe.

If the person has done the psychological work, he won't be or feel swallowed up or diminished by this inclusion in the universal. He maintains individuation, *perceiving* his unity with the Divine Mother with his individuated "I am" consciousness even as he experiences it. It is not the extended narcissism of the child perfected, but what you might call the expanded individuation of the adult. That is, as a person frees himself of constraints and begins to be more and more his true Self, he begins to be more than himself. As he releases himself from the forces of contraction, his whole being expands. The love of the Good Mother expands with it and he at once gives and receives this love with every breath.

Some people who are actually quite spiritual, may object to some of the language used to describe it. A nineteen-year-old surfer, for instance, virtually gags at the expression "Divine Mother," but wrote in an essay about surfing: "As I sit here on my board, I have an uncanny sensation of being part of everything around me. The water, of course; it surrounds me, makes its every movement my movement, and it talks to me, challenging me one time, then silently divulging its secrets of strength and solitude. And the sun, with whom I arose, has grown with me and stays to share the morning. Strangest of all, I feel a part of the other surfers, too, even those who will 'snake' my waves, for they, too, arose with the sun and are conversing with the sea."

It isn't the language that is important. Just as the experience of Self is uniquely personal, so will be the expression of it.

8. **The transpersonal experience leads one into the "land of paradox" wherein nothing is really as it appears.**

For a person to have the experience of the transpersonal, he must have some inkling that it is possible. Yet, if he has some concept of what the transpersonal experience is, then his experience will be limited by that concept. The paradox, then, is that one is limited if he knows, yet might never have the experience if he doesn't know he can. This dream, offered by a client, illustrates the paradoxical nature of life in the transpersonal:

> I had a marvelous book that had all the mysteries of life written in it. When I opened it I couldn't read the language. But I knew that if I gave the book away, I would know everything in the book and how to read it, but I would no longer have the book to read.

And, from Lao Tsu in the *Tao Te Ching*:

> Look, it cannot be seen— it is beyond form.
> Listen, it cannot be heard— it is beyond sound.
> Grasp, it cannot be held— it is intangible.
> These three are undefinable;
> Therefore they are joined in one.
>
> From above it is not bright;
> From below it is not dark:
> An unbroken thread beyond description.
> It returns to nothingness.
> The form of the formless,
> The image of the imageless,
> It is called indefinable and beyond imagination.
>
> Stand before it and there is no beginning.
> Follow it and there is no end.
> Stay with the ancient Tao,
> Move with the present.
>
> Knowing the ancient beginning is the essence of Tao. [10]

9. Doubt is the only thing that gets in the way of anything and everything's being possible.

If we open our minds to the idea that there need be no rules and that anything is possible, then we can rearrange our life structures and assumptive systems so that anything *is* possible. We can create our own reality with the only limitation being our perception of what reality is. A young child does this in play. Give a child a large cardboard box and see how many realities he creates. We recently watched a three-year-old turn her trike upside down, then crank the pedals around and around with her hand. The other hand she held out as if she were holding something as she waited. At last she stopped cranking the pedals and offered her daddy what was in her hand: "homemade ice cream, Daddy!"

As we grow older, we lose our faith in imagination and begin to trust only tangible reality and the reality of repetition and consistency. It may be only in a crisis that we can relinquish our learned doubts, our destructive and limiting behavior patterns, and re-enter the world of the Self, in which anything is possible. People with severe, life-threatening illnesses occasionally defy the pessimistic medical prognoses and decide to make themselves well. They set about participating in their own healing with an understanding they never had while participating in their own illness.

If we accept the assumption that we create our reality according to our beliefs, then it follows that whatever we believe to be true will be true, and whatever we are skeptical of will not be true for us. Sometimes we hear people joking about another's success, saying, "The only reason he could do it is that he was too dumb to know it was impossible." Ignorance sometimes does allow a clarity that too much structured knowledge inhibits. Once we know all the rules, we doubt, and doubt is the interruptive force to the transformative process.

> All knowing comes from the unknown —
> From the deepest despair a new being can be born.
> There is no end, only beginnings —
> And death is not the destroyer, but doubt.

What we see and call reality is only a tiny portion of the total reality. . . a fraction of the infinite made manifest through our perception. The more extended our perception, the more infinite is made manifest.

If it is your wish to go beyond the narrow pathway that most travel, to walk amongst the stars, you must first walk toward your fears, cast off your closed armor of lies and then risk the terrifying dazzle of truth.

Rev. Daniel Panger [11]

10. Here and now is all there is.

In the shift to the transpersonal, people begin to experience a different sense of time. When someone first truly experiences the moment, the eternal Now, it comes as a great insight. The past becomes just a memory that exists in and is created by the present. We are dealing, ultimately, with time and space. When time is conquered, we have only *Now*. When space is conquered we have only *Here*. The awareness of here and now is deceptively simple and relatively profound.

A shift in the conceptualization of time occurs in the body. Time stops being linear and starts being both eternal and immediate. One client described this shift when she said, "Oh my God, there is no ultimate anything! This is it! It is all happening in this moment." Many such insights occur to clients as they do the breathing work. These insights are often extremely profound internal experiences and are almost always difficult to articulate.

With the shock of this revelation, often there comes a disturbing loss of short-term memory and some details of the past. People who normally don't forget things find that living intensely in the here and now makes past and future blur. They may forget conversations, misplace their keys, or lose their cars in parking lots. As the shock wears off, though, memories of the past become clearer and their short-term memory improves because they are able to be present in their lives as they live them.

11. The masculine and feminine principles are discovered at this time.

The balancing of these energies now becomes important work. When a person re-owns or reclaims the anima/animus on the interpersonal level, he might be precipitated into the transpersonal realm. There, one loves not only individual men and women, but Man and Woman. We see the love relationship in a much larger context, no longer simply romantic in nature but infinitely more profound, universal, and spiritual. We quote from Robert Jonson in *She*:

> Jung, in one of his most profound insights, showed that, just as genetically every man has recessive female chromosomes and hormones, so too every man has a group of feminine psychological characteristics that make up a minority element within him. A woman likewise has a psychological masculine minority component within her. The man's feminine side Jung called the *anima*; the woman's masculine side he called the *animus*. [12]

The awareness of the awakening anima/animus principle often sends people into projective experiences of trying to find this in the outer world. Many people leave marriages, have affairs, or in other ways search in the external world to find their lost knight on a white horse or the princess in a tower. What the client must realize is that the journey is inward, that we can each find his masculine or feminine side within. Without this realization, one might fall into the trap of finding the anima/animus outside oneself and marrying it. This can be just as unsatisfactory and mutually devastating as other projections. Far better that one should take on the task of finding one's own inner counterpart. Then instead of projecting it onto someone in the outer world and falling in love with it, he can honor it within himself. This way he can enter any relationship as a whole being, with no need to make unreasonable demands of a partner for his own self-fulfillment.

We talk later about another trap, the trap of denying one's "shadow side." If a person doesn't accept the male or female side of his nature, it is perceived as evil in the outside world. A woman, for instance, denying her animus, would be quick to see brutality and lechery in the actions of men with charisma and power. A man, denying any "feminine" intuition or tenderness in himself, would have a distorted view of such traits in women and see them as attempts to trap or harm him. The obvious danger in this trap is that the person must protect himself against the evil he sees. At times in the past, all that was necessary was to proclaim someone a witch or a demon and he or she would be drowned, stoned, or burned by a fearful, hysterical crowd.

> Know the strength of man,
> But keep a woman's care!
> Be the stream of the universe,
> Being the stream of the universe,
> Ever true and unswerving,
> Become as a little child once more.

> Know the white,
> But keep the black!
> Be an example to the world!
> Ever true and unwavering,
> Return to the infinite.

> Know honor,
> Yet keep humility.
> Be the valley of the universe!
> Being the valley of the universe,
> Ever true and resourceful,
> Return to the state of the uncarved block.

> When the block is carved, it becomes useful.
> When the sage uses it, he becomes the ruler.
> Thus, "A great tailor cuts little."
>
> Number 28
> *Tao Te Ching* [13]

12. All of life is in flux, with everything either dying or being reborn.

Another indication that someone is changing perspective is his having an experience of symbolic death and rebirth and beginning to see life as changeable and impermanent. There is, in the Buddhist philosphy, the doctrine of impermanence— nothing is lasting; there is no ultimate or permanent anything. Everything that rises must also fall, so that everything is always in some phase of this process. This process is life. The Hindu philosophy is similar. The following passage from *The Tao of Physics*, by Fritjof Capra, expresses the integration of the Eastern and Western points of view:

> The Dance of Shiva symbolizes not only the cosmic cycles of creation and destruction, but also the daily rhythm of birth and death which is seen in Indian mysticism as the basis of all existence. At the same time, Shiva reminds us that the manifold forms in the world are maya— not fundamental, but illusory and ever- changing — as he keeps creating and dissolving them in the ceaseless flow of his dance. . .
>
> Modern physics has shown that the rhythm of creation and destruction is not only manifest in the turn of the seasons and in the birth and death of all living creatures, but is also the very essence of inorganic matter. According to quantum field theory, all interaction between the constituents of matter take place through the emission and absorption of virtual particles. More than that, the dance of creation and destruction is the basis of the very existence of matter, since all material particles "self- interact" by emitting and reabsorbing virtual particles. Modern physics has thus revealed that every sub- atomic particle not only performs an energy dance, but also *is* an energy dance; a pulsating process of creation and destruction. [14]

And from Jack Rosenberg:

> Speak not to me of dying,
> For life will never begin until the old is gone.
> We each die every time we change.
> And each death is accompanied by mourning and sorrow,
>   with fear of what will become of us.
> And we go on, and we go on —
> Onward to each new life, each new way of being,
>   each new exciting moment.
> Speak not to me of dying —
>   for life begins anew each moment.

Carlos Castenada in *Journey to Ixtlan* speaks of death as residing always above the left shoulder; this awareness enhances one's experience of and involvement in the present moment. [15] The breath itself illustrates the death/rebirth process in the exhalation/inhalation. One of the traps of this experience is that some people may begin to believe that since their death is being physically experienced, the physical body is really dying. They become afraid or ill, and manifest the change in a physical way. They confuse the death of old habits with physical death because of too great an identification with the character structure within the body.

"To suffer one's own death and be reborn is not easy," Fritz Perls says in *Gestalt Therapy Verbatim.* [16] Though this experience of dying is symbolic, it *feels* like a real death and can cause anxiety attacks and other severe physical symptoms. Many people in the transpersonal process become ill, but it is the death of the old identity in the body that they are experiencing. While these illnesses may or may not be serious, they are the symbolic way of acting out this "death." It is important then to define and reframe the whole idea of death into terms as natural, for instance, as the breath process itself. Our lives can be transformed within the body; *we do not need to die to be reborn!*

During this process of change, we work with the body, preparing it to contain and channel the energy released as attachments are broken and muscular holding patterns are relaxed. As consciousness of the Self develops, the body is made ready to be the temple within which the Self resides. As we become more in touch with our dying, we become more in touch with our living.

The insights of the meaning of the death and rebirth experience often occur through the breathing work when people have "out of body" experiences in which they realize that death is no more than consciousness leaving the body. This "out of body" experience is very valuable because it allows one to actually *feel* the separateness between the body and one's essence. Similar experiences are reported by Raymond Moody (*Life After Death*) [17] and Elisabeth Kubler-Ross, (*On Death and Dying*) [18]. For example, a person may feel himself floating near the ceiling, looking down at his own body. When one realizes that consciousness exists apart from the body, he usually loses his fear of physical death. This temporary stepping out of the body lets him see that *we are more than our bodies*. Initially, in IBP, we use the breathing to help a person re-identify with his body. As the work continues, he is able to identify the Self with more than his body. Only then can the integration of body, Self, and soul be sustained.

Often these occurrences of profound internal change caused by the emergence of the Self in one's life will demand change in the external life as well. If the person resists these changes and attempts to bottle up or hold back the emerging Self, serious illnesses may occur. When the insights for growth occur and a person makes the decision to resist the necessary changes, then it is as though the body has to give the person a stronger message from inside that these changes need to take place. Often we will see people with life-threatening diseases who ignored these messages at a certain point and decided not to change their lives in accordance with the needs of the emerging Self. Within a short time after this decision, illness may occur. The profound awarenss of the seriousness of this process to one's physical aliveness is emphasized by the body. When we work with this, people often become aware of the very moment in which they made the decision not to change, and now review that decision. On the energetic level, the denial of this awareness creates blocking of energy, and referring to our assumption that "blocked energy creates disease," we can see exactly how one creates illness in the body. This is an area that deserves more serious study and systematic research to better understand the relationship between illness and conscious awareness of one's emotional patterns and one's willingness to take responsibility for positive change.

13. **Learning to surrender to the Self and its demands is essential to this journey.**

As we give up whatever attachments or habits hold us back, our journey ceases to be a journey *to* the Self and becomes a journey *of* the Self. Our identity— however we have come to know ourselves — merges with our essence and everything trivial and extraneous is sloughed away. It's like the deathbed awareness of Dr. Rosenberg's mother when she suddenly knew who she was and what she wanted and how unimportant everything was that she had allowed to stand in her way.

Dreams and Myths

At this juncture, our dreams are valuable signals of our progress in the transpersonal experience. They can tell us not only how far we have come, but also where to go from here, as this client's dream did:

> I was standing in a place that was gray and ephemeral. I was wearing a diaphanous gown and there were soft shapes like sand dunes around me. Suddenly there was a demarcation that was so clear. On the other side were flowers and green grass and it was full of life and brilliant color. I was on the gray side of the line. I knew that I had to step over the line. I also knew that my husband would not be able to follow me there. I am not on the other side of the line, nor am I still on the gray side. I

I am afraid if I cross over the line, I will have to leave my husband behind.

This was an individuation dream. It showed her that she had made great progress in finding her Self and pointed the direction she had to take next. It wasn't a message to leave her husband, but that she would have to give up her dependence on him before she could step into the fullness of her life as an individual. Nor was it an urgent message, telling her to act immediately. *One doesn't simply step out of an old life and into a new one.* It may look that way sometimes, to an outsider, but the process of change leading up to that step occurs over a period of time. This dream showed that the woman was still growing and changing, still in the process of crossing the line into personhood. Her fear indicates her resistance to taking total responsibility for herself, at least on an emotional level, but not her refusal to do so. She is moving in that direction. She hasn't denied the process by turning her back on the opportunity offered on the other side of that line.

A trap here is in misunderstanding the dream's content and message. The woman felt that it might mean she would have to leave her husband in order to grow. She only partly understood that individuation, at this level, is an internal process. The changes start there and may not affect the external world directly. She may or may not leave her husband, but this isn't the issue of the dream. The issue is, rather, the giving up of her dependence and the realization of her being able to live fully in her essential aloneness. It is not her marriage per se that matters, but her need to feel whole.

The process of change is like being on a great ocean liner in which the captain stands at the helm and changes course very quickly with a flick of a switch, a spin of the wheel. The ocean liner doesn't appear to move at all; it cannot whip through the water to point in a new direction. It takes a long time for it to move to the new setting, and when it does, the horizon may appear as before. It takes a very seasoned captain to feel when the course is correct.

Paying attention to dreams will help keep the ship on course, for dreams may serve as guides in the journey to the Self. At this time, dreams become extremely important, as important as objective reality. Working with the body opens the channel to the unconscious, and previously hidden or overlooked material begins rising to consciousness. The client can learn to live with his dreams and listen to the messages they bring. The journal becomes a helpful tool in integrating his conscious and unconscious realities. A person grows clearer and clearer as he moves inward — a process greatly facilitated by the body work— and he begins paying attention to the emerging unconscious material.

Keeping close track of dreams as well as waking events lets a person become aware of the synchronicity between both realities, as well as the message from each reality. That is, he will see many coincidences of content and pattern that have significance for him. He may see in them messages of approbation, encouragement, warning, or they may be clues for solving current problems. Whatever they might be, he should honor the coincidences as evidence that the unconscious reality is as important as the conscious reality.

Dreams take on a different quality now. They may be visionary, more vivid, real, and brilliant. They are not easily forgotten as former dreams may have been. Often dreams and reality become so fused that people are more profoundly affected by their dreams. The body work is essential at this time so the dreams can be integrated into physical reality. The confusion that arises when one doesn't do the body work is similar to what happens when one spends a lot of time in meditation and becomes lost in a trance. One client said, "After intense periods of meditation, I began to see that what I thought was waking reality had a very dreamlike quality and that the clarity of my meditation had become more real to me." This could have been a problem had she not been grounded in the body. Because she had done the body work, she was able to see the drama, the illusions of her everyday life more clearly.

There is a useful exercise that stesses the importance of dreams. We ask a client to "imagine that you are dreaming all of the activities that led to the moment of coming to this room. See yourself getting up in the morning. What did you do first? Now you are showering, brushing your teeth, eating breakfast. Dressing. Driving here. Now you are entering the room. Now open your eyes. Which is the dream?" The point of the exercise is to emphasize the concept that the unconscious is as important as the waking reality.

Another client's dream follows:

> I had a dream in which I was to take a vacation. I had two choices: one was to go east, the other, west. I wanted to go to Hawaii, but I couldn't afford it, So I asked a travel agent if there wasn't some cheaper way to go and she laughs and says, "Yeah, you could swim." So I go to a sporting goods store and buy a wetsuit and I march into the ocean. I am going to swim. I have a little waterproof pack on my back with water and food. Soon I am out beyond the sight of land, swimming and floating to rest and I begin to have a dialogue with some fearful part of myself.

"Come on. You can't do this. This is stupid. You are going to die."

"I am all right. Why should I die? I am a good swimmer. I know how to rest in the water. I am not in a hurry. I'll do what I have to do and enjoy the trip."

"The sharks will get you."

"Why should the sharks get me? I am not going to hurt the sharks. The sharks aren't going to hurt me. There is nothing to be afraid of." I swim on.

The fear increases as this inner voice gets stronger. I was aware as I dreamed that this was going to have to be acted out. This fear seems to be creating, drawing in the sharks to prove its point.

The sharks come. I turn around and look at the other doubting side of myself and say, "Oh, no, I am not going to get my vacation. We have to act this one out because of your belief, your fear."

The shark cuts me off at the waist.

I said to the doubting self, "So what has happened? I am still here. Essentially nothing has changed." I continue swimming.

But the other part of me has become the shark and is intent on convincing me of its point. The shark cuts me off at the neck.

I am still here. Everything is the same. My reality is exactly the same. I am aware, however, that as a head I cannot sustain physical reality for very long. I look around at the sea and the sky and take in as much as I can before the head disappears.

"Okay, now what?" I say. "Where will I go, and how? Am I just going to sit here? Where? There is no here or where or place to go. There is just me and the remaining impression of time and space that I had been occupying. My ideas are what remain and they are going to dissolve soon," I say to myself. "Where can I locate myself so as not to dissolve with these ideas, for these are not me. How to identify myself with that which never changes?"

"In the heart," comes the answer.

"Well, how do I find my heart, without my body how do I locate it, without my breath how do I find my way?"

There was now a communication of some kind going on with a number of folks — Jesus was the main one I could relate to, but others were there to help me find my way.

The dream suspends itself in this struggle to reach my heart.

I work very hard to move into this reality. At last a memory triggers the movement of consciousness into the state of all-encompassing love, and in an instant I explode into light and speed. My whole mind screen is an explosion of light of the brightest sort. And a sense of movement so fast that I was everywhere at once.

We work on dreams at three levels. The first is on the Scenario level where we do the psychological interpretations of the unconscious. The second level is the reality level where a person might be working on a current life problem. The third level is the deepest. Here dreams are vivid and clear, filled with light, brilliant colors, and archetypical symbols such as doors, bridges, gates, stairways, and so on.

Robert Johnson explains in *He: Understanding Masculine Psychology* how closely related to dreams are archetypical myths:

> Mythology was sacred to primitive people: it was as though their myths contained their very souls. Their lives were cradled within their mythology, and the death of their mythology, as happened with the American Indians, meant the destruction of their lives and spirits.
>
> To most modern men, however, the word myth is almost synonomous with false or illusion. This is because of the misguided idea that myths were the childish way ancient man had of explaining natural phenomena that science explains so much better. But certain psychologists and anthropologists are now helping to see myth in another light, to understand that mythology reflects underlying psychological and spiritual processes taking place in the human psyche. C. G. Jung in particular, with his theory of the collective unconscious, has pointed out that myths are spontaneous presentations from the unconscious of psychological and spiritual truths. For Jung, myths have meaning for everyone because they represent in story fashion "archetypes," that is, patterns of life that are universally valid.
>
> A myth stands in relationship to mankind in general as a dream does to the individual. A dream shows the individual an important psychological truth about himself. A myth shows an important psychological truth that applies to mankind as a whole. A person who understands a dream understands himself better; a person who grasps the inner meaning of a myth is in touch with the universal spiritual questions life asks all of us. [19]

Here we would like to introduce the monomyth which helps an individual get more clarity in the understanding of the unconscious process, because he can begin to interpret dreams using this model. J. Campbell explains this myth in *The Hero with a Thousand Faces.*[20]

Figure 32
The Hero's Journey

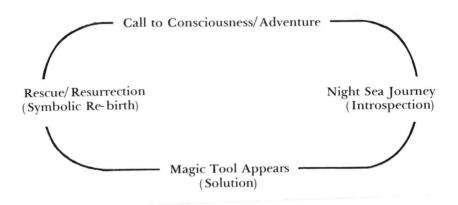

As people move into the transpersonal level, their dreams will begin to erupt with archetypical images which allow us to track them in terms of their journey to the Self, the myth, and their own individual stories. In the model above, the dilemma is presented: a problem must be solved that requires the dream-hero to leave the castle on a dangerous journey. He enters a night sea journey, a dark forest, or encounters a dragon (symbolizing introspection). Then, when it seems he can't go on, a magical tool appears, or he meets a wise person with the key to the solution of the problem. After being rescued from danger (symbolic rebirth, awakening, or individuation), the hero returns to the castle with the problem solved.

In working with dreams and their effect on the energy of the body, we have a person build a charge and then tell his dream in a Gestalt manner, playing all the parts in it. He also interprets the dream through the "hero's journey" model. Thus we find meaning in the dream, and then we find the meaning reflected in the holding patterns of the person's character structure in the body.

In addition, dreams should always be recorded in the journal. Then as the person reads over his dreams, he can begin to see his unconscious process according to the monomyth in a sequence of dreams. He can see individual dreams as steps in the fairytale, and can even predict the next step in his process. Combining the monomyth with the journal work helps a person live with his dreams, and to understand them on an archetypical level, rather than simply interpreting them in a psychological manner.

Body Experiences in the Transpersonal Process

Centers of Energy (Chakras)

As the transformational process develops, people may become conscious of centers of energy throughout the body, known to the Hindus as chakras. Although the Sufis, the Hopis, and the Kabalists all have different descriptions of these energy centers, they agree that the energy field emanates from and circulates through major centers, nodes, or plexes of energy concentration. Reich himself labeled segments of the body (chapter 5) which correspond to the energy centers. Abraham Maslow, who founded the school of humanistic psychology (*Toward a Psychology of Being*), labeled a hierarchy of needs. These ranged from survival needs at the bottom to peak experiences. People progressed from one to the next and became self-actualized. Maslow's model correlates perfectly with the Indian chakra system (below).

Figure 33
The Chakras

We don't identify the levels or the centers for a client, preferring to encourage whatever personal experience evolves for him in therapy. If a person knows any one system, his experience will correspond to that system because our beliefs and expectations shape our experience. If he has no preconceived idea, he will describe his awakening to the Self and to the energy of the body in his own unique terms. Although we encourage this unique expression and understanding in therapy, it is helpful here to discuss these experiences in terms of the Kundalini energy of the Indian chakra system.

There are seven chakras or energy centers located from the base of the spine to the crown of the head. They correspond to physical organs in the body, but are features of the energy field, and not the organs themselves.

The Kundalini energy (the energy of the Unverse, embodied) rises by developmental levels through the energy centers, from survival to spiritual. The energy at the higher levels seems to be more refined. This rise of energy occurs on a lifetime scale and in response to meditation, awareness through trauma, maturation, and Integrative Body Psychotherapy. As it reaches each of these energy centers, the total existence of the person changes: his whole psychological existence in the world, his world view, the way he functions in the world, and the way his energy is manifested. We will describe each of these energy centers briefly, because they offer the most convenient metaphors for the sense of the different levels of consciousness, particularly the transpersonal levels.

One reason for presenting the chakra system here is that as a person opens his body and experiences the transpersonal in the body, his body reactions change markedly. He stops having the tingling and muscular vibrations and begins to feel heat traveling up the spine, a sensation very similar to the awakening of the Kundalini in the chakra system. We present the chakra system as a way of understanding what is happening, lest these dramatic body experiences prove frightening.

The devotee of Kundalini yoga tries to stimulate the flow of energy up the spine to activate the different centers or chakras. He does this by meditation, breathing (pranayama), and movement and body asanas or positions that stimulate the energy flow up the spine. Each chakra or center has a picture that goes with it; there is color, a sound and a whole atmosphere about it. The chakras are viewed as lotuses opening, and as the yogi brings his energies to these centers they being to tingle within the body. It is interesting to note that the chakras correspond closely to the neuroplexes of Western physiology.

The realms of the spiritual and the physical in Eastern thinking are so intimately interrelated that one can hardly separate the two. To the Oriental, the psychological way of being and the physical way of being are two manifestations of the same thing. There is no difference between the two.

The first chakra is the Muladhara Chakra, located at the base of the spine. This is the root or base chakra. The person whose energy is tied up here has a kind of hanging-on existence. . . not moving out into the world. The picture is one of the serpent biting its tail. There is no joy; there is no zeal for life. There is simply a hanging-on to life. Joseph Campbell, the eminent authority on mythology, describes this state in terms of dragons. He said that dragons have a curious function. They tend to guard things, and the things they guard are gold and beautiful girls. They can't make use of either; they just hang on. This is the way their Kundalini or psychic energy is at this first level, and it corresponds to how some people are throughout life. They won't "give up" and enjoy life. . . they are just hanging on and existing.

The second center is at the genitals. It is the Svadisthana Chakra. This is the favorite resort of the Kundalini, the life energy. Here one's whole existence in life is centered around sex. One in turn interprets all of one's existence in terms of sexual energy. This is the "Freudian" chakra. . . the conception of man as basically erotic. In therapy, interestingly enough, as one begins to come to life, to let go and to move, the first thing that opens up many times is sexual desire and sexual energy.

The next stage or chakra is the Manipuraka Chakra. It resides at the level of the navel. Here the energy is directed at power. . . to turn things into the self, taking in. This is the area of Adlerian psychology or Nietzschian philosophy. The main goal of life at this level is to be on top, to be in control, to incorporate, to consume, to achieve power, to be a winner. Some politicians are an excellent example of life at this stage.

These first three chakras typify the way most of us live in the world. We manifest different forms of these chakras at different times, although it's possible to get stuck with only one focus of energy. These, then, are man's major uses of life energy. The way we control these energies, centers, or ways of being in the world is determined by social custom and laws.

The next three chakras are the spiritual chakras. The first of these is the Anahata Chakra, which is at the solar plexus or heart center, and is the chakra of love. It is also the chakra of transformation, of the "coming together" or the loss of duality. At this point opposites come together. . . desire and aggression, terror and fear are extinguished. The reason is that at this point there is a loss of the sense of ego, a loss of selfness. One acts without a sense of self, yet with love. The central theme in Jungian psychology is this union of opposites with man's spiritual origins. It is interesting that when we feel affection, love, and warmth for someone, we want to reach out and bring them to our breast, to hold them close to the chest. The way of being in the world when operating from this chakra is one of reaching out with love.

The next chakra is the Visuddha. This is the chakra right at the base of the throat. At this chakra one's energy is directed toward purifying the contaminants of the lower chakras on the trip to higher spirituality, and coming to the light directly, turning into the inner sound of God. This is the monastic level. Here are the disciplines of the spiritual level, moving out of the world and turning to the inner world. One's energy is directed inward spiritually to ease one's consciousness on to the next higher level.

The sixth chakra is Ajnna, located between the eyebrows at the "third eye". It is the center of spiritual power and knowledge, the highest sphere of inner authority that you can attain. When the energy or serpent is here, you have reached the point of beholding the image of the world of God. This is the realm of heaven and bliss on earth.

The final chakra is the Sahasrara, located at the crown of the head. Here one is past all pairs of opposites and at one with God.

There are a great many texts written about the chakras. Sir John Woodruff's *The Serpent Power* is a very authoritative text on Kundalini yoga.

Often, these chakras are confused. For example, if the first and second chakras are confused, the person has to have sex to feel secure (constellation around sex); if first and third chakras are confused, the person must be in control in order to feel secure (constellation around power); if second and third chakras are confused, the person uses sex for power; if second and fourth are confused, the person confuses sex and love. A person stuck in the second chakra or level of consciousness often can experience sex, but not love, while conversely, limiting oneself to the fourth chakra level of consciousness may lead to experiencing love, but not sex. In this way, one can see that it is important to maintain access to all levels of functioning. The first three chakra levels can also be seen to correspond to the subsequent three levels; for example, first and fourth are gateways, second and fifth are creativity centers, and third and sixth deal with worldly and intuitive power, respectively. These are all ways of using the chakra system to understand how people relate to the world, other people, and themselves.

There are a number of ideas common to Eastern philosophy (particularly the Kundalini yoga system) and IBP

- The fate of the individual is in his own hands and is a function of his own psychological attitude. You are responsible for your own evolution. Only you can help yourself.
- The images of mythology are projections of the psyche; all gods in heaven and hell are in you.
- The psychological attitudes can be transformed by concentrating on these energies. As one pays attention to the manifestations of these energies, it is possible to own the projections and work through them. For example, we described in chapter 8 people who project sexual energy and imagine that everyone else is interested only in sex. By looking out and focusing on what he projects, a person can work backwards to own the projection. The yogi focuses on chakras to transform his consciousness.
- Work with the breath and the holding in the body can change the psychological structure of the person.

All four of these essential yogic principles are at the core of IBP.

The process one may go through with a guru is very similar to what happens between therapist and client. In IBP, as the therapist introduces a client to altered states of consciousness through the breathing and body work, he is often looked upon as magic (see Transference, chapter 7). With a guru, the same sort of transference can occur. A guru who doesn't claim to be magic knows he is only a reflector for the energy of the Universe. The guru must continually reflect back to the person the qualities of the Self he has projected, much as the therapist does in the transference relationship. The guru must be solidly established in his Self so that he can be an impeccable mirror of the greater Self.

The concepts of yoga are not new. The Yogasutras of Patanjali are five thousand years old. The word "yoga" means "to yoke, to link together," and it is our individual consciousness that is linked with the Source of Consciousness. Yoga also means "to make straight the path to which God is realized or realizes herself." ("Herself" is consistent with Divine Mother image and with Shakti, feminine principle, creative energy force of the universe of which we speak throughout this book.)

Physical Manifestations of the Transformational Process

Landmarks in the transformational process may come in mental, emotional, or physical experiences. Some of the physical or energetic manifestations that occur in the body can be very disturbing to some people. They are so similar to symptoms of a psychotic episode that a person having them might think he is going crazy. If, indeed, he presents himself to a doctor or hospital because he is having hallucinations, hearing voices, or operating under outlandish delusions, he is likey to be misdiagnosed and mismanaged. A true psychotic episode could actually be a person's desperate attempt to establish the sense of Self.

IBP therapists are trained to recognize these physical symptoms as part of the transformational process. Support and guidance through the labyrinth to the Self is probably what is needed, not medication and hospitalization.

When excessive amounts of energy in the body are released in therapy, the person may feel nervous or anxious if he attempts to contract around that energy. Other body sensations include tingling, vibrating, and shivering. This is often referred to as the "Kundalini" rising; however, as we saw in chapter 4, these are symptoms of a charge. At this time in therapy, these symptoms may change to an experience of heat in the body as the charge deepens.

The body experiences create problems only when the person resists them. When allowed to flow, the symptoms are never greatly disturbing. This is true of the psychological processes as well. One must learn to surrender and go with these experiences and not try to stop them or hold them back. When people resist the flow of energy, they commonly have severe muscular contractions, particularly in the neck, or diaphragmatic spasms, or cramps in the feet or legs. We treat the severe contractions in the same way we treat contractions that occur in the breathing session (chapter 4).

The fact that these experiences can occur between therapy sessions when the person is alone may make them even more frightening. Some people will go to physicians to eliminate these symptoms. Physicians will prescribe Valium, Thorazine, or other sedative drugs; the symptoms will go away; and the transformative process is interrupted. Some women may think the sensation of heat in the body is premature menopause because of the similarity to hot flashes. Heat is released during a body session, but it continues to be released outside of the sessions. This often misleads women as to the nature of this experience.

Changes in women's menstrual cycles are extremely common,

due to hormonal changes related to energy releases. Even though men are not as aware of their biological rhythms, they too may experience similar symptoms and discover during this process that they have monthly biorhythmic cycles. Women, being accustomed to mood shifts every month, are better able to ride out any that occur now. Men, however, are not used to periodic moodiness and are more likely to be overwhelmed and fragmented by it than are women.

A hypersensitivity to certain foods may occur and diets may change dramatically. People may find that they can no longer tolerate alcohol or red meat, preferring light foods and fewer spices than before. Timing of food intake changes; people may eat smaller portions more frequently, becoming more attentive to their internal clocks. Blood sugar levels may change so that one may not be able to tolerate refined carbohydrates and may become hypoglycemic during this process. People should be counseled to be extremely careful of their diets at this time, since hypoglycemic reaction is more likely to occur, especially with people who practice fasting to heighten their experiences. Fasting may instead produce psychotic-like reactions.

There may be changes in sleep patterns. People may need far less sleep. They may have been used to eight or ten hours a night and now require only two or three. Others may increase their sleeping hours. For those who sleep less and become worried about insomnia, it may help to explain that they are functioning with much greater levels of energy than ever before. It becomes a problem only when one focuses on the insomnia rather than the energy pattern. If he were to focus on the energy rather than the loss of sleep, he could use those extra hours to work in his journal or pursue creative activities he never had time for before.

Some of the most profound changes may occur in the area of sexuality. Some people become less interested in sex. Some believe that they can heighten the transformative process by becoming celibate. They then believe that the celibacy is sustaining the experiences that occur, but this is a false assumption. It may even inhibit the process, since the energy levels will actually decrease if they eliminate sexual activity. People become so fulfilled by the heightened experience of energy in the body that sex becomes less important in their lives. This will be a problem if the celibacy— imposed to heighten psychic experiences— closes down the pelvis, causing physical blocks and endangering health. *It is important to keep all chakras open and functioning.*

In contrast to those who choose celibacy are those who become more interested in sex at this time, possibly because of the great explosion of energy in the body. A number of spiritual practices include sexual rituals to heighten the transformative process. If people begin to equate sexuality with the transformative process, they may center their interest around heightening the orgastic experience, and, for them, orgasm becomes the only road to enlightenment. Orgasm and heightened sexuality are part of the transformative experience, but become a trap when seen as the only means to achieve it.

Some men may become impotent, and this can be extremely frightening. This is a temporary situation caused by an inability to focus the energy into the genitals (See chapter 8). However, if a man believes his condition is permanent, he may panic and try to shut off the transformative process. This and other physical changes are simply exaggerations of a person's physical blocks that have not been totally cleared.

Other symptoms of this energy overflow in the body may be changes in perception such as visions, altered perception of colors (which may seem much more vivid than before), the ability to see colored auras around people and objects, and alterations in figure/ground perception. These visual perceptions seem to be similar to the psychedelic experience. These changes and the loss of preconceived reality can be frightening if the person does not understand that he is now able to *see* the energetic composition of matter, the flow of the universe in matter. There are many different systems for the interpretation of colors and of the auras and we avoid them all, since assigning meaning makes people see what they expect to see, and invalidates the individual's experience. As with all the transformative experiences, we are more concerned that the person discover his own meaning and see through the experiences to the Self.

The most frequent and important reaction of all is the feeling that the body is not solid, but is an energy field extending beyond the boundaries of the physical body. When this occurs, people become very sensitive to their own and to other people's energy fields. One woman had this dream:

> I was a slave in Egypt and I was kept captive by wearing a very stiff coat. I escaped and fled to Israel where I found my husband, but I was afraid to be with him because I knew I would have to take off my coat. Between my body and the coat was a layer of feces and I didn't want him to see it.

At the body level, the dream is about her body armoring and the feared feelings underneath which she is afraid to reveal. Later in therapy the same woman could no longer have her hair done at her usual beauty shop because she couldn't stand to be under the dryer or to have the hairdresser come near her. She felt smothered by the dryer and she felt as though her hairdresser was walking upon her as he approached her. She had lost her armoring and was able to experience her energy field, which was very frightening to her. These experiences need not be frightening if one is grounded in the Self. That is why we do such extensive psychological work with clients to prepare them for these experiences. When one has a solid sense of Self, there is no confusion or need for interpretation. All is clear and unfolds in its own way.

As the flow of energy gets stronger through the breathing, it may be felt as heat moving up the spine and elsewhere in the body. It has also been described as hot light, or vibrations like radio waves or radar. The person may move automatically, assume spontaneous yoga postures, twitch, and so on as the energy clears its path through the body. Other symptoms may be flushing and red eyes. There may be paraesthesia (numbness) or hyperaesthesia (oversensitivity) of parts of the body that were formerly blocked.

As the energy flows through there is a simultaneous clearing of the intuitive channel. This results in ESP and precognitive knowing and dreaming. One client, whose husband was a very traditional psychiatrist, had been having precognitive experiences regularly. One day she called him from home and proceeded to describe the contents of that day's mail at his office. He wasn't in the least fascinated for he was frightened and disturbed and thought she was hallucinating. Similarly, physicians will treat the hot flashes as menopause, despite the lack of other symptoms.

The person who is grounded in the Self will be able to tolerate these experiences and not fear for his sanity. As many of these symptoms occur during breathing sessions in therapy, they can be explained or dismissed on the spot. A client feeling bizarre patterns of heat coursing through his body might ask the therapist if something is seriously wrong with him. When the therapist reassures him that many unusual symptoms are normal in the transformative process, he is unlikely to panic over the symptoms that occur outside the sessions.

The emergence of a spontaneous spiritual guide from the individual's psyche may occur at this time, and it is important to honor this. It is for this reason that we don't recommend meditations on spiritual guides because they may be premature to the experience that eventually emerges from the individual. When such an archetypical force comes from within, it is a powerful source of growth.

Accompanying all these experiences is the desire to take good care of the physical body, to feed it well and give it exercise. This desire grows with the understanding that the body is the temple within which the Self resides and breathes, and through which the conscious energy of the universe flows.

Traps in the Transpersonal

All along the way we have pointed out certain traps that go along with each transformational experience. These "traps" sidetrack a person in his journey. Now we would like to point out several we haven't already mentioned.

What You Believe Is What You Get

This is the paradox that what you believe is what you get, that is, if you know, you can't know. This is precisely why we eschew all spiritual belief systems. If a person has been introduced in some external way to a particular form that he is supposed to look for, then the spontaneous experiences become limited by these previous beliefs.

The "Messianic Explosion"

We believe that all religions are based upon projections of the Self that are then put outside the Self and worshipped. When psychic channeling and other such experiences occur, some people believe that they are the only ones who have ever had this experience — that they are "chosen" and their connection with God is so personal and unique that no one else could have possibly had the same experience. Consequently, they form their own "religion," teach people their "message," and make "converts" to the new "religion," thereby limiting the potential spiritual experience of the "convert." This shows a lack of ability to contain in the "teacher" who tries to "teach" the message instead of "being" it. Ira Progroff in *The Well and the Cathedral*[21] gives a very good analogy. He says that spirituality (or the Transpersonal) is a river flowing very deep inside and each person drills his own well, tapping into the same river. The individual thinks that his own well is unique and builds a "church" over the well to honor the river, but basically each one is tapping into the same source. This results in their honoring the well and not the water.

One major way to inhibit the transpersonal experience is the lack of containment mentioned above. Especially in the realm of healing, we see may "healers" who have not really made that deep inner connection to the source of all energy. They do their healing, not from that tapped river underneath, but from their own personal and rather limited source of energy. Thus they get drained and often become ill. Healer, heal thyself! It is important not to become a teacher or healer unless the experience of Self is well established within. A healer doesn't exorcise or take anything away from the person, but changes the person's energy vibrations with his own. One client said he wanted to become enlightened so he could teach and heal others. He pursued his transformation as methodically as if he were working toward a degree. He had mapped out a curriculum and was taking courses to satisfy his goal of enlightenment. The trouble was that no one can learn from the outer world how to be a healer. The more he tries, the more it will elude him, for it can only be learned within.

The Entrance of the "Demonic"

What we are referring to here is a projection or misunderstanding that comes from the individual's disowned aspects of his personality (see chapter 6, Polarizing) and needs to be worked through on the psychological level as one would any projection. A good explanation comes from Johnson's *He: Understanding Masculine Psychology:*

> The individuation process involves the individual in psychological and spiritual problems of great complexity. One difficult problem is always the matter of becoming reconciled with the shadow— the dark, unwanted, dangerous side of ourselves that conflicts with our conscious attitudes and ideals, but with which everyone must somehow come to terms if he or she is to become whole. Rejection of the shadow personality results in a division within the personality and establishment of a state of hostility between consciousness and the unconscious. Acceptance and integration of the shadow personality are always difficult and painful but result in the establishment of a psychological balance and unity that otherwise would be quite impossible. [22]

The demonic, then, is equivalent to Jung's "shadow" and is a projection. This projection needs to be owned as an archetype of the evil that exists in the world and inside each of us. This can be frightening, but it is a lot less so when it's owned as a projection and acknowledged as a part of life.

Transference and Countertransference Traps

The client may project onto the therapist all the positive and negative beliefs about the energy experience he is going through. If the therapist has not worked through his own grandiose needs, then both the client and the therapist are in trouble. This is exactly like the "magic" stage of the psychological transference except that the client projects divinity instead of magic. He also disowns and projects his own unique experience of his essence and power, greatly slowing down his transpersonal process. Love, too, is a central part of the unfolding of the Self and, if it is projected out instead of contained within, it will dissipate and misdirect the energy that has been released.

The power of this type of transference is so great that the therapist sometimes believes it. The trap for the client is that he needs to contain his power and divinity for himself, and he will never be able to do this if the therapist takes on the projection and owns it. The therapist impedes his own personal growth, too, if he accepts the projections since he will no longer be working on his own process, believing he has already "arrived."

Constellation Around Psychic Powers

Attachment to the side effects of the transformational process may take the person off the track. Psychic openings and healing powers are some of the side effects that occur, and a person may become identified with or constellated around these powers, events, and capabilities, losing his path to the Self (this is the Messiah Complex). People often confuse the spiritual experience with the occult. Occult powers, however, are developed on the route to the spiritual and are defined as "magic," not to be confused with the spiritual.

Rather than *allowing* these psychic experiences to happen, the person may become terrified and run away from them, thereby interrupting the transformative process. This is also a trap. To give an inkling of how strong that fear is, here is a story:

> A mysterious and compelling woman walks the land and tells people who approach her, "I can give you a pill that will allow you to read other people's minds and give you a direct connection to healing energy and psychic powers. But, if you once take this pill," she cautions, "you can never turn these powers off. Now, would you like one of my pills?" No one has ever taken one, and the mysterious lady walks on.

Some people become enamored of these powers and have the opposite reaction: fear of losing them. It is only the *attachment* to these experiences and powers that gives one the sense that they will disappear. The Self is neither astonished, impressed, nor frightened by itself or its manifestations. The Self simply *is*, and it easily accepts unity with all else that is. These events, which may or may not occur, are simply signs that one is on the right road. One does not wrap himself around the signpost, but is simply grateful for the indication that the course is good and that he may continue down the road.

Satsang Effect

Many people choose to leave therapy at this time in order to affiliate with a spiritual group that will provide support for the unfolding Self. If a spiritual group is used as an escape from the reality of everyday life, this becomes a trap, but it is possible to find support for these new experiences in a group of others undergoing the same process.

As a pole supports the upward growth of a sapling into a tree, so the "satsang effect" provides support for the new awareness of Self to take root and grow strong in a person. A community of similarly growing individuals and a teacher can hold one's sights steady and stabilize him in the midst of the turmoil that might occur as the Self emerges in his life. The problem or trap here may come in the belief system that goes along with a spiritual group, which, as we said earlier, may limit one's own individual growth.

Head Trip

Often people move into the transpersonal experience before the psychological level is fully explored and they are unable to contain or remain grounded in the process. If a person cuts off the body experience, the transpersonal experience will be difficult and painful because of muscular contractions instead of a relief from difficulties and pain, which is the way it should be. If a person splits off from the experience, he will only have a mental understanding or idea of it ("head trip") and not the full experience itself. Any experience not felt in the body is merely a mental construct and not an experience; it is a map, but not the territory itself. We feel it is important, therefore, to direct the therapeutic experience through the psychological work and the melting of the body armor before the full transpersonal unfolding begins.

Fallen Angel

Sometimes people have sudden bursts of spontaneous or drug-induced psychic experiences, and they feel that they were chosen by God. Since they have not done the psychological work (owning the Self and detaching from the Scenario) to support or ground these experiences, they lose their briefly-held powers. Then they feel as though God has deserted them. This is one of the traps when the transpersonal enters in a rush unsupported by the psychological work. It's necessary then to go back and do some psychological work in order to put this experience into some proper perspective. A person who had this happen began to see synchronicity in every part of her life. Her view of reality was dramatically altered. Her therapist happened to be out of town when this experience hit her, so she went to see a psychiatrist. The psychiatrist thought she was having a psychotic break and hospitalized her for ten days. If her own therapist, who understood such happenings, had been there he would have been able to put the experiences into perspective for her, so she could have begun to use them in her own growth work. Instead, she believed that she was having a psychotic episode. What really happened was that she was flooded with the transpersonal experience.

Sane/Insane/Unsane

Bob was standing on Mt. Tamalpais when God spoke to him and told him to clean up the environment. He came down from the mountain and started washing himself with somebody's garden hose because God had told him to clean things up and he figured it was a good idea to start with himself. The homeowner called the police and the arresting officer took him to a psychiatric hospital. At the hospital he refused to eat the food, because he claimed it was poisoned. He would eat only raw vegetables that hadn't been sprayed with pesticides (was he wrong?). They thought he was crazy and shot him full of Stelazine (a strong tranquilizer). Dr. Rosenberg happened to be the therapist assigned to Bob — lucky for Bob — and he helped him understand that one of the traps of being enlightened is that you can't really tell other people about it. What Dr. Rosenberg taught him is that you can be sane, insane, or unsane. If you're sane, you agree with consensual reality (it's okay to eat poisoned food in this case). Sanity becomes insanity when one considers that under this definition it's okay to drop bombs on people, pollute the atmosphere, and so on. If you disagree with that, you are called insane! If you are insane (that is, disagree with consensual reality) you get locked up! What you have to do when you enter the transpersonal experience is become *unsane*. You can see what's happening — that although your reality doesn't fit with what most people agree is reality, you can live in a manner that doesn't get you locked up. Bob later became a park ranger, where he could happily live out his life unsane!

Another example: the Maharaji was hunting and he saw a monkey up in a tree, so he got out his bow and arrow and shot at the monkey. The monkey deftly grabbed the arrow, broke it over his knee, and threw it back at the Maharaji. The Maharaji then signaled his troops and a thousand arrows were shot at the monkey, killing him. The point is that, although the monkey had power, he shouldn't have flaunted it if he wanted to survive. One must contain power and not flaunt it, otherwise he will be destroyed.

Meditation

One of the most valuable ways of centering, of contacting the sense of Self and well-being, and of working in the transformational process is through meditation. The problem we commonly see is that most people take meditation too seriously; they work at it, trying too hard to make something happen. This over-seriousness tends to make a person rigid and to defeat the purpose of meditation, which is to let go and to become a witness of yourself. If you are too serious, you interrupt the process of surrendering and of allowing and of fusion with the cosmos.

Meditation is not "doing" anything; it is a state of "being," that is, a state of consciousness. This state of consciousness is a body experience: the art of being "present." Meditation is a "listening-within." You don't "do" meditation; meditation comes to you.

There is a distinction between the practice of meditation and the state of meditation. The practice of meditation is like a train that takes you to another state of consciousness, but later returns you to the consciousness of everyday life: work, relationships, and so on. Meditation allows one to be "present" in his life. It is a process of clearing the route to his essence and of becoming in touch with all that he can be.

Fixation. Now, we are going to focus on the train — the vehicles, techniques, or practices of meditation which are merely methods or systems to assist you in developing a certain atmosphere or attitude. Many of the techniques of meditation involve the "fixation" of one or more of the senses. By fixation, we mean that if one focuses on a particular function over a long enough period of time, he moves out of his mind and into his sensations.

First, let us look at the sense of sound and using a mantra. Saying the mantra is not meditation; it is simply the vehicle to reach a meditative frame of consciousness. The mantra is provided by a guru or teacher who is said to be able to read a person's vibration. Then the repeated sounding of the mantra may actually change the person's vibration to another level. Unfortunately, most people do not have gurus who can read their vibrations, so the mantra may be chosen at random out of a book. Even this can work perfectly well, because it turns off the mind. Mantras are very ancient religious traditions, very often repeating the name of God. What they actually do is fixate the sound (repeating it again and again), and by doing this, the person moves into a "state" of meditation. The Good Mother messages and the rosary, for example, are forms of mantras.

Another form of meditation is the "mandala," which will fixate the visual sense. If, for example, one looks at a circle, he can become so fixated that he moves into the feeling of closure that comes with the circle mandala.

The sensory isolation tank is a method of fixating the sense of touch. Since the sense of touch is lost, one goes into a state of meditation. Za-Zen (Zen sitting meditation) is another method of fixating the sense of touch or the kinetic sense, since one sits in one position without moving for a long enough time that he loses the sense of sitting and moves into a state of meditation.

Sufi dancing, which is whirling and twirling, fixates the inner ear, so that the dancer can no longer sense where he is (kinesthetic sense) and then goes into a state of meditation. Alpha training through biofeedback is another method of achieving the same results. The above methods are all forms of "fixation" meditation.

Developing the "Witness". Developing the "witness" is another form of meditation. This particular technique stresses the intellectual as opposed to the sensory function. Vipassana, or thought-watching meditation, is one form, as is Gestalt "awareness continuum." Counting the breath to a certain number and then starting over again is another form of thought-watching exercise. The counting gives one something to do with his mind so he can develop the witness consciousness. This practice is like the story of the genie who was driving the guru crazy, asking what to do all the time, so the guru gave the genie a task to keep him busy and out of the way. "Build a tower seven stories high," he told him. The genie was back in a short time. "It's done," he said, "Now what?" The guru replied, "Now go climb up and down the stairs, over and over and over."

By using the "witness" we give the mind something to occupy it while we shift to another level of consciousness — the state of meditation. It is important for the person to notice as he uses this practice how he interrupts himself. For instance, if he observes that he is past-oriented, it is an indication that his work is to finish unfinished business. If he is future-oriented, it indicates anxiety or insecurity, that he is having difficulty letting go and flowing with the here and now.

Body Energy. In Body Energy meditations, the person focuses on the energy centers of the body (chakras) for purification, contemplation, and balancing. If he is low in one center, he can focus on symbols associated with that center (see figure 33) and bring that center into balance.

Cleansing or Preparatory. There are also exercises which prepare a person for meditation, such as "Pranayama" (breathing exercises), a cleansing meditation, Here is an example of a typical breathing exercise:

Put first two fingers on forehead, thumb on one nostril, fourth finger on the other nostril. Breathe in one nostril to a count of eight, hold for a count of eight, breathe out opposite nostril for a count of sixteen, then breathe in that same nostril and continue the process, using finger and thumb to close alternate nostrils.

Rules. There are some simple rules to follow which will facilitate the practice of meditation:

1. Always meditate in the same place.
2. Meditate at the same time each day.
3. Choose times that have the best flow with the universe — sunrise or twilight are best.
4. Be sure to sit in a well-grounded position, for example, the lotus, half-lotus, or with feet on the floor.
5. Create an environment that will affect the lower brain. For example, use incense (to stimulate the olfactory lobe) or a gong or bell, which will set up a conditioned response in you and facilitate the state of meditation.

Traps Along the Way to the State of Meditation. The problem that most people seem to have is that they get fascinated by the vehicle they are using. It is important to remember that the vehicles are only crutches to help one get started. Eventually, he will be able to reach a state of meditation without using a vehicle to get there. People have a tendency to get involved with and attached to the forms they are using. People get stuck watching the "movie"; that is, they get engrossed in seeing colors, imagery, and so on. It is as though they are riding a bicycle to get to the train, and they get so engrossed with the scenery that they never get to the train (which takes them on a trip right back to where they were — the state of meditation). In other words, they get so fascinated with the scenery, or what's happening in their heads, that they never allow the experience, which would move them out of their minds and into the feeling in the body where the sense of Self and well-being reside.

The Journey of Life

The journey of life is never a simple one, nor is any one journey just like another. We cannot define the inner sojourn, nor predict the individual's path, but as therapists, we see many similarities between our clients' journeys and our own.

At the beginning, especially, there is always pain, the pain that brings a person into therapy. There is the pain of a physical, psychological, or spiritual crisis, and the pain of knowing that one's journey has come to a standstill and can't proceed without outside help. For many, it is difficult to accept this help, and they decline repeatedly the therapeutic alliance before they accept it. Once they accept it, they can begin the transference process, through which they can re-experience and re-structure injuries of childhood and make up the deficiences of their development.

We see how they stumble forward and how their boundaries work (if they have any) and how they fragment and pull themselves together again. We see them gradually develop the healthy narcissism they need for a constituted Self. As this happens, we see them depend less and less on their defensive character structures and more on the growing sense of well-being in their bodies. They confidently engage in a trial-and-error process with the outside world.

The early pain gives way to joy as a person realizes his newly constituted Self. Often, at this stage, he may move into the transpersonal process, but not always. One person may go into the transformation of his consciousness and another may not. It seems to happen almost as a matter of grace or, perhaps, of timing. The transformation process may not be for everybody, at least not at the particular time he is working at constituting his Self.

One who does broaden his perspective changes his consciousness and begins to understand his life in relation to death. He is able to sustain his sense of Self and bring it into his life. This change of consciousness is so profound that it affects not only the person who goes through it, but often everyone he comes into contact with.

The transpersonal experience and its attendant transformation of consciousness is like a gift. Without changing the character structure lodged in the body, though, a person can't keep this gift because the openness that comes with the expansion of consciousness cannot be supported or sustained.

As the body is the vehicle through which we express our being, it is important to include it in any process of growth that we choose to follow. The body, Self, and soul are all manifestations of consciousness. The body is the physical expression, the Self is the individual psychological expression, and the soul is the expression of our essence as it merges with universal consciousness.

We call the life process the path of Uniqueness. There is nothing to "do"; we cannot make it "happen," but it will happen if we desire it. We must make a commitment to our essence, and it will start to unfold in our life. Once the seed of the transformative process has been planted, we have no choice but to let it grow and to nurture it. The degree and kind of nurturance we provide determines the quality of the experience we have.

Glossary

ARMOR, ARMORING — The pattern of holding or tension in the muscles that originally served to protect an infant or child against the pain of not having his needs taken care of in a loving and timely manner; any muscular holding pattern developed to ward off pain, even when older. Differs from boundaries in that it is muscular, actually part of the body, whereas boundaries are energetic and extend outward from the body and serve to keep people at a desired distance or to contain the Self. Armor is one's personal "shell" that protects the Self from further injury. Armoring is localized in particular body segments, for example, an armored chest area (where the heart lies) might mean a person would separate his loving, emotional life from his sex life.

BLOCK, BLOCKAGE — Anything, but usually a muscular tightness or holding, that restricts the normal free flow of energy through the body, as well as draining a certain amount of energy itself to maintain the block.

BOUNDARIES — Boundaries are the energetic limits of the Self. A Self boundary is the sense (or experience or awareness) of the Self that is separate from the world yet exists in harmonious relationship with it. It is flexible, so that others can be allowed closer in at will or be kept further out. A defensive boundary is a rigid substitute for the flexible Self boundary, developed as a result of improper reflection and/or early emotional trauma. As in armoring, a defensive boundary develops to protect or defend the Self. Because it is a product of poor mirroring, it is rigid instead of flexible, keeping all others out. To draw an analogy, boundaries are to armor as the moat is to the castle walls. In therapy, the boundaries are important in that the therapist must honor them and not invade, waiting instead for an invitation. An individual can be induced to relax his boundaries long before the therapist has reached his armor, which can be softened with body work.

BREATHING — Breathing is the essence of the body work. Through systematic breathing we reveal muscular holding patterns or armor, which puts people in touch with their deep down, gut-level emotions, giving them a chance to (re) experience their sense of well being. Breathing work helps people to integrate their growing cognitive understanding of themselves with a physical sense of well being, i.e., redeveloping a sense of Self and healthy narcissism. Sometimes we say that we "breathe" a client, meaning that we guide him through the breathing exercises. Breathing allows one to expand his body and, thus, his capacity for containing feelings of excitement, joy, sexuality, etc.

CHARACTER, CHARACTER STRUCTURE — Character is an outgrowth of childhood experiences. It is a rigidified pattern of behaviors determined by the various injuries suffered during the early years of life. Character structure is a combination of armoring and the repetitive patterns set up in the Primary Scenario. It is physical in that it is lodged in the body.

CHARGE — Intensification and expansion of the excitement in the body, coming from the free flow of energy. It can be developed through breathing work, and is decidedly necessary for orgastic release.

CONSTELLATE, CONSTELLATION — Constellating behavior is the seeking of one's identity through revolving about outside sources, such as other people, activities, roles, jobs, personality characteristics, etc. That is, one's identity comes from what one revolves around, not what one *is*. This comes about through improper mirroring, i.e., when a small child receives insufficient, inaccurate, or inconsistent feedback about who and what he is he turns to the outside world to find that information. This is the characteristic defensive style of relating of the "Never-Enougher," whose longings come out of an early injury and cannot be satisfied in the current event.

CONTAINMENT — Containment is the holding or sustaining of energy and feelings of excitement within one's body. A person who can contain has a strong sense of Self and no need to project his good feelings away from himself. He has flexible boundaries and no armoring, and therefore has the physical ability to expand and contract his body to allow for containment of increased excitement and energy. This gives him great potential for total orgastic experience. A person who cannot contain may dissipate energy, project away from himself and onto others, or engage in energy draining behaviors such as spending money, telling secrets, etc. He may be heavily armored and unable to expand and contract his body enough to contain. He cannot build sufficient charge for true orgastic release, and may have premature ejaculations.

DEFENSES, DEFENSIVE CHARACTER STYLE — Defenses are, in general, any body structure, habit, or character style that protects the Self. They develop in the face of injury to prevent further injury, and include armoring, rigid boundaries, and splitting off from one's feelings so as not to feel any pain. A defensive character style is a manner of relating to others so as to protect the Self from further injury. There are several different styles. The Split-Off, As-Iffer and Sleepwalker have to varying degrees separated themselves from their bodies and are not connected to their feelings. The Never-Enougher had an early primary relationship which didn't give him sufficient sense of identity, resulting in his eternally seeking "enough" from all further relationships, activities, food, drugs, work, anger, etc. The Super-Trouper has responded to the inundation of his primary relationship by walling off his undeveloped Self within rigid body armor and forming rigid boundaries to keep others at a distance.

DISCHARGE — Attempt to eliminate discomfort by getting rid of the charge by physical activity or emotional catharsis.

EGO, FUNCTIONING EGO — The ego, as we use it, is the cognitive part of the Self, the verbal structure that comes later in development than the basic sense of well being that exists in the body as free flowing, unimpeded energy.

ENERGY — We, as human beings, are constellations of energy. The energy that each thinks of as his essential "Self" is contained in his physical body, itself a mass of energy more or less contained in a solid form. We also are a field of energy outside our bodies.

ESSENTIAL SELF — The energetic expression of the soul.

FRAGMENTATION — Reversion to the undifferentiated mass of energy that is the primitive or potential Self. An individual knows his Self initially as the free-flowing energy, then gradually differentiates body, emotions, other people. Through bonding and mirroring he gets an increasingly consistent, complete picture or image of himself, a piece at a time, forming a cohesive whole. When an emotional injury occurs, he loses sight of this image. All the separate pieces fly apart and his cohesive image is no more — he is fragmented. This is the sense of being annihilated, of losing one's sense of identity.

GESTALT, GESTALT DIALOGUE — Gestalt therapy was founded by Fritz Perls. It differs from other therapies in that it deals with the whole picture of the person within the context, contact boundaries, organismic self regulation, existential awareness, and centeredness. IBP grew out of Gestalt, and added direct contact with the body, long term depth work with the core concept of the Self and spirituality, and an emphasis on the past and the transference. Gestalt dialogue is a technique of conducting a conversation between or amongst all parts of a person and/or a person with his environment, for greater under-standing of the internal dynamics. For example, a person with a chronically stiff neck might ask the neck why it was stiff and then, speaking for the neck, tell the person why it tightened up.

GOOD MOTHER, GOOD FATHER — The Good Mother and Good Father work is a way of helping a person re-enter the developmental stage in which his Self-development was interrupted so that he can become his own ideal parent, completing that stage in a manner designed to form a complete sense of Self. It involves excising the residual "bad" parent and replacing it with the good parent. This involves internalizing the Good Mother "messages" so that the person becomes his own source for love, reassurance, comfort, validation, and sense of identity.

GROUNDING, GROUNDED — Grounding is presence and containment of energy in the body. A person who is not grounded is not in touch with reality. Although we do not let clients leave therapy session without grounding exercises (Chart A), someone leaving ungrounded would be spaced out, trance-like, walking on air. There would be no physical energy in the feet or pelvis, it would all be concentrated in the head.

HOLDING, HOLDING PATTERNS — As in armoring. . . a person tightens muscles to protect the Self from pain. When this happens consistently, a pattern develops. These patterns are body manifestations of tension, as in muscular armoring, but the effect is largely upon relationships.

IDENTITY — Sense of Self. Knowing who one is, as learned through proper and sufficient mirroring. Identity is a body as well as a cognitive experience.

INJURY — We deal essentially with psychic injuries, those actions or circumstances that generally lead to fragmentation and thence to armoring or the establishment of rigid boundaries. Injuries in therapy are actions on the part of the therapist, inadvertent or otherwise, that cause a client to fragment and/or to regress in his therapeutic stage of transference (empathic failures).

INTERRUPTION — A break in a process. In development of the Self, an interruption is usually an injury that causes a child to develop defensive armoring and/or defensive character styles to prevent further injury to his immature Self. It also prevents or inhibits further growth of the Self. That's why we have to go back to the point where development was interrupted to resume development. In breathing work, interruptions occur when a client can't tolerate the excitement of a charge or the hidden feelings. The early interruptions are physical ones, such as itching, giggling, yawning, or symptoms of hyperventilation that all vanish as he gets used to the sensations and learns to contain them. Later interruptions are psychological ones that occur when, again, client and therapist get too close to painful, hidden feelings.

INTROJECTS, NEGATIVE AND POSITIVE — Introjects are parts or aspects of a person that he has internalized from external sources. Usually we speak of the Negative Introject as the internalized criticism of the parent. We say that a person "swallows whole" his judge or persecutor and keeps him with him the rest of his life, allowing him to limit his pleasure and hamper his growth. The Positive Introject is our replacement for the Negative Introject. When the Negative Introject is released, it is replaced with the parental experience the person should have had but didn't. This is the Good Mother and the Good Father.

NARCISSISM, HEALTHY — A healthy narcissism is the product of a healthy introversion, that ability for a child to go within himself to verify his identity, to get reassurance that he is okay, no matter what experiences he has in the outer world. The healthy narcissism is essentially the internalization of the mirroring process once performed for the child by the mother. At first, she contains for him his Self, flashing it back to him when he needs to know who he is. Then he contains it for himself. It includes self trust, integrity, confidence.

OPENING (as in "opening" the chest or pelvis) — Opening part of the body is the same as releasing it, i. e., inducing it to let go of the energy or tension tied up in muscular holding patterns. One opens the ocular segment of the client's body so as to make contact with him possible.

ORGASM, ORGASTIC RELEASE — As orgasm is usually a a genital release. An orgastic release is a total body release which may or may not be accompanied by a genital release.

PRIMARY SCENARIO — The total environment or ambience into which a child is born, especially the relationship patterns in his immediate family. The relationships in the Primary Scenario determine the repetitive patterns an individual will follow much of his life.

RELEASE, RELEASE TECHNIQUES — Relaxing or opening of the holding patterns in the body (or the muscular armoring) so that the emotions underlying the armoring (or the block) are freed for expression and examination; spreading the energy or charge evenly throughout the body.

RE-LIVING EXPERIENCES — The process of going back into a time and place and experiencing it again with all of one's senses. This is a technique for reaching old injuries and retroactively nullifying or re-experiencing, and then desensitizing oneself to them.

RETROFLECTED — Turned back on the self. For example, a person who is angry with another but is afraid to confront him may hurt himself in some way rather than express the anger directly. It's unconscious, as in the spitefulness of the child in a solipsistic relationship.

SELF OBJECT — In a solipsistic relationshp, the person who is the extension of the other. Originally, it is the child who is the self object of the parent but, when the solipsistic relationship is repeated in later iterations, the self object is anybody who plays the part of the child. The self object is looked at and treated as an extension of the Self, not as a separate being. It is a tool, a way of getting satisfaction, fulfillment, and identity second hand, through someone else. In Self Psychology it is spelled "selfobject" (one word).

SELF, SENSE OF SELF — Feeling of identity and continuity experienced in the body, as well as the cognitive/ verbal structure of the mind. The awareness of one's Self comes from the proper mirroring of the child's growing awareness of his individuality and personal worth, validity, and self esteem. It also develops in the body as un-blocked or unimpeded energy flow. The Self is different from the soul in its individual identity expressed in a unique body/ mind.

SOLIPSISM, SOLIPSISTIC RELATIONSHP— A relationship in which a parent considers the child an extension of the parent, a tool, perhaps, for fulfilling old, unfilled desires of the parent. The child learns that his own feelings are irrelevant and may react variously by splitting off, cutting off, or armoring against invasion, spitefully hurting the parent despite the cost to the Self.

SOUL— The basic energy of some sort of universal source that, when embodied in a human being, becomes the Self.

SPLIT OFF— Separation from one's body in order to avoid feelings of pain but resulting in avoidance of all feelings, good and bad. Happens when a child's feelings aren't honored and/or when he is expected to be an extension of the parent as in a solipsistic relationship. This defines a defensive charater style as well as a reaction to momentary sensations that are intolerable, i.e., people may split off when the going gets touch in therapy or in a relationship.

SUPER TROUPER— A defensive character style of relating that involves cutting oneself off from one's feelings through rigid body armor, with the help of inflexible boundaries. The Super Trouper is self-reliant, cold and distant in relationships.

TAO— The flow of Universal Energy in Eastern philosophy. Could be thought of as a synonym for God.

TRANSFERENCE— The projected and actual therapeutic relationship (between client and therapist).

TRANSFORMATION— Transformation of the Self is the removing of learned patterns and defensive character armoring that keeps one locked into ways of the world that are not supportive of the expression of one's inner essence (Self or soul).

TRANSPERSONAL— Beyond the Self, especially, beyond the Self into the Cosmic Consciousness, the Oversoul, the Tao, or whatever spiritual Universal Source one accepts.

UNFINISHED BUSINESS— Situations in the Primary Scenario that never led to satisfaction, that are compulsively repeated through life in attempts to get satisfaction or closure, e.g., to get 'Mother" to love one at last, to get it done in a way that constitutes the Self rather than causing fragmentation. Unfinished business comes about as a result of interruptions.

Appendix
Chart A:
I. B. P. Release Techniques

Segment	Fixed Muscular Patterns and Associated Affect	Major Muscle Groups	Muscle Release Techniques
I. Ocular **Band I**	Fixed look of wonder. Questioning. Worry, fretting, furrowed brow ("What will I do now" look) Anger, aggression (temporalis) Depression, despair Surprise (raised eyebrows and forehead) Suffocation feelings (associated with birth trauma and anesthesia) Skeptical, interested	Back/top of head and forehead (frontalis to occipatalis) Side of head (temporalis) FMP creates wrinkles because muscles do not move	Massage occipitalis to release frontalis (work back to front). Constant pressure of palms on forehead and base of skull while stretching scalp releases fascial sheath. Pressure of palms on both sides of head (temporalis) with rocking motion Stroke brow from center outward to over ears. Caution: gentle massage; nerves can be traumatized easily (see *Total Orgasm*, pp. 132 – 135).
Band II	Inadequacy, shame, shyness Anger (wide-open, glaring look) Terror (wide-open eyes, infra-orbital foreamen) Tears, free-floating sadness (red, moist, constricted, misty eyes) Laughing eyes Tension expressed by fluttering eyelids Flat affect (no one's home) Blank stare, "dead" eyes, split off	Sphincter muscle surrounding eyes (obicularis oculii) corrugator supercilli procerus levator palpebrae superioris (eyelid muscle) nasalis depressor septi dilatator naris	Stroke under eyes, over cheek to temple. Cup hands over eyes (avoid pressure directly on eyes). Massage occipitalis to reduce ocular constriction. Massage temporalis

Energetic Release Points	Movement/ Stress Release Techniques	Associated Somatic Manifestations	Comments
1 – 9 relate to whole head and face (4 – 9)	Exaggerated facial expressions causes muscle fatigue and releases fixed muscular patterns Screaming, yelling, biting, crying (blow his top) releases repressed emotions and tension in forehead	Tension headaches Migraine Pressure in head	Sensory awareness and visualization create sense of space inside head Face is a very delicate area and must be massaged with care: there is no fascia; muscles attach directly to skin; stretches skin; many nerve fibers, great subtleties of movement and expression possible FMP creates wrinkles — muscles do not move look for hand/face gestures; caution with face — respect boundaries — "unmasking" person
Medium pressure on infra/ supra orbital foramen notches (4 a, b)	Weave random patterns with penlight varying distance and speed until voluntary visual control is relinquished Roll eyes to top of head; open eyes wide.	Myopia (withdrawal from contact) Hyperopia (repressed anger, keeping others away) Sinusitis	Contact withdrawal exercises — open and close eyes ("I'm going away, I'm coming back") Remove hard contacts and eyeglasses Respect boundaries — do not "unmask" a person

Segment	Fixed Muscular Patterns and Associated Affect	Major Muscle Groups	Muscle Release Techniques
II. Oral **Band III**	Aggression (masseter) Dependency: helplessness Sexual feelings (oral sex play) Sucking feelings that were prevented— longing, insecurity. Fixed smile, disgust, desire Anger (tight masseter jaw, clenched teeth, compressed lips) Holding on— maintaining control (masseter) Defiance, stubbornness (jutting jaw)	JAW: temporalis (affects ocular and oral bands) Masseter (mastication) External, internal pterygoid (resistant to release— causes hard eyes) MOUTH: obicularis oris— sphincter muscle surrounding mouth zygomaticus (corners of mouth) quadratus labii superior (upper lip) risorius caninus (beside nose)	Massage mouth and lips (obicularis oris) Masage masseter by holding muscle between thumb inside mouth and forefinger outside mouth Massage temporalis to release mouth Massage external pterygoid at posterior retromolar area of maxilla (behind last molar on top) Bucinator (cheek)
Band IV	Sucking Pitifulness (mentalis) — quivering chin. Worry, doubt Tears— swallowing back. Dismissal, negative feelings ("So now what?")	CHIN: Mentalis Platysma (wide sheet-like, extends from clavicle to chin) Trapezius Quaclatrus labii inferior Triangularis (pulls corners of mouth down) Hyoglossus (underneath tongue)	To stimulate crying: a) Massage mentalis and then hold until it trembles b) Gently stroke platysma toward mouth c) Massage under mouth, pressing up into floor of mouth
III. Cervical	Crying Anger Withholding expression	TRAPEZIUS: Back of neck to center of spine STERNO-CLEIDO-MASTOID: Behind ear to clavicle and sternum	Press at center of shoulders and back of neck and massage Hold SCM between fingers to pinch and massage Apply intermittent pressure to throat as client makes vibratory sound with breathing Stretch and pinch trapezius

Energetic Release Points	Movement/ Stress Release Techniques	Associated Somatic Manifestations	Comments
Pressure at temporalis and masseter (1, 2, 3)	1 To release anger: 　a) biting, holding, releasing with towel 　b) yelling, screaming 2 To release throat: 　a) stimulate gag reflex by touching uvulae 　b) spitting 3 Sucking thumb or web of hand 4 Clench and relax jaw 5 Reaching with lips	Infantile oral patterns: Thumb sucking, lip biting, tongue thrusting, nail biting Overeating Alcoholism Drug addiction Smoking	Check for incongruity of mouth and eyes (sad eyes— smiling mouth) Functions of mouth: communication, nourishment, swallowing, expression, laughing or crying, aggression (biting), respiration, sucking, gagging, vomiting Remove prosthesis before biting exercises
9 10	6 Exaggerate jutting jaw		Gagging— expressive and retentive functions of throat Includes tongue and floor of mouth
Back of neck, clavicle, jaw (10, 11 a, b, 12) 16	Hang head over end of table to open throat Roll head from side to side to loosen trapezius Protrude tongue and inhale for throat, jaw, chest release Coughing elicits crying and opens throat Yelling, gagging, swallowing may release throat Barrel roll (see below) Roll neck on tennis ball	Chronic throat infections Neck tension Speech defects Sexual dysfunction (see pelivc segment and "Comment" column)	Because of the jugular vein, thyroid gland, carotid arteries, trachea, parathyroids, and carotid sinus in this region, it is important to treat throat very carefully and to avoid use of anterior pressure altogether The cervical and pelvic segments are functionally, muscularly, and energetically related. Tension in one may be displaced in another Notice catching or rasping of breath to locate throat block

Segment	Fixed Muscular Patterns and Associated Affect	Major Muscle Groups	Muscle Release Techniques
IV. THORACIC	Self-protection (round shoulders, concave chest)	CHEST-UPPER BACK (includes arms and hands)	Press down on upper chest on exhalation, then release on inhalation
	Sorrow, wanting, pity, longing (heartbreak), fear, anxiety	intercostals (between ribs)	Massage between intercostal muscles
			Massage pectoral (avoid mammary tissue)
		pectoralis major/ minor (chest to shoulders)	
	Joy, compassion		Shoulder lift: pull up on shoulder blade while person is on side
		latismus (back around sides of chest)	
	Trust		Rolling tissue alongside the spine to shoulders for calming effect
	Self-esteem, pride	rhomboids (short, thick muscles behind shoulder blades)	Release knots in back muscles by firm finger pressure
	Withholding anger (barrel chest)	trapezius	Press rhomboids
		teres major	Massage paraspinal muscles toward center of spine
	Doing, expressing (arms)		
			Hold, squeeze and massage dead (cool) areas to energize.
	Raised rigid shoulders indicate fear		Thump fist on spine
	Rounded shoulders indicate overburden		
V. Diaphragm	Power, assertion, rage	Thick band of muscle, attaches directly under ribcage, below lungs and above stomach, extends around to spinal column	Deep massage of diaphragm under ribcage on exhalation (while holding shoulder points)
	Kundalini yoga — excessive diaphragmatic breathing		Abdominal massage relieves tension in diaphragmatic segment also
	Professional singing, wind instrument playing — creates diaphragmatic rigidity		Hold one hand on diaphragm, other on back under diaphragm
VI. Abdominal	Assertion, aggression, anger	(Diaphragm to pelvis) contains major vital organs	Knead rectus abdominus
			Abdominal massage in clockwise direction
	Strong "gut" emotions	Rectus abdominus (originates at pubis and inserts at thoracic 5, 6, 7)	Abdominal breathing
	Deep sobbing		Pressure on lumbar area releases abdominal tension
		Psoas (attaches to lower spine, crosses over pelvic bone to upper leg); connects leg to trunk	Abdominal massage stimulates parasympathetic— elicits crying release

Energetic Release Points	Movement/ Stress Release Techniques	Associated Somatic Manifestations	Comments
16 (6 points) 11 a, b, c 19 20 a, b 21, 22, 23, 24 31, 33	Hitting Reach arms downward on expiration Reach arms out (longing) Barrel roll: arms extended overhead, roll on barrel from shoulder to hips, sound with breath Twisting a towel (exaggerate imploding anger) Exercises that arch back	Respiratory disorders (asthma, bronchitis, etc.) Circulation, blood pressure Chronic tension of hands and arms (caused by repressed anger) Angina Tachycardia	Much holding in back; treat back vigorously for best effect Functions: ARMS, HANDS: Extending into world and protection from world: hitting, giving, taking, holding, grasping, manipulating, stroking Heart center: Sense of Self and Well-being Nipple erections (male and female) is a sign of parasympathetic release Eye-chest connection (work with splitting-off in chest also Put pillow under back to elevate chest

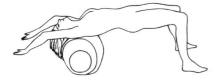

13 11 a, b, c	Barrel roll Bridge Gag reflex originates here and stimulating gagging or vomiting will release block in diaphragm Arms lift on inhalation (arch back), down on exhalation	Back pain Respiration disorders Digestive disorders (peptic ulcer, nervous stomach) Hiccoughs	Regulates respiration Gateway to ANS Separates two halves of body (top-bottom splits); restricts expression of all feelings which rise from abdomen Resistant to change— difficult to approach

14	Barrel roll (to hips) Bridge: on back, feet on floor, fists under heels, lift body to shoulders off the floor (only shoulders and feet on ground), breath (also releases pelvis)	Digestive disorders (ulcers, food allergies, colitis, etc.) (Held back emotions: - implosion of emotional energy - causes tension) Lower back pain	Center of gravity of body— storehouse of energy according to Eastern views "Feeling and power center" Seat of chi, ki

331

Segment	Fixed Muscular Patterns and Associated Affect	Major Muscle Groups	Muscle Release Techniques
VII. Pelvic	Emotions of sexuality Vulnerability Fear Anger, rage Pleasure Charisma Loss (abortion, miscarriage) Childbirth traumas Chronic tightness in suprapubic muscles Pelvic-heart split (see Chapter 5 on sex) Containment (see Chapter 5 on sex) premature toilet training causes pelvic blocks: lack of muscle differentiation leads to chronic anal sphincter tension, tightening of pelvic floor	Rectus abdominus Psoas Inguinal (suprapubpic) Pelvis is a hinge between legs and torso Pubococcygeus muscle (PCG) (vaginal muscles) Levator ani Sphincter ani externus Transverse perinae Bulbocavenosus Sphincter urethra Gluteus maximus	Massage neck (see Comments) Lightly massage inguinal area Massage lower abdomen to stimulate ovaries and uterus Massage sacrum Massage buttocks if tight

Energetic Release Points	Movement/ Stress Release Techniques	Associated Somatic Manifestations	Comments
15	1 Pelvic rock: on back, feet grounded, cock pelvis back (arch back) with	Sexual dysfunction (premature ejacu-	Pelvic blocks recipro- cally related to neck,
17	inhale, rotate forward with exhale. (Neck moves reciprocally back on	lation, orgasmic dysfunction,	throat, mouth and shoulder blocks
18	inhale, forward on exhale)	impotence)	*See Chapter 5 on
32	*2 Pelvic bounce: on back, feet grounded, bounce pelvis vigorously	Urinary dysfunc- tion (cystitis ureth-	sexuality.
34	to open anus and awaken pelvis	ritis)	*Avoid vigorous invasive techniques*
	*3 Pelvic lift: on back, feet on floor or on wall, lift pelvis off floor and rock while breathing	Gynecological dis- orders (chronic menstrual cramps,	*Approach with caution*
	*4 Bridge	dysmeorrhea, yeast infections, vagini-	*Highly vulnerable area*
	5 Knee-chest position: chest and knees on floor, breathe into abdo- men (good for menstrual cramps, tipped uterus)	tis) Hernia	Make energetic con- nection between pelvis and eyes (maintain eye contact) — to associate
	*6 Knee spread (inner thigh): on back, knees together, feet on floor—	Retraction of scrotum	sexual excitement and pelvic opening with here and now contact
	inhale, cock pelvis back and bring knees together; exhale, roll pelvis forward and drop knees apart (10 times)	Enlarged penis (due to inadequate discharge)	*Avoid vigorous invasive techniques.* Never touch genitals. Mouth-
	7 Genital breathing — breath as though exhaling with genitals and/ or anus; abdominal and pelvic	Hemorrhoids Constipation	genital or breast- genital connection, especially in females.
	muscles relaxed		
	8 Squat: feet flat on floor, arms be- tween legs, reach forward and breathe		
	9 Little bird: sitting, feet flat, soles together, close to body, raise and lower knees while breathing (stret- ches adductors [inner thighs])		
	*10 Hold legs open while person tries to close		
	*11 Hold legs closed while person tries to open		
	*12 Hold pelvis down while person pushes up		
	13 Sucking (see stress positions in segments II, III)		
	14 Kegel exercise (PCG contraction and relaxation) — increase genital feeling for men and women		
	*15 Kicking (releases anger)		

Segment	Fixed Muscular Patterns and Associated Affect	Major Muscle Groups	Muscle Release Techniques
Legs, Feet	Inflexibility (hyperextended knees, rigid ankles)	LEGS: Adductors (coccygeal and sacral vertebrae contain nerves which vitalize pelvis and legs)	Massage vigorously adductors, abductors, calves and feet— pull on toes
	Anal retentive— personality— holding on may be expressed also in tension in feet(clenched toes)	Abductors Calves Long muscles of legs	
	Insecurity, self-support, stability (grounding functions)		
	Defiance, stubbornness(digs heels into ground)		
	Charisma associated with knees		

Energetic Release Points	Movement/ Stress Release Techniques	Associated Somatic Manifestations	Comments
17	Grounding Exercises: 1, 2, 3, 4, 8	Flat feet (fallen arches), weak knees	Grounding: It is important to ground energy (get it into feet) when pelvis opens — energy will remain stuck in pelvis otherwise
18	16 Bioenergetic bend: stand erect, knees flexed, toes in, heels out, lean back, fists on small of back, breath	Sciatica	
25			
26		Leg cramping	Energy exchange with the earth
27	17 Stepping out: stand against wall, tilt pelvis forward with one foot, then other foot, step out		Contact with reality
28			
29			
30	18 Lean hands against wall, push feet into floor, knees flexed, breathe		
35			
34			
36 (below knee)			

Other New Books From Humanics New Age

Body Conditioning: A Thinking Person's Guide to Aerobic Fitness
Kenneth France, Ph. D.

Heart attacks killed author/runner Jim Fixx and cut short the career of tennis player Arthur Ashe. Many exercisers are running a similar risk. *Body Conditioning* shows how to evaluate any kind of workout and how most aerobic exercisers can decrease their risk of heart attack. Improved performance and enhanced enjoyment in exercising are common side effects of this method, but best of all, you'll be sure your exercise is *totally* beneficial by checking first with *Body Conditioning*.

Midlife Myths and Realities
William H. Van Hoose

Most people have some fears as they approach midlife— fears that surface when they hear the words "middle-age crazy" or "midlife crisis." But these catchy terms are only misleading myths, Dr. Van Hoose explains. In reality, midlife is a time of life that's ripe with opportunity for personal fulfillment. Most midlife adults are reaching the peak of productivity, and they occupy most of the positions of power and influence in our society. Nevertheless, there are problems unique to the middle years, and Dr. Van Hoose provides realistic guidelines for handling them.

The Tao of Leadership
Lao Tsu's Tao Te Ching Adapted for a New Age
John Heider

This adaptation of one of China's best-loved books of wisdom will be valuable to anyone in a leadership position, whether within the family or group, the church or a school, business or the military, politics or government. Anyone who is concerned with more effective decision-making and leadership or who seeks a new understanding of the nature of things will find inspiration in *The Tao of Leadership*. "This is a particularly readable and accessible version of a great but difficult work." — *Publishers Weekly*

These books and other Humanics New Age publications are available from booksellers or from Humanics New Age, P. O. Box 7447, Atlanta, Georgia 30309, (404) 874-2176. For orders only, call toll free, 1 (800) 874-8844. Visa and MasterCard accepted. All prices subject to change.

14.95